P

Pu...
the I...
...eries ...itor: ...o Ca...

BASW

Social work is at an important stage in its development. The profession is facing fresh challenges to work flexibly in fast-changing social and organisational environments. New requirements for tra..ing are also demanding a more critical and reflective, as well as more highly skilled, approach to practice.

The British Association of Social Workers has always been conscious of its role in setting guidelines for practice and in seeking to raise professional standards. The concept of the *Practical Social Work* series was conceived to fulfil a genuine professional need for a carefully planned, coherent series of texts that would stimulate and inform debate, thereby contributing to the development of practitioners' skills and professionalism.

Newly relaunched, the series continues to address the needs of all those who are looking to deepen and refresh their understanding and skills. It is designed for students and busy professionals alike. Each book marries practice issues and challenges with the latest theory and research in a compact and applied format. The authors represent a wide variety of experience both as educators and practitioners. Taken together, the books set a standard in their clarity, relevance and rigour.

A list of new and best-selling titles in this series follows overleaf. A comprehensive list of titles available in the series, and further details about individual books, can be found online at :
www.palgrave.com/socialworkpolicy/basw

Series standing order **ISBN 0–333–80313–2**

You can receive future titles in this series as they are published by placing a standing order. Please contact your bookseller or, in the case of difficulty, contact us at the address below with your name and address, the title of the series and the ISBN quoted above.

Customer Services Department, Macmillan Distribution Ltd, Houndmills, Basingstoke, Hampshire RG21 6XS, England

Practical social work series

New and best-selling titles

Robert Adams *Social Work and Empowerment (3rd edition)*

Sarah Banks *Ethics and Values in Social Work (3rd edition)* **new!**

James G. Barber *Social Work with Addictions (2nd edition)*

Suzy Braye and Michael Preston-Shoot *Practising Social Work Law (2nd edition)*

Veronica Coulshed and Joan Orme *Social Work Practice (4th edition)* **new!**

Veronica Coulshed and Audrey Mullender with David N. Jones and Neil Thompson *Management in Social Work (3rd edition)* **new!**

Lena Dominelli *Anti-Racist Social Work (2nd edition)*

Celia Doyle *Working with Abused Children (3rd edition)* **new!**

Tony Jeffs and Mark Smith (editors) *Youth Work*

Joyce Lishman *Communication in Social Work*

Paula Nicolson and Rowan Bayne and Jenny Owen *Applied Psychology for Social Workers (3rd edition)* **new!**

Judith Phillips, Mo Ray and Mary Marshall *Social Work with Older People (4th edition)* **new!**

Michael Oliver and Bob Sapey *Social Work with Disabled People (3rd edition)* **new!**

Michael Preston-Shoot *Effective Groupwork*

Steven Shardlow and Mark Doel *Practice Learning and Teaching*

Neil Thompson *Anti-Discriminatory Practice (4th edition)* **new!**

Derek Tilbury *Working with Mental Illness (2nd edition)*

Alan Twelvetrees *Community Work (3rd edition)*

sarah banks

ethics and values in social work

third edition

palgrave
macmillan

First edition 1995
Reprinted six times
Second edition 2001
Reprinted five times
Third edition 2006
published by
PALGRAVE MACMILLAN
Houndmills, Basingstoke, Hampshire RG21 6XS and
175 Fifth Avenue, New York, N.Y. 10010
Companies and representatives throughout the world

PALGRAVE MACMILLAN is the global academic imprint of the Palgrave Macmillan division of St. Martin's Press, LLC and of Palgrave Macmillan Ltd. Macmillan® is a registered trademark in the United States, United Kingdom and other countries. Palgrave is a registered trademark in the European Union and other countries.

ISBN-13: 978–1–4039–9420–2
ISBN-10: 1–4039–9420–X

This book is printed on paper suitable for recycling and made from fully managed and sustained forest sources.

A catalogue record for this book is available from the British Library.

A catalog record for this book is available from the Library of Congress.

10 9 8 7 6 5 4 3 2 1
15 14 13 12 11 10 09 08 07 06

Printed in China

To past and present community and youth work and social work students at Durham and York Universities

Contents

List of figures, tables and lists

Figures

Tables

Lists

Preface to the third edition

It is both an honour and a challenge to be asked to prepare a third edition of this book. The decision about what to add, alter or remove demands consideration of the changes that have taken place in social work and the organisational and policy contexts in which it is prac- tised. The process of revision is also influenced by new themes, theo- ries, models and approaches developed in recent literature in the fields of moral philosophy, professional ethics, social work ethics, social policy and social work practice. Furthermore, producing a new edition of an existing text provokes a sometimes uncomfortable reflexivity on the part of the author. How have my ideas changed? What assumptions, prejudices, cultural and educational influences do I now see in the previous editions? How ought I to re-write this book in order to take into account all these changes, while still retaining the book's integrity and coherence? Having met and talked to some of the readers of the earlier editions, how can I ensure that this edition of the book is more relevant to them and to future readers, while remaining clearly written and easy to understand?

Constantly changing social work

The Introduction to the first edition of this book, published in 1995, started with the statement: 'Social work is currently in a period of change.' I have retained this statement in this, the third edition. In the preface to second edition, I noted the editorial comment in the magazine *Community Care* (1999/2000) that ushered in the new millennium with the headline 'A new century of uncertainty', and claimed that: 'Few professions have changed more than social work in a decade.' This comment relates to the UK, but similar shifts in the organisation and practice of social work are also occurring in many other countries as the introduction of market principles, the mixed economy of welfare and the increasing concern with quality assurance and standards take hold (see Clarke, 2004; Donati and Folgheraiter, 1999; Lorenz, 2001; Soulet, 1997). These changes are having profound effects on the nature of the roles and tasks performed by social workers and on the status and identity of social work as a profession. What this means for professional ethics is one of the questions the book has to address, even more so now than when it was first published in 1995.

At the time of writing, major changes are continuing in the UK in the field of social work, social care and social services generally. These include the establishment of general councils as regulatory bodies in the countries of the UK, which are registering social care practitioners and have developed new codes of practice for social care work (see, for example, GSCC, 2002). Social services departments in local authorities are being transformed, with the formation of new children's trusts and health and social care trusts based around inter-professional working with health, education and other professionals. Mechanisms for surveillance and tracking, particularly of children and young people, are being introduced, based on new information technology systems, designed both to protect the public from young offenders and young people from neglect and abuse. These developments have inevitably informed some of the changes that have been made to the first and second editions of this book, although they have not been dwelt upon in depth, as by the time the book is published, another new policy initiative will probably be in place and it is the broader trends that are more important when looking at ethics and values.

Some of the trends towards fragmentation and specialisation of the work, the growth of procedures and protocols and the concern to involve service users as partners in decision-making noted in Chapters 5 and 6 are still there and intensifying, with an even greater focus on inter-agency partnerships, inter-professional working and surveillance. More literature is emerging on 'postmodern social work', which takes account of this fragmentation of practice and recognises the diversity of the values and needs of service users. While ethics is only just beginning to be considered in the context of this literature (for example Rossiter et al., 2000), the implications for professional ethics could be profound, depending on whether a 'sceptical' or 'affirmative' view is taken, to use the distinction made by Rosenau (1992, pp. 15–16). There are those who announce the 'end of ethics' as a system of universal principles of right/wrong, good/bad (see McBeath and Webb, 1991), others who argue that certain value choices are superior to others and see the possibility of emancipatory action for social change (Ife, 1999; Leonard, 1997). Some of this literature on postmodern perspectives on social work has been incorporated into Chapter 3.

The 'ethics boom'

In addition to the changes in social work practice, there has also been what Davis (1999) has termed an 'ethics boom', particularly in the field of professional ethics. This was noted in the second edition, and is continuing, marked by a growth of publications on ethics in public policy and the professions. Some of this has to do with changes in technology, particularly in the field of medical ethics, where new issues relating to genetics, for example, are subject to intense debate. But there is also a much broader concern in all professions with 'standards in public life' as a number of high-profile cases of corruption, lying or malpractice have come to light. Ethical issues in social work are no exception, with many more publications coming out in recent years than previously with a specific focus on ethics (for example Beckett and Maynard, 2005; Clark, 2000; Hugman, 2005; Hunt, 1998; Payne and Littlechild, 2000; Wilmot, 1997).

While the focus of professional ethics in the past tended to be on developing lists of principles and how to handle conflict between principles (say between respecting the self-determination of a service user and promoting her welfare), the interest noted in the second edition in what I have called character- and relationship-based ethics ('virtue ethics' and the 'ethic of care') is intensifying even further, as outlined in Chapter 3. The growing emphasis, particularly by feminist ethicists, on diversity and difference, context and relationships, narratives and discourses is highly relevant to social work and is increasingly being used by social work academics and practitioners.

Situating ethics

I have been exercised by the fact that the earlier editions of the book have been used in a number of different countries. This has heightened my awareness of the national and cultural specificity of some of the language, concepts and approaches used and has caused me to question how a book about ethics can be relevant across a range of different cultural, legal and practice contexts. In a desire to make such a text more relevant to different parts of the world, it is tempting to remove the contextual specificity and keep the discussion at a more general level – the level of universal and abstract principles. Yet one of the developing themes in the ethics literature is the importance of context – the richness of everyday life in which decisions and dilemmas are located. In the sociological and social work literature, the recognition of cultural diversity and the specificity of responses demanded is a key feature.

The tension between the universal and particular; abstract principles and contextualised relationships; universal human rights and particularised caring relations is, of course, a recurring theme in sociological and moral philosophical literature. These distinctions are often presented as in an 'either/or' relationship – for example either we focus on abstract principles as the core of ethics or on contextualised relationships. They may also be presented as dualisms, that is, separating what should be regarded as an indivisible whole into two parts and focusing on the differences rather than the whole picture or the dynamic relationship between the two. However, such distinctions do not necessarily entail a dualism in thinking or acting. We can regard abstract principles and contextualised relationships as different aspects of ethical thinking and acting.

In the first edition of the book, the focus was on what has been termed 'principle-based' ethics, with an emphasis on ethical decision-making as essentially about prioritising and then acting upon ethical principles (such as respect for self-determination or the promotion of welfare). In the second edition, a new chapter was added covering 'character- and relationship-based' approaches to ethics, reflecting the recent revival of virtue ethics (based on qualities of character rather than principles of action) and feminist and other situated approaches to ethics with a stress on the importance of care, responsibility and relationships between particular people. I argued that ethical being and acting could plausibly be regarded as based on a plurality of values of different kinds (including principles, qualities of character and particular commitments to people). I acknowledged that in real life interactions, where the actual verbal and non-verbal communication can be heard and felt and emotions come into play, then situated ethics is paramount. However, in a textbook and in the context of teaching, I suggested it was easier to continue to analyse case examples of ethical problems and dilemmas in terms of principles. The exercise of analysis, although artificial, does in itself play an important role in developing ethical awareness and reflection. However, in this third edition, I have added further coverage of character and relationship-based approaches, attempting to weave these aspects into some of the discussion of cases in the final chapter.

Once we expand the domain of ethics to include aspects of moral perception, motivation and commitment (in addition to moral judgement and reasoning), then we begin to move into the terrain of moral psychology. If we regard the study of ethics as about the webs of relationships, responsibilities and cultural beliefs that form the rich textures of people's lives (that is, as about more than just the articulation and examination of the implementation of abstract ethical theories and principles about the nature of right action or justice), then we also start to encroach into the fields of sociology and anthropology, which adopt empirical as well theoretical modes of study. This worries some moral philosophers, who argue that this is not doing 'ethics' in the traditional sense of moral philosophy (the latter is necessarily abstract, theoretical and/or analytical). The fact-value distinction may be invoked to argue that such social science studies of ethics are doing something different (investigating the facts, what people actually believe and do) to moral philosophical studies (which articulate and prescribe ethical principles about what people ought to do and believe). But, as with the other distinctions mentioned earlier, this one does not really make sense in practice (although as a conceptual distinction it may be useful).

If we accept the embeddedness of ethics in all aspects of life, and in particular in social practices, then it is important to study how certain ethical beliefs and qualities of character are constructed and performed during the course of everyday encounters in social work. Such ethnographic studies add to our practical understanding of social work ethics, although we do need to bear in mind that they originate within a different disciplinary and methodological framework compared with the more philosophically oriented approaches that have been common in the professional ethics literature (the relationship between philosophical and social scientific studies of ethics is discussed further in Banks, 2004a). The development, especially by feminist philosophers, of situated and contextualised ethics, perhaps offers a bridge between the philosophical and ethnographic approaches to the study of ethics. This book does not aim to offer or give accounts of empirical studies of what social workers do in practice, but is based on a developing view of ethics as comprising both abstract philosophical theorising and as situated within policy and practice contexts. I have tended to use illustrative case studies based on real accounts given by practitioners in order to maintain a closeness to the practice experiences of social workers.

Changes in the third edition

The Introduction and Chapter 1 remain broadly the same, although some small but significant changes have been made. For example, the definition of social work used as a starting point is that of the International Federation of Social Workers (IFSW, 2000). Although this is a very generic and de-contextualised description of the nature and purpose of social work, it is at least internationally recognised and I have used it in preference to the more specific UK definition offered in previous editions. Organisations like the IFSW that exist at an international level for social work and social workers operate on the basis of commonalities, while recognising distinctiveness and difference. The concept of international social work seems, in fact, more akin to a social movement than to an organised profession or specific job. Professions and jobs exist in specific national and local contexts and are heavily influenced by legal and cultural traditions as well as current policies and organisational norms and practices. Whereas social work as a social movement is based on international solidarity around a shared purpose of challenging poverty, promoting human rights and social justice.

Following recent trends, especially in codes of ethics, I also distinguish more clearly in this edition between 'values' and 'ethical principles'. Although very often in the context of discussions in professional ethics, the term 'values' is used synonymously with 'ethical principles', in this edition I use the term 'values' more broadly to encompass ethical principles, moral qualities (or virtues), ideals and commitments.

I have deliberated over the use of the term 'welfare state' as it occurred in earlier editions. While many commentators continue to use the term to refer to state-organised systems of welfare, it is recognised that in some countries there has never been a 'welfare state' as such and in most others it is in a situation of change or decline. While references are still made to 'welfare states', more often the term 'welfare systems' is used.

Several new short case examples have also been included in these early chapters to illustrate the discussions, including a case from a student about professional boundaries and relationships – an issue taken up further in later chapters when the theme of personal–professional conflicts is discussed.

Chapter 2, on principle-based approaches to ethics, has been expanded to include a section on radical/anti-oppressive perspectives, in addition to Kantian, utilitarian and common morality approaches. Although radical perspectives on social work were covered in the previous editions, they were not presented as an approach to ethics, but rather as either an extension of utilitarianism or as a denial of ethics as a bourgeois illusion. This account was largely influenced by the Marxist and neo-Marxist literature on social work of the 1970s and 1980s. The anti-oppressive, structural and critical approaches to social work that have developed from the 1980s and 1990s do have an explicit value-base and this has been taken into account in a separate section of Chapter 2.

Chapter 3 on character- and relationship-based approaches has also been extended to include a short separate section on 'postmodern' and constructionist approaches to ethics. Again, while the influence of postmodernist thinking was discussed in the second edition, particularly in relation to the fragmentation of social work knowledge, some of the more positive and practical approaches that are now appearing in the social work literature have clearly articulated values based on diversity, difference, partnership, building strengths and reconstructing selves. As such, their influence needs to be taken into account in discussions of ethics and values in social work.

In the first two editions, the fourth chapter of the book included discussion of the relationship of social work values to the 'knowledge base', taking account of some of the recent literature on social work practice and theories. In writing this new edition, I felt this chapter was no longer needed, as texts on social work theories are much more likely now to integrate coverage of values and ethics (for example, Healy, 2005; Payne, 2005). It was also in danger of becoming too unwieldy, as different theoretical approaches multiply, as exemplified in Payne's (2005) *Modern Social Work Theory*, a constantly expanding book as it moves through several new editions. This chapter was, therefore, removed, with parts that covered radical social work and postmodernism being transferred to Chapters 2 and 3.

The chapter on professionalism and codes of ethics (now Chapter 4), has been revised to take account of the latest versions of codes of ethics supplied by the professional associations in membership of the International Federation of Social Workers. There is a continuing trend for codes to become longer and more prescriptive and some emergent new themes are noted, although codes of ethics tend to be slow to reflect actual changes in practice. For example, in some cases the concern with the rights of citizens and service users is now beginning to encompass the notion of their reciprocal responsibilities, and several codes have extended their sections on confidentiality, sometimes explicitly to take account of multidisciplinary work.

The structure of the next two chapters (5 and 6), on service users' rights and social workers' duties and responsibilities, is broadly the same as in the earlier editions, taking into account some of the intensifying trends towards service user responsibility, 'consumerist' approaches, user participation in decision-making, empowering practice, increasing standardisation and regulation of the social work task and a concern with 'evidence-based' practice. However, in both chapters, additional sections have been added on 'relational rights' and 'relational duties' respectively. This is to take account of the fact that rights and duties have traditionally been interpreted as belonging to abstract, isolated individuals. However, the notion of 'relationship' is important not only in the ethics of care, but also ethical approaches of non-western religions and cultures. Rights and duties may make less sense in these contexts and may be regarded as unhelpful. Alternatively, it may be possible to reframe these concepts as embodying an element of relationship within them – a move that seeks to take us beyond the dualisms of individual–society, rights–responsibilities, the right–the good, justice–care, distance–proximity and so on.

Chapter 7 starts, as in the second edition, with a discussion of the nature of ethical judgements. However, a new section has been added acknowledging that ethical judgements are simply one part of the domain of ethics, which can also be characterised as including moral sensitivity (perceiving the ethical dimensions of a situation); moral motivation (prioritising moral concerns above other non-moral ones); and moral character (qualities such as courage and commitment). A new case example has been added, raising complex issues of power in the student–supervisor relationship and in being a black male in a white agency working largely with women. The final case example is an account from a very experienced team manager of difficult ethical decision-making in a multi-professional context. The multi-professional aspect of the case has been high-lighted in the third edition, as inter- and multi-professional working is becoming increasingly common. This case shows that the tensions and value conflicts that may occur in these contexts require the professionals involved to have clarity about their distinctive roles and courage to stick to their values and principles.

As in the previous editions, the main aim of the book is to encourage critical thinking, reflection and reflexivity about the ethical problems and dilemmas encountered in social work practice, hence this last chapter is one of the most important in the book. It highlights the importance for both trainee and experienced social workers of discussing and debating ethical issues in their practice with others and the usefulness of a variety of types of case example to stimulate this process.

Acknowledgements

The main stimulus for writing this book has been the dialogue and discussion generated through teaching ethics to trainee social workers and community and youth workers, particularly at the Universities of Durham and York in the UK. I have also benefited greatly from periods as a visiting lecturer in higher education institutions in several other European countries, especially Amiens, Lisbon, Malmö and Oulu, where students have generously shared their dilemmas and problems and staff their ideas on teaching ethics. The continuing work with colleagues in the European Social Ethics Project since 1998 has also been a constant source of inspiration and I would like to thank all past and present members of that group for their companionship and stimulation.

I would like to thank the social workers who were prepared to discuss their ethical dilemmas with me – particularly trainee social workers from the Universities of York and Durham, and social workers from several social work agencies in the north of England. I am also grateful to the International Federation of Social Workers and the professional associations across the world that sent copies of their ethical codes; to Kate Boardman, Lieve van Espen, Marie Sanders and Mea Wilkins for their translations; to Katie Appleford and Vic Jupp for research assistance; and to the *International Journal of Youth and Adolescence* for permission to use sections in Chapter 3 from an article concerning virtue ethics and the ethics of care. Many colleagues and friends have offered encouragement and been prepared to discuss aspects of the first, second and third editions of the book with me, including: Margaret Bell, Tim Bond, Lorna Durrani, Ken Fairless, Umme Imam, Tony Jeffs, Juliet Koprowska, Kate Leonard, Una McCluskey, Audrey Mullender, Alf Ronnby, Muriel Sawbridge, Maria Rosàrio do Serafim, Mark Smith, Fritz-Rüdiger Volz and Robin Williams. I have also benefited from working with Arne Grønningsæter and Richard Hugman, and others from across the world, who joined in the dialogue on the drafting of the new statement on ethics in social work for the International Federation of Social Workers and International Association of Schools of Social Work. I am grateful to Jo Campling for her enthusiastic support, to Catherine Gray at Palgrave Macmillan for her usual patience and to three anonymous referees for their helpful comments on the first and third editions.

Finally, I would like to thank Robin Williams for listening to my repetitive reflections on the process of creating new editions, Esh Winning women's book group and Durham yogis for broadening my mind and sustaining body and soul and Fred Banks for first pointing me in the direction of philosophy.

SARAH BANKS

Introduction

Current context of social work

The occupation of social work is currently in a period of change – both in the UK and in many other countries – as the role of the state as a direct provider of services declines, resources for welfare are being reduced and new styles of management and accountability are introduced. This makes it not only difficult to look at the ethics and values of social work (because old values may be becoming irrelevant and new ones are beginning to emerge) but also particularly important. Social work has always been a difficult occupation to define. It is located within and profoundly affected by diverse cultural, economic and policy contexts in different countries of the world. Social work embraces work in a number of sectors (public, private, independent, voluntary); it takes place in a multiplicity of settings (residential homes, area offices, community development projects); practitioners perform a range of tasks (caring, controlling, empowering, campaigning, assessing, managing); and the work has a variety of purposes (redistribution of resources to those in need, social control and rehabilitation of the deviant, prevention or reduction of social problems). This diversity, or 'fragmentation' as some have called it, is increasing, which raises the question of whether the occupation can retain the rather tenuous identity it was seeking to develop in the 1970s and 1980s.

In such a climate of fragmentation, there are some who argue that it is the values of social work that should hold it together. Yet the values traditionally stated – self-determination of the service user, acceptance, non-judgementalism and confidentiality, for example – are neither unique to social work nor do they seem to be complete for social work. Similar statements of values or ethical principles are made for medicine, nursing and counselling, for example. It is precisely because these values are so broad ranging that they can encompass the variety of tasks and settings that come under the umbrella of 'social work'. They are relevant to the 'caring professional' who is in a relationship of trust with a service user in need of help. Yet this description has never adequately characterised social work, which may also be about controlling people in the interests of social order. So, not only do the traditional social work values fail to characterise social work uniquely, they also fail to encompass social work itself completely. Other values also seem relevant, such as fairness in the distribution of resources and the promotion of the public good. As state-sponsored social work changes, with the emphasis less on the individual helping relationship and more on the distribution of resources and on social control, this is becoming more apparent. State social workers who are involved in the criminal justice system, community care, child protection and mental health are finding themselves working to an increasing number of legal, governmental and agency procedures and guidelines. This brings ethical issues around justice and fairness to prominence. At the same time, workers in specialist services that are often located in the voluntary (not-for-profit) sector, such as child advocacy or AIDS/HIV counselling, can operate more easily within the traditional casework value system that emphasises the self-determination of service users (or its modern development, 'empowerment') and the rights and welfare of individuals.

Terminology: 'social work', 'social workers' and 'service users'

There are many definitions of social work. These vary in emphasis according to the purpose for which they are written, the ideological viewpoint of the authors, the country and/or organisation of origin and the level of generality or detail. As Healy (2001, p. 80) comments, there are both striking similarities and differences in social work practice around the world. Some of the similarities are due to the influence of American and western European education programmes and literature in countries where social work developed later or was influenced by former colonial links. The establishment of international professional organisations and the growing ease of global communications have also contributed to an increasing awareness of common and inter-connected issues and problems. Yet, at the same time, as social work has become established in a range of countries, so its methods and approaches have adapted to the local conditions and culture. So while it is possible for the International Federation of Social Workers (IFSW) to produce a definition of social work that is designed to be applicable worldwide, it is a very general statement of purpose and principle. It is acknowledged that the priorities of social work will vary between countries and time periods, depending on cultural, historical and socio-economic conditions. The IFSW (2000) definition will, however, be used as a starting point for this book:

> The social work profession promotes social change, problem solving in human relationships and the empowerment and liberation of people to enhance well-being. Utilising theories of human behaviour and social systems, social work intervenes at points where people interact with their environments. Principles of human rights and social justice are fundamental to social work.

The purpose of this statement is to unify social workers around the world and to provide a common starting point for presenting social work to governments and other international and national agencies and bodies. The term 'profession' is used to describe social work, which instantly gives the occupation a status and implied unity. Reference is made to the use of theories relevant to social work interventions, which again serve to legitimise social work as a profession, based on a body of knowledge. Implicit in this is the fact that the theories need to be learnt through an educational process and applied through expertise. The definition also focuses on the purposes of social work, which include the terms 'social change', 'empowerment' and 'liberation'. These terms indicate that social work is about more than just helping people to adapt to their environments. It is about enabling them to take action for themselves. The fact that the definition explicitly refers to principles as fundamental highlights the importance of social workers having a commitment to a set of core values. The mention of 'human rights' and 'social justice' covers both issues of individual freedom of choice and action and the distribution of power and resources in society.

The term 'social worker' is used in this book to refer to people who are paid in a professional capacity to undertake the work just described. The IFSW definition is followed by a commentary, which includes a fuller description of social work practice, suggesting that 'interventions range from primarily person-focused psychosocial processes to involvement in social policy, planning and development'. It is important to note that some of the activities that form part of these interventions (such as counselling or helping people obtain services and resources in the community) may be carried out by people who are not social workers (volunteers, family members, other welfare professionals). But the location of the interventions undertaken by social workers within a rubric of theory and specialised terminology indicates that the practices will only be recognised as social work if they can be constructed in this way.

I have tended to adopt the term 'service user' or simply 'user' to refer to the people who use social work services. I prefer this to 'customer' or 'consumer' as these terms have connotations of choice and market-based relationships that are not necessarily appropriate in social work. Occasionally the term 'client' is used, as this was until recently in common usage and some of the social work literature uses this term. I have tended to use 'she' when I am referring to a social worker instead of the more cumbersome 'he/she'.

Terminology: 'ethics' and 'values'

It is also important to clarify the terms in the title of the book – 'ethics' and 'values'. People use the term 'ethics' in a number of different ways, but perhaps the most important distinction to make is between ethics as synonymous with moral philosophy and ethics as moral norms or standards. Within each of these two broad types of usage there are also many variations, depending on what aspects of moral philosophy are stressed and whether 'moral norms' are seen as habits, preferences, rules, standards, principles or character traits, for example.

If we take the first usage of ethics, as moral philosophy, it is a singular term, used to describe a branch of philosophy concerned with the study of 'morality, moral problems and moral judgements' (Frankena, 1963, p. 3). This is the way most moral philosophers writing on ethics use the term. For example, Warnock (1998, p. 7) talks of 'ethics (or moral philosophy, as I prefer to call it)'. The nature and remit of moral philosophy is, of course, disputed. But often philosophers distinguish three types of ethics as follows:

1. *Metaethics* – comprises critical and analytical thinking about the meaning and use of moral terms such as 'right', 'good' or 'duty', about whether moral judgements can be justified or what the nature of morality is, for example.
2. *Normative ethics* – attempts to give answers to moral questions and problems regarding, for example, what the morally right course of action in a particular case is, whether someone is a morally good person or whether lying is always wrong.
3. *Descriptive ethics* – studies what people's moral opinions and

beliefs are and how they act in relation to these – for example, whether people in Britain believe abortion is always morally wrong.

Some philosophers confine moral philosophy to metaethics only (for example, Urmson, 1975, p. 99), but generally it is regarded as comprising both metaethics and normative ethics, although some philosophers may inevitably spend more of their time on the former than the latter. Descriptive ethics, however, is usually regarded as outside the realm of moral philosophy, although not irrelevant, in that it comprises the kinds of empirical and historical inquiries that might be conducted by anthropologists, sociologists or historians. Clearly in the context of professional ethics, we are interested in all three aspects of ethics, including descriptive ethics (what moral views social workers actually hold and how they behave in practice), although the purpose of this book is not to conduct an empirical inquiry.

The second usage of the term 'ethics' is as a plural term referring to the norms or standards of behaviour people follow concerning what is regarded as good or bad, right or wrong. Commentators vary according to whether they regard ethics as norms, standards, rules, principles or character traits and whether they regard them as internally developed by the moral agent or externally imposed by an outside authority. A common use of this second sense of ethics is in the expression 'code of ethics' – which is usually regarded as a set of principles, standards or rules of conduct for ethical practice. A variant on this usage of ethics is to use the term synonymously with 'morality' to mean a system of moral norms or standards.

In English we often use the terms 'ethics' and 'morals' interchangeably in this second sense. Indeed, as Edwards (1998, p. 41) points out, 'morals' is derived from the Latin (*mores*) and 'ethics' from the Greek (*ethos*), both meaning habits or customs. It is in this interchangeable sense that I will use the terms 'ethics' and 'morals' in this book, along with the adjectives 'ethical' and 'moral'. However, it is important to point out that some commentators do distinguish between the two. Osborne (1998, pp. 221–2) makes the following distinction:

> Moral systems are systems of interdiction; they are ideologies, codes to which individuals must relate themselves. Ethics, on the other hand, might be considered in a more positive sense, not as codes of interdiction, not as external norms to which individuals must relate themselves, but as constructed norms of 'internal

consistency' (cf. Deleuze, 1988: 23; Foucault, 1984). Morality, one could say, is about doing one's duty to others or doing one's duty by some moral norm; ethics is about doing one's duty to oneself.

This has resonances with the distinction made in some of the French literature between 'la morale' and 'l'éthique'. Bouquet (1999, p. 27) defines 'la morale' as 'a set of universalisable values, absolute and imperative; it comprises duties'. She suggests that the term has become discredited through being confused with moralising and through the recent rejection of a prescriptive morality, of dogmatism and universalism. Common usage is now substituting the term 'éthique' for 'morale'. She regards 'l'éthique' as equally normative, but not categorical. It is principally associated with the subject and interior to the subject (that is, the moral agent) who is autonomous, free and responsible to herself for her acts. Bouquet defines 'l'éthique' as 'the set of principles which are at the foundation of each person's conduct'.

However, such distinctions in the English-speaking literature are less common and great care must be taken to ascertain how commentators are distinguishing 'ethics' and 'morals', if at all, since they do not all follow the same broad distinctions made by Osborne and Bouquet. For example, Bauman frequently talks of 'ethics' as the externally imposed codes prescribing correct behaviour universally (1995, p. 11) and the 'moral impulse' or 'morality' as internal and 'autonomous' (1993, p. 46). No such distinctions will be made in this book.

The term 'values' is equally problematic. 'Social work values', 'the value-base of social work', 'social work as a value-laden activity' are all common phrases in the social work literature. Yet what is meant by 'the values of social work'? 'Values' is one of those words that tends to be used rather vaguely and has a variety of different meanings. Timms (1983, p. 107) cites a literature review that discovered 180 different definitions. In everyday usage, 'values' is often used to refer to one or all of religious, moral, cultural, political or ideological beliefs, principles, attitudes, opinions or preferences. For our purpose, 'values' can be regarded as particular types of belief that people hold about what is regarded as worthy or valuable. In the context of professional practice, the use of the term 'belief' reflects the status that values have as stonger than mere opinions or preferences.

Clearly there are many different types of thing that can be regarded as valuable. Seedhouse (1998, p. 78) lists: physical objects (for example furniture); aesthetic qualities (for example beauty); intangibles (for example creativity); principles (for example truth telling); or ideologies (for example communism). In the literature on professional values, it is frequently principles, and particularly ethical principles, relating to how people should be treated, what ideas or actions are worthy or unworthy, good or bad, right or wrong that are regarded as values. For example, the IFSW (2000) definition of social work includes 'respect for the equality, worth, and dignity of all people', 'human rights' and 'social justice' under the heading of 'values'. However, some of the literature also includes what Seedhouse calls 'intangibles' as professional values, such as creativity or integrity, which we might regard as 'virtues' or character traits of workers. Furthermore, there is an increasing tendency to distinguish 'values' from 'principles' in some statements on professional ethics (for example, Australian Association of Social Workers, 1999; British Assocation for Counselling and Psychotherapy, 2001; British Association of Social Workers, 2002), with 'values' being used to encompass broad beliefs about the nature of the good society and the role of social work within this (belief in human dignity and worth, integrity in social work practice) and principles being general statements about actions that promote these values (treating people with respect, placing service users' needs first). I will use the term 'social work values' in a very broad sense to encompass this whole range of beliefs about what is regarded as worthy or valuable in a social work context (general beliefs about the nature of the good society, general principles about how to achieve this through actions and the desirable qualities or character traits of professional practitioners).

Professional values can be distinguished from personal values, in that personal values may not be shared by all members of an occupational group. For example, a person who works as a social worker may have a personal belief that abortion is wrong, but this is not one of the underlying principles of social work. Insofar as professional values are located within and influenced by broader societal values, then they may reflect particular ideological or political positions (for example liberalism). But lists of professional values do not usually include direct or overt statements of ideological or political beliefs. Employing agencies' values are usually similar to those of the profession as a whole, although some specialist organisations may include explicit religious or ideological beliefs. A worker's personal values, however, will encompass all of Seedhouse's range of categories and may include religious as well as aesthetic and ideological beliefs.

Rationale and aims of the book

The discussion thus far suggests that it is both timely and difficult to explore the nature of the ethical and value issues inherent in social work practice. It is timely not just because the old values are under threat, but also because social workers themselves are increasingly under moral attack from the press and public for the outcomes of their actions. Controversies over the handling of child abuse cases, for example, raise ethical questions about the duties and rights of social workers and the extent to which they should be blamed if a child dies or if children are removed from their families unnecessarily. Many social workers feel a sense of guilt and anxiety when having to make a difficult ethical decision. While such feelings are inevitable for anyone who makes difficult decisions and has a sense of moral responsibility, should social workers take all the blame for bad outcomes? One of the purposes of this book is to encourage social workers to be clear about their own value positions and hence to reduce some of the unnecessary feelings of guilt, blame and anxiety in making difficult ethical decisions.

In the course of collecting material for this book, I have found that when social workers are asked to describe ethical dilemmas in their practice, there is never any shortage of examples and there is no need even to define what is meant by an 'ethical dilemma'. If we do define what is meant by the term 'ethical dilemma' – a choice between two equally unwelcome alternatives relating to human welfare – then it is immediately apparent that the occurrence of ethical dilemmas in social work is serious and common. There is never any shortage of cases where the rights of parents have to be balanced against the rights of children or the social worker's duty to the agency conflicts with a duty to the service user, for example.

There are no easy answers to the ethical problems and dilemmas in social work practice. It is not possible (or desirable) to produce a rulebook that would enable social workers easily and quickly to resolve these dilemmas. Even if it were, the resolution of the dilemma will still entail making a choice between two unwelcome alternatives, perhaps by careful consideration and deciding that one alternative is less unwelcome than the other. Having made the choice, the impact of the dilemma does not go away, for even the least unwelcome alternative is still unwelcome. The resolution of a dilemma often leaves a residue of guilt, blame or regret. This is where some of the main stresses for social workers lie; not just in having to make difficult choices and decisions, but having to take responsibility for the unwelcome nature or outcomes of the decisions. For example:

> Peter is a 10-year-old boy whose parents are still barely able to control him after a lot of support from a social worker and a range of professionals from other agencies. Should the social worker recommend that Peter be removed from the parental home, a decision that would go against the wishes of Peter and his parents and might cause further disruptive behaviour as a result of the move? Or should she recommend that he stay at home, a course of action that is contrary to the demands coming from neighbours and the school and risks further violent and disruptive behaviour towards other children and neighbours?

Both solutions have unwelcome consequences. The process of investigation, taking into account the legal and moral rights of different parties, the risks involved in both courses of action and the legal, procedural and moral responsibilities of the social worker is a complex one. Whatever course of action is taken, somebody's rights may be compromised and some of the consequences may be unwelcome.

The aim of this book is not to tell social workers how to make such choices – I believe that would be both impossible and undesirable. It is impossible because of the complexity of social work decision-making; no rulebook could cover the variety of situations. It would be undesirable because it would suggest that social workers would simply have to follow the prescribed rules applying in each case and could in effect abrogate their individual responsibility for decision-making. Rather, the book aims to encourage critical thinking, reflection and reflexivity through exploring the nature of the ethical problems and dilemmas in social work, how and why they arise and what might be some alternative ways of tackling them according to different ethical theories and approaches. Through gaining a clearer understanding of what the problems and dilemmas are about, social workers should be able more readily to decide where they stand on some of the important ethical issues in the work and will have more confidence in justifying the decisions they have made and may feel less obliged to take the blame for the inevitable unwelcome outcomes of social work intervention.

At the end of each chapter, exercises have been included that can be used by readers to focus their thoughts around particular issues or by tutors/facilitators teaching or working with groups of social workers. Case studies drawn from accounts given by social work students and practitioners have also been used, mainly in Chapter 7, to illustrate how ethical problems and dilemmas arise and can be tackled in practice. Details of the cases and all names of people involved have been changed to preserve anonymity.

1 | Ethical issues in social work

There is general agreement among social work practitioners and academics that questions of ethics, morals and values are an inevitable part of social work. The majority of social workers, when asked, have no difficulty in offering examples of ethical problems and dilemmas. The literature of social work is also very clear: 'Moral issues haunt social work', says Jordan (1990, p. 1); according to Pinker (1990, p. 14), 'social work is, essentially, a moral enterprise'; while Reamer (1999, p. 3) states: 'social work is among the most value based of all professions'; and Healy (2001, p. 101) concludes: 'value commitments and ethical principles are at the core of social work as a profession'.

This chapter will explore the nature of the ethical issues inherent in social work and how and why questions of ethics arise. It will also consider the guilt and anxiety felt by social workers and whether the blame allocated to them for outcomes of what are essentially moral decisions is justified.

The ethical, the technical and the legal

Frequently in the social work literature, values are distinguished from knowledge and ethical/moral issues from legal and technical matters. Such distinctions can be useful, as long as it is not implied that knowledge can be value free or that legal and technical decisions can be made without recourse to ethics. For example, a social worker might say, 'it is essentially a legal question whether to detain this person in hospital under the Mental Health Act'. Yet, as Braye and Preston-Shoot (1997) point out, the law is rarely clear and has to be interpreted by the social worker. The law tells us that if we make the technical (and ethical) judgement that the person concerned is suffering from a 'mental disorder' such that it is in the person's interest to be detained in hospital, then we have the legal powers to bring that about. Laws do not tell us what we ought to do, just what we can do. The laws in operation nationally and internationally themselves reflect certain values and norms in the societies where they apply, some of which we may regard as immoral – for example, in the case of laws that regulate immigration, abortion or human cloning. Most decisions in social work involve a complex interaction of ethical, political, technical and legal issues all of which are interconnected. Our values will influence how we interpret the law.

Giving another example, when asked to assess a person's eligibility for a disabled person's parking permit, a social worker might say: 'It is a technical matter to decide whether this person is eligible for a disabled person's car parking permit.' The social worker assesses the person according to the defined criteria and makes a decision using her professional skill and judgement. The social worker might only judge that moral issues were involved if she had to consider whether she ought to give the person a permit although the person did not quite meet the criteria. This is a helpful distinction between the technical and the ethical. However, a decision might be regarded as a technical one not because only technical questions of measurement and assessment were involved, but because the social worker chose to see it in that way – as she might if it were a relatively straightforward case that did not present any ethical problems or dilemmas. The process itself, assessing needs for a parking permit, is not devoid of ethical content. The criteria of need that determine who should get permits will be based on ethical judgements about social duties to reduce some of the disadvantages caused by disability or about how to distribute a scarce resource efficiently and fairly, for example. The social worker may judge that the criteria are not fair or do not result in resources being allocated to the most needy people.

In the light of this discussion, it may be useful to distinguish between ethical issues, ethical problems and ethical dilemmas as follows:

- *Ethical issues* – pervade the social work task (including what appear to be 'legal' or 'technical' matters) in that social work frequently takes place in the context of state systems of welfare premised on principles of social justice and public good and the social worker has professional power in the relationship with service users. So, although deciding whether to give a parking permit to a person with a disability in a case that is straightforward may not involve the social worker in agonising over a moral dilemma, it is not devoid of ethical content.
- *Ethical problems* – arise when the social worker sees the situation

as involving a difficult moral decision, but is clear what is the right course of action – for example, when she decides to turn down the application of a very needy person for a parking permit because this person does not quite fit the criteria.

● *Ethical dilemmas* – occur when the social worker sees herself as facing a choice between two equally unwelcome alternatives, which may involve a conflict of moral values, and it is not clear which choice will be the right one. For example, should she bend the criteria for issuing parking permits in order to help a very needy person or stick to the rules and refuse a permit to someone who really needs it? She is faced with a conflict between the interests of this individual and the public interest in having rules and criteria that apply to everyone.

Thus what is a technical matter for one person (simply applying the rules) may be an ethical problem for another (a difficult decision, but it is clear what decision should be made) or a dilemma for a third person (there appears to be no solution). It depends on how each person sees the situation, how experienced they are at making moral decisions and how they prioritise different values (see Banks and Williams, 2005 for a detailed discussion of practitioners' accounts of ethical issues, problems and dilemmas).

What are the ethical issues in social work?

In collecting examples of ethical difficulties experienced by qualified and trainee social workers in the UK and various countries in Europe, I identified four main types of issue, which frequently result in ethical problems and dilemmas:

● *Issues around individual rights and welfare* – a service user's right to make her own decisions and choices; the social worker's responsibility to promote the welfare of the service user.
● *Issues around public welfare* – the rights and interests of parties other than the service user; the social worker's responsibility to her employing agency and to society; the promotion of the greatest good of the greatest number of people.
● *Issues around equality, difference and structural oppression* – balancing the promotion of equality, with due regard to diversity; the social worker's responsibility to challenge oppression and to work for changes in agency policy and in society.
● *Issues around professional roles, boundaries and relationships* – deciding what role the social worker should take in particular situ-

ations (counsellor, controller, advocate, assessor, campaigner, ally or friend); considerations of issues of boundaries between personal, professional and political life.

Any categorisation is obviously artificial, and does not do justice to the complexity of the issues within each category and the overlap between them. Frequently there are conflicts between rights, responsibilities and interests both within and between these categories. However, this framework may be a useful starting point for exploring issues of values and ethics in social work practice. Quotations from four social workers talking about their practice may illuminate our discussion.

Rights/welfare of the individual

An 80-year-old woman, Mrs Brown, was recently referred to a social work agency by a local hospital after a fall at home. A social worker visited her in her home to assess her needs and felt that Mrs Brown was finding it hard to look after herself – her house was dirty and untidy and it was clear that she was not eating much. She lived alone and her son visited twice a week to deliver shopping. The social worker suggested that she should consider having a home care assistant to help her on a daily basis, but Mrs Brown refused categorically. The social worker commented:

> It was difficult to know how far to try to persuade or even coerce
> Mrs Brown to accept the offer of a home care assistant, or whether
> just to leave her alone and hope she would manage to survive.

Here the focus of the worker's concern is the service user's welfare. The social worker wants to respect Mrs Brown's own choices about how to live her life, yet the worker also wants to ensure Mrs Brown feeds herself properly and is checked on regularly in case she falls again. There is a conflict between the promotion of the service user's welfare and her right to make her own choices.

Public welfare

A residential social worker spoke about Sally, a 12-year-old girl who had recently come into a care home because her parents felt her behaviour was out of control. She had been having sexual relations with a 50-year-old man who supplied her with money in return for sexual favours:

The police were near to catching the man, and asked staff to lift restrictions on Sally leaving the [residential care] unit in the hope of catching him in the act. Should we have refused because we were allowing Sally to put herself at risk, or was catching the culprit and preventing further risk to herself and other girls a priority?

The social worker sees that it will be in the best interests of everyone if this man is caught, yet feels uneasy about using the young girl in this way, because of both the deception involved and the responsibility if any harm comes to Sally when she is allowed out of the care home. This case is presented as involving making a decision about whether the public interest in catching the man outweighs the deception involved and the short-term risk to Sally.

Structural oppression

A social worker visited a travelling family who had recently moved their mobile home to a site in her area. They had requested that their children attend a local playgroup. When the worker arrived to discuss how to provide financial support, she was told that the children had been refused access on the grounds that it may cause other local families to remove their children and hence threaten the viability of the playgroup. During the visit the social worker noticed that the children had been playing with an electric fire and plugs while the worker was talking to their parents:

> I realised that in another situation I may well have challenged the parents in allowing their children to play with such a dangerous appliance. Given that I felt they were being treated very shabbily by the wider community, I found it very difficult to challenge any of the ways in which they cared for their children.

The social worker is aware that the travellers are being discriminated against by both the local community and wider society. She does not want to collude in this, but is not sure how to react. This is a case of a social worker recognising she is working with members of an oppressed group, not wishing to oppress them further by challenging their standards of childcare, yet concerned about the safety of children.

Professional boundaries and relationships

A student social worker was undertaking a fieldwork placement in an agency working with families and children in the UK. A recently arrived Ethiopian woman with two young children was referred to the agency by the asylum seekers' unit in the local social services department. This woman, A., had recently been relocated to the area as part of a government policy of dispersal of asylum seekers and seemed very depressed and isolated. Her 7-year-old daughter was reported to be withdrawn and unhappy at school and both mother and daughter cried during most of the first home visit. The student also felt that the family was being subjected to 'low level racism' in the area where they lived. The student visited the family at least once a fortnight over the next three months, during which time the situation improved and mother and daughter appeared much happier. When the student's placement was due to end, she reported feeling some discomfort about how the family viewed their relationship with her:

> I was aware that A. viewed me as a friend, and although she was aware that I was a worker, when I told her that I would be finishing the placement soon she became upset. A. made a number of comments on numerous occasions asking me to visit her whenever I was in the area and invited me to her son's birthday party in four months' time. I felt that I did not deal with this effectively, as I tended to use the fact that I did not live in the same city as an excuse for not being able to maintain contact, and I felt that this blurred the professional boundaries. I found it extremely difficult to maintain these boundaries and although I felt guilty for giving the impression of being a family friend, I also felt that it would be extremely harsh to tell A. that she was a 'service user' rather than a friend.

This student obviously developed a good relationship with a very vulnerable family. As a student, she may have had a relatively small caseload and so could afford to spend time and energy with this family and to develop what was perceived (and/or desired) by A. as a close and caring relationship. This case highlights the dangers of the caring role of the social worker being misunderstood and misinterpreted by service users and the importance of clarity at the outset and honesty during the course of a relationship. This situation was still concerning the student after the placement ended and had clearly caused her to reflect on what she might have done differently, as she commented: 'I didn't sit down and explain in an honest way.'

These descriptions have simplified the issues arising in each case. In many cases, issues in all four categories arise and some of the problems and dilemmas workers face are about balancing different sets of rights, interests, responsibilities and commitments. Social work is a complex activity, with many layers of duties and responsibilities (for example to one's own moral integrity, to service users, to the agency and to society). These often conflict and have to be balanced against each other. There are no easy answers to questions such as these. They are part of the everyday life of social workers. Some will handle them more easily than others – depending on experience, moral sensitivity and their own value positions. Often it helps to discuss difficult cases with colleagues or in supervision sessions, to gain a range of different perspectives on the issues involved and possible courses of action. Short vignettes can be useful as a focus for reflection and student discussions, to encourage rehearsal of issues and actions (see Chapter 7; also Banks, 2001b, 2005; Banks and Williams, 1999).

In discussing these cases, many people would probably state that the dilemma identified in the second case (whether to respond to the request of the police) would not arise for them. For it would be clear that the strategy proposed by the police was inappropriate (it could be regarded as 'entrapment' and hence might not stand up in court) and/or unethical (it involved treating Sally as a means to an end and breached the social work relationship of trust with her). Similarly in the third account, many social workers in this situation might not pay particular attention to the children playing with the electric fire (they might notice other features of the living conditions or family interactions) and/or might not regard this as particularly dangerous. Others might be less concerned about the discrimination faced by the family or more concerned and also more aware of the role of 'cultural competence' in working with people with a range of different backgrounds and lifestyles.

In the remaining sections of this chapter we will explore how and why questions of ethics are an integral part of social work practice.

Social work as a human services profession

Social work may be regarded as a 'human services' profession along with the health care, teaching and legal professions. The social worker has special knowledge and expertise and must be trusted by service users to act in their best interests. The relationship between social worker and service user is an unequal one, in that the social worker is more powerful. Social work, therefore, along with law, medicine, nursing, counselling and other similar professions has a code of ethics designed, among other things, to protect the service user from exploitation or misconduct. Some commentators describe the social worker–service user relationship as a 'fiduciary' one – that is, based on a relationship of trust (Kutchins, 1991; Levy, 1976, pp. 55ff.).

While there are many similarities between social work and professions such as law and medicine, there are also several ways in which social work is different. Some have argued that social work is a 'semi-profession', partly because the individual autonomy of social workers is more limited than that of doctors and lawyers. Many social workers are either directly or indirectly employed by the local state; they may have a social control function and therefore their primary aim is not straightforwardly to work in the best interests of the service user. In many countries, social work is part of a 'welfare state' or at least a state-organised system of welfare, which is itself based on contradictory principles and undergoing a process of questioning and change (Roger, 2000), as is the role of the professions generally (Southon and Braithwhaite, 2000).

Social work and state welfare systems

Social work may be delivered by public, voluntary/not-for-profit or private sector organisations. Its services may be offered as part of the provision of state welfare or control or as services motivated by independent philanthropic concern or as services to be purchased directly by customers/service users. In the UK and many other western European countries, from its charitable origins in the nineteenth century, social work grew rapidly in the mid-twentieth century largely as part of a state-organised and state-funded system for distributing goods and services to meet certain types of social need of individuals, families, groups and communities and to cure, contain or control behaviour that was regarded as socially problematic or deviant. It became part of a welfare state that oversees and funds a range of other social services, including education, health, social security and housing and other public services such as the police, the army, roads and refuse collection. These are collective services, which, in principle, benefit the whole community. However, social services are often regarded as different from public services in that they are seen as a means of transferring resources to people who are dependent – through sickness, old age, childhood, unemployment or disability, for example.

Welfare states are allied to capitalist economies and have a redistributive role through taxation, compulsory social insurance and direct provision of services. They can be seen as compensating for defects in the market system in the allocation of goods and services. Even in countries like the USA and Japan with relatively weak welfare states, state social workers are employed in a range of settings from welfare offices to hospitals and courts of law.

Many commentators have analysed the nature of welfare states in terms of contradictions. Marshall (1972) saw the tensions inherent in welfare capitalism between the values of social justice and equality and the competitive individualism of the market, although he recognised that the aim of the welfare state was not to remove inequality of income, rather it was to eradicate poverty and give everyone equal status as citizens in society. According to O'Connor (1973, p. 6) welfare states have two contradictory functions in capitalist societies – accumulation (enabling private capital to remain profitable) and legitimation (of the existing economic and social order). Moon (1988, p. 12) succinctly summarises the contradictory principles upon which the welfare state is based as follows:

> The welfare state embraces the market, but at the same time seeks to limit and control it; it incorporates ideas of rights, especially rights to property and the fruits of one's labor, but asserts a right to welfare, a right to have one's basic needs met; it is based on a conception of the person as a responsible agent but recognizes as well that many of the conditions of one's life are due to circumstances beyond one's control; it is premised upon sentiments of sociability and common interest, but its very success may undermine those sentiments; it seeks to provide security, but embraces as well a commitment to liberty.

Moon suggests that this is one reason why the concept of the welfare state appears to be so vulnerable to criticism. Others might disagree that it is the contradictions per se that make it vulnerable (Offe, 1984, ch. 5), but there is no doubt that the whole concept of the welfare state – its aims, its functions, its methods and its outcomes – is the subject of questioning and criticism from various quarters, both right and left (Pierson, 1998; Roger, 2000). The economic recession of the mid-1970s gave rise to a sustained critique of state welfare provision from rightwing politicians and theorists and this was reinforced by the recession of the late 1980s/ early 1990s. First, the burden of taxation and regulation imposed on capital was claimed to serve as a disincentive to investment. Second, welfare benefits and the collective power of trade unions were said to amount to a disincentive to work. The argument has also been made from a communitarian perspective that family values and responsibilities, a sense of community and moral obligation may, in fact, be undermined by systematic state welfare provision (Etzioni, 1995, 1997). Criticisms from the left tend to focus on the ineffectiveness and inefficiency of the welfare bureaucracies, which have done little to redistribute income between classes and do not tackle the fundamental causes of poverty and unemployment. Feminist and anti-racist critiques have been increasingly vocal as many aspects of the state welfare systems have been shown to reinforce gender and race stereotyping, discrimination and oppression. The welfare state is also seen as a repressive instrument of social control (through individualising problems and distinguishing between the deserving and undeserving). These critiques have led to changes in welfare systems across the world, often resulting in an increasing role for markets, private provision and new forms of management and governance, including service user and citizen involvement (see Clarke, 2004 and Chapters 5 and 6 for further discussion).

This account of social work as part of the state-organised welfare provision is important as it helps us understand how some of the ethical issues are inherent in the role of the social worker. Insofar as social work is what Johnson (1972) called a 'state-mediated profession', it is based on contradictions and societal ambivalence. Social work contributes towards expressing society's altruism (care) and enforcing societal norms (control); it champions individual rights as well as protecting the collective good. Social workers are regarded as wimps (caring for those who do not deserve it) and as bullies (wielding too much power over individuals and families). As the welfare state is questioned, undermined and reformed, so the role of social work is also subject to question and change (Langan, 2000; Roger, 2000). While systems of state welfare vary enormously in different parts of the world, and in some countries the majority of social workers are not employed by the state, social work is very often at least partially funded and hence controlled through government sources.

Blame and guilt in social work

The position of social workers working with people who are needy and vulnerable, often at the interface between the state and civil society, means that they frequently bear the brunt of blame for certain unpalatable societal problems such as child abuse. One of the most publicised areas of social work is child protection. In this context, if a bad outcome occurs, social workers usually get the blame. A bad outcome can be either that children left at home suffer or die or that children are removed from home unnecessarily. Franklin (1989) demonstrates how the press often portray social workers either as indecisive wimps who fail to protect children from death or as authoritarian bullies who unjustifiably snatch children from their parents. Either way, the social workers are to blame. As Franklin comments:

> Press reporting of child abuse, paradoxically, rarely focuses upon the abuse of children. It quickly regresses into an attack on welfare professionals, particularly social workers who, in their turn, seem to have become a metaphor for the public sector. (Franklin, 1989, p. 1)

Social workers can be seen as symbols of state welfare, simultaneously representing two of its much criticised facets – bungling inefficiency and authoritarian repression. Although Aldridge (1994, p. 70) argues that 'social work and its vicissitudes are not singled out for vilification' by the press, it nevertheless offers a soft target when its interventions fail. Social workers, Franklin claims, seem to have a unique place among professionals in being regarded as culpable by the press for the fate of their service users. This may be partly connected with the more ambivalent and morally charged role that social workers play in society. For example, doctors treat people who are sick; and sickness might be regarded as an unfortunate state that generally affects individuals through no fault of their own. Social workers are often working with people whom society regards as 'undeserving', idle, feckless or deviant. Social workers have a control as well as a care function. It is their job to protect society from deviant or morally dangerous people; if they fail to do this job, they are committing a moral crime. Physical and sexual abuse of children, particularly by their parents, is a threat to social stability and the idea of the family as a good and caring setting. Child abuse in families, therefore, must not happen. It must either be prevented by social workers (and therefore barely exist) or not exist at all. Social workers' vilification by the press and public is partly due to their role as welfare professionals in a society that is ambivalent about state welfare. It also reflects the particular role they play within state welfare systems, which includes both the care and the control of people whom the family or other state agencies cannot help and who may be regarded as difficult or deviant.

Taking the child protection role of social workers as an example, social workers tend to feel that they should not always take the blame in cases where children are abused or die. The situation is complex: resource constraints mean that social workers cannot always provide the services required; decisions regarding how to handle children at risk are usually taken by inter-professional groups at case conferences and are a shared responsibility; assessing the nature of risk of child abuse is an uncertain art and even the most skilled and competent professionals who follow all the guidelines and procedures may find a child dies. Obviously if workers fail to follow the procedures correctly or neglect to carry out specified duties, then they are culpable. Yet if a worker does the best she can in the circumstances, surely she should not be blamed? This is certainly the line taken by Macdonald (1990) and seems to make sense to most social workers. However, this is not the view of Hollis and Howe, who claim that it is justifiable to blame social workers for bad outcomes (such as child deaths) even if they have done their well-intentioned best. Social workers must accept this as part of their role, which involves a high level of moral risk. They suggest that:

> the social worker would receive better sympathy, if her respon-
> sibility for bad outcomes was understood to be personal yet, at the
> same time, a function of the role rather than of self-evident
> personal incompetence. (Hollis and Howe, 1990, p. 548)

Their view, they suggest, helps explain why professional social workers are troubled by guilt even when they have done their best.

Hollis and Howe are, in a sense, putting social work decision-making back into the sphere of the moral, suggesting that the more comfortable retreat into the bureaucratic and technical (following procedures and making technical 'risk assessments') is not an appropriate response to public blame. Yet, in order to do this, is it necessary for Hollis and Howe to go so far as to say that social workers should always be blamed for a bad outcome? Their view depends upon accepting the premise that the outcomes of an action/decision determine the nature of the action/decision. If the child survives and thrives, the action was morally right; if the child dies, the action was morally wrong. It appears that such decisions are what Nagel (1976, p. 143) would describe as 'decisions under uncertainty', where the overall moral judgement can shift from positive to negative depending on the outcome. While we might agree that the death of a child is a negative outcome and that the social worker involved in the case might have made a technically wrong decision not to remove the child from the family, was it also a morally wrong decision? Surely not, if the social worker gained as much information as possible, assessed the risk and made the judgement that the risk to the child was low? We might even question whether the decision was 'technically' wrong. The social worker may have been right – the risk was one in a hundred and the fact that this case was that one in a hundred does not prove the social worker wrong – one might say she was unlucky. Risk assessment in social work is not a precise, scientific or straightforward business. It might be the case that the technical decision is a 'decision under uncertainty', so we would, in fact, say that the social worker's assessment was correct or incorrect according to the outcome. However, to say that it is *morally* right or wrong according to the outcome is surely going too far.

That social workers feel 'guilt' for a bad outcome is not surprising. Yet in the same way that my friends would tell me not to feel guilty for running over a young child who unexpectedly leapt out in front of my car, surely we would say the same to the social worker. We may torment ourselves by blaming ourselves and thinking 'if only I had reacted more quickly; if only I had visited the family an hour earlier', but what we should feel is regret, not guilt. I imagine Hollis and Howe would respond that the cases are not analogous. In fact, they liken the social worker to the driver of a car who nevertheless drives knowing the brakes are faulty. Had I run over the child while driving with faulty brakes, then I would have been morally blameworthy.

According to Hollis and Howe, in taking on the job of social worker, the worker knows that she is being asked to drive a car with faulty brakes. Therefore she must expect and accept moral blame when bad outcomes occur (as they inevitably will). Yet this analogy does not capture the complexity of social work practice. First, while this may not exonerate the social worker, it is important to note that it is not her job to service the car. Second, while she may be in the driving seat, there are plenty of others in the car map-reading or directing. Third, while objective observers like Hollis and Howe may claim that the brakes are faulty, the rest of society regards such a state as the norm and is certainly not prepared to pay to improve the brakes. If social workers take moral responsibility, they are, in effect, allowing others to scapegoat them and avoid taking blame and hence to avoid recognising the variety of contributing factors that caused the child's death and the need to change some of these factors. Also, if social workers always take the blame for outcomes that are largely outside their control, they become personally and professionally undermined and stressed. It may be appropriate to take some responsibility, and hence blame, but certainly not all of it. Otherwise the retreat into 'defensive' social work (following rules and procedures) becomes even more necessary and appealing as a survival strategy.

One of the purposes of this book is to enable social workers to gain an understanding of the nature of ethical decision-making and hence to feel less unnecessary guilt and blame for the outcomes of decisions and actions with which they are involved. Very often in connection with moral and ethical issues in social work (and indeed the caring professions generally) the term 'dilemma' is used. As has already been noted, a dilemma is usually defined along the lines of 'a choice between two equally unwelcome alternatives' – which seems to sum up quite well how it often feels to be a professional in a 'no win' situation. Let us imagine a child protection case, briefly outlined as follows:

> The father of a young baby has been violent to his partner (the baby's 17-year-old mother) on several occasions in the past. Recently the baby has suffered bruising three times. The mother explains that the baby fell from his cot twice and on one occasion her partner accidentally dropped him. Despite input from a social worker and health visitor, it has not proved possible to support the parents to any great extent in coping with looking after the baby. A case conference of the various professionals involved is called to consider what to do to ensure the baby is protected.

Very many factors will be taken into account during the case conference in coming to a decision about what level of intervention is necessary and possible as well as legally and ethically justified in order to protect the baby. The conference participants will be very mindful of the infringement of parental rights and the potential damage and unhappiness that may be caused if the child is removed from the family. Yet, if the child remains with the family, there is a chance that the child will suffer physical abuse from the father and may be injured or even die. The simple way to resolve the dilemma as identified here is to try to work out whether one of the alternatives is more unwelcome than the other and then act on that. Of course, members of the case conference also need to try to work out how likely it is that each of the unwelcome outcomes will occur, using various protocols and procedures for assessing and predicting risk. They might decide that it is more unwelcome (indeed, it would be tragic) for the child to die than to be unhappy.

However, let us assume that the consensus of opinion at the case conference is that it is highly unlikely that the father will seriously injure or kill the child. Participants also judge that there is scope for more intensive work with the parents to improve their parenting skills and to cope with some of pressures that may lead to the baby suffering further harm. Therefore it is decided to leave the child with the family. The professionals involved know it is a risk – a moral risk as well as a technical one – which is why the situation is described as a dilemma. There are no welcome outcomes, only less unwelcome ones; when the choice is the lesser of two evils, whichever one chooses is an 'evil'. This is a constant problem for the social workers and other professionals involved such cases. If the professionals have carefully thought through all aspects of the dilemma and made a decision to act in order to try to avoid the worst outcome, then they have acted with moral integrity.

I will return to this important issue of the guilt and blame felt by social workers and will explore further how these can be counteracted at the end of the book, in the light of the more detailed discussion of ethical and value issues in the next few chapters.

Conclusions

In this chapter, I have set the scene for our discussion of questions of ethics in social work. I have argued that ethical problems and dilemmas are inherent in the practice of social work. The reasons for this arise from its role as a public service profession dealing with vulnerable service users who need to be able to trust the worker and be protected from exploitation; and also from its position as part of state welfare provision based on contradictory aims and values (care and control; capital accumulation and legitimation; protection of individual rights and promotion of public welfare) that cause tensions, dilemmas and conflicts. The current 'crises' of the welfare state, which entail a questioning of both its legitimation function and its capital accumulation function, are increasing the tensions and dilemmas for social workers, who very often find themselves the victims of media attacks and public blame. I argued that this blame is often unjustified and it is important that social workers both understand the essential tensions in their role and consider how moral decisions are actually made in social work, in order that they are not consumed by unnecessary guilt about the unfortunate, tragic or unwanted outcomes of cases in which they have been involved.

putting it into practice

Exercise 1

Aims of the exercise – to encourage readers to identify ethical issues in their own practice and to reflect on and clarify their own ethical stance.

1. Briefly describe a situation/incident/event in your experience as a practitioner that raised ethical issues for you.
2. List the ethical issues that were raised.
3. What does your view of this situation/event tell you about the important values and ethical principles that underpin your practice as a social worker?

Further reading

Dominelli, L. (2004) *Social Work: Theory and Practice for a Changing Profession*, Oxford, Polity Press. An overview of the nature of social work, taking a global perspective, in the context of current uncertainties and challenges. Dominelli argues for a new relationship between social workers and service users based on ideas of citizenship, solidarity and reciprocity.

Smith, R. (2005) *Values and Practice in Children's Services*, Basingstoke, Palgrave Macmillan. This book offers a useful discussion of the different value positions inherent in laissez faire and interventionist approaches to child protection, an account of practice dilemmas and a framework for action.

Warnock, M. (1998) *An Intelligent Person's Guide to Ethics*, London, Duckworth. A book written by a moral philosopher, who has herself been involved in the UK public policy-making process, designed to introduce the lay person to ethical thinking covering topics such as death, birth, rights and freedom.

2 | Principle-based approaches to social work ethics

This chapter and the next will explore a number of approaches that have been or could be taken to theorising about ethics and social work. There are many ways of categorising approaches to ethics. For the purposes of this discussion, I will divide the approaches into two broad kinds: those that focus on principles of action, which will be the subject of this chapter; and those that pay more attention to the character of the moral agents and their relationships with each other, which will be covered in the next chapter. I will draw on some of the theories of ethics developed by moral philosophers and on literature in other areas of professional ethics, particularly health care, to develop ideas as yet underexplored in the context of social work. Some caution must be exercised in relating theories of moral philosophy to professional ethics. When writers on professional ethics talk of 'Kantian' or 'utilitarian' approaches, they are not necessarily taking on board the whole of the ethical theories of Kant or utilitarianism, but rather suggesting that their approaches to professional ethics have connections with some of the basic orientations to morality found in those theories. The aim of these two chapters is to point out some of these connections to help to clarify the nature of different approaches to social work ethics.

Principles

The most common approach to professional ethics is to articulate a set of general ethical principles which give guidance about how we should act. According to Beauchamp (1996, pp. 80–1), a principle is:

> a fundamental standard of conduct on which many other standards and judgements depend. A principle is an essential norm in a system of thought or belief, forming a basis of moral reasoning in that system.

It is important to distinguish a principle from a rule, which is much more specific and narrower in scope. For example, 'respect people's rights to self-determination' would count as a principle because its scope is broad, in that it applies to all people in all circumstances, whereas 'respect the rights of service users to consult files' is more specific in that it applies to people in a social work context who wish to see their files and would therefore be regarded as a rule. Principle-based theories of ethics usually construe ethical reasoning and decision-making as a rational process of applying principles and derived rules to particular cases and/or justifying action with reference to relevant rules and principles (for clear examples of such approaches in medical and nursing ethics, see Beauchamp and Childress, 2001, pp. 385–91; Edwards, 1996). We will briefly look at three principle-based approaches, the first two of which can be loosely linked with Kantian and utilitarian approaches in moral philosophy and the third with radical and anti-oppressive approaches in social work.

The number of approaches to ethics that could be covered is potentially very large, as most of the world's religions have sets of principles of right action, all of which are slightly different and often reflect major differences in worldview, including the nature and role of God/gods, human nature, moral duties, the moral law and the individual–social relationship (see Holm and Bowker, 1994; Singer, 1993). However, in this book I will focus on the kinds of principle found in the international statements on social work, which tend to be rooted in Judeo-Christian and humanistic traditions and reflect the universal human rights approach of organisations like the United Nations, as summarised in international declarations and conventions on human rights and the rights of the child. These principles, based on the assumption of the individual as the fundamental unit in society, do not reflect the religious and cultural beliefs of people in many parts of the world where the extended family, tribe or community is the focus of attention and the notion of individual rights makes much less sense. Arguably, some of the approaches to ethics outlined in the next chapter (based on qualities of character and inter-personal relationships) fit better with more communal approaches to ethics, as do elements of the radical and anti-oppressive approaches in social work, covered towards the end of this chapter (for a brief discussion of social work values and religion, see Beckett and Maynard, 2005, pp. 48–62; for a useful discussion of African-centred worldviews relevant to social work see Graham, 1999, 2002).

Respect and autonomy in the social work relationship: Kantian principles

Much of the literature on social work values and ethics has focused on lists of principles about how the social worker ought to treat the individual service user. Such lists of principles are often under-pinned by one basic or ultimate principle formulated as 'respect for persons', which, it has been argued, is the foundation of social work ethics and, indeed, any system of moral thinking (Plant, 1970). In western secular literature this principle tends to be linked with Immanuel Kant, the eighteenth-century German philosopher. However, a similar kind of 'golden rule' can be identified in many religious traditions worldwide, ranging from Judaism's 'What is hateful to you, do not do unto your fellow human' to the Sikh principle 'No one is my enemy, and no one is a stranger. I get along with everyone' (Inter Faith Network for the UK, 2004).

Kant and respect for persons

Kant formulated his principle as a categorical imperative (that is, a command that must be adhered to), one version of which is: 'So act as to treat humanity, whether in your own person or that of any other, never solely as a means but always also as an end' (Kant, 1964, p. 96). By this he meant that we should treat others as beings who have ends (that is, choices and desires), not just as objects or a means to our own ends. The individual person is intrinsically worthy of respect simply because she or he is a person, regardless of whether we like the person, whether they are useful to us or whether they have behaved badly towards us. According to Kantian philosophy, a 'person' is a being who is capable of rational thought and self-determined action, where 'rational' means the ability to give reasons for actions; and 'self-determining' entails having the ability to make decisions and acting according to one's own choices and desires. 'Respect' can be regarded as an 'active sympathy' towards another human being (Downie and Telfer, 1969, 1980).

It is this aspect of Kantian moral philosophy, the principle of respect for persons, that has been the most influential in social work ethics. It focuses on the content of morality, explicitly stating how we should treat other people. Other features of Kant's theory are also important in relation to professional ethics. He did, in fact, formulate several other versions of his categorical imperative, one of which focuses on the importance of consistency and universalisability in the form of moral judgements: 'Act only on that maxim through which you can at the same time will that it should become a universal law' (Kant, 1964, p. 88). The example of promise-keeping can be used to illustrate this point. In order to get a loan, I may be tempted to promise to repay the money borrowed, although I have no intention of doing so. The maxim I might act on in this case could be something along the lines of: 'I will make a false promise if it will get me out of difficulty.' However, if I ask whether I could consistently will that this should become a universal principle applying to everybody, Kant's answer would be 'no'. For if everybody made false promises, the whole institution of promise-keeping would collapse and there would be no basis for getting loans at all. So if I could not will that everybody should do this, then such an action would be morally wrong. It is important to stress that for Kant, making false promises is not wrong because of the consequences if everyone did so, but rather that it would be logically inconsistent to will that everyone should do it, because I would then be making a promise in a world where promise-keeping no longer existed. This highlights a very important feature of Kantian ethics, the stress on rationality and the importance of the will. According to Kant, the only good action is that which is done from a sense of duty (as opposed to inclination). We work out what is our duty through a process of logical reasoning. We are, like all our fellow human beings, rational and autonomous – that is, we are free to make our own decisions and choices; we ourselves make the moral law and give it to ourselves. However, this does not entail absolute freedom to act on desires or whims or on choices that are solely beneficial to ourselves as individuals, rather to act on principles that we could will as universal laws – what O'Neill calls 'principled autonomy' (O'Neill, 2002, pp. 73–95).

There have been numerous criticisms as well as many defences and developments of Kantian ethics (for brief summaries see Arrington, 1998, pp. 262–94; Norman, 1998, pp. 70–91; for the debate in social work see Downie, 1989; Webb and McBeath, 1989, 1990). Many of the criticisms have tended to focus on Kant's formalism (his stress on the form of moral judgements as universal-isable and consistent) at the expense of the content of morality, and on his moral absolutism (for example that lying is always wrong) and his stress on doing one's duty for its own sake as the only morally worthy motive. However, few have developed in any detail a wholly Kantian approach to social work ethics – although Bowie's (1999) application of Kantian moral philosophy to business ethics gives some idea of how it might be achieved. 'Discourse ethics', as developed by the contemporary German philosopher and social theorist Habermas, is occasionally mentioned in the social work literature (Blaug, 1995; Hugman, 2005, pp. 125–39). Discourse ethics is also a formal system, developed from Kantian ethics, based on universal principles of moral reasoning enabling us to reach consensus on generalisable maxims (Habermas, 1990, pp. 116–94). However, Habermas's theory moves on from the Kantian notion of moral agents as individuals working out their moral duties in isolation, to a recognition of the inter-subjective nature of morality, seeing universal moral principles as those that are validated in an ideal system of rational discourse, which would allow everyone concerned a 'fair' hearing and remove the distorting domination of wealth and power (see Banks, 2004a, pp. 81–2 for a brief discussion of Habermas in relation to professional ethics and the social professions).

Respect for persons and social work

In social work, as I said earlier, the main element of Kantian moral philosophy that has been influential is the principle of respect for persons that has been used to underpin a set of general principles relating to the relationship between the individual social worker and service user. The lists of principles of the social worker–service user relationship developed for social work are often adaptations or modifications of the seven principles developed by Biestek, an American Catholic priest, in the late 1950s (Biestek, 1961, first published 1957). These principles have been surprisingly influential, especially given two factors. First, Biestek did not intend them as ethical principles per se. Indeed he seemed to regard them primarily as principles for effective practice – instrumental to the social worker's purpose of 'helping the client achieve a better adjustment between himself and his environment' (Biestek, 1961, p. 12). Second, his emphasis was primarily on the voluntary one-to-one casework relationship, where the service user initiates the contact by coming to the agency and relates individually to a social worker. This is somewhat removed from the complexities of modern social work, which may include compulsory intervention within a statutory framework and work with families, groups and communities. However, since the principles have been so influential, it may be useful to summarise them here.

List 2.1 Biestek's casework principles, 1957

1. *Individualisation* is the recognition of each service user's unique qualities, based upon the rights of human beings to be treated not just as a human being but as this human being.

2. *Purposeful expression of feelings* is the recognition of service users' need to express their feelings (especially negative ones) freely. The caseworker should listen purposefully without condemnation and provide encouragement when therapeutically useful.

3. *Controlled emotional involvement* is the caseworker's sensitivity to service users' feelings, an understanding of their meaning and a purposeful, appropriate response to them.

4. *Acceptance* entails the caseworker perceiving and dealing with service users as they really are, including their strengths and weaknesses, congenial and uncongenial qualities, maintaining throughout a sense of their innate dignity and personal worth.

5. *Non-judgemental attitude* entails that it is not part of the casework function to assign guilt or innocence or degrees of service user responsibility for causation of problems, although evaluative judgements can be made about the attitudes, standards or actions of service users (that is, the caseworker does not judge service users themselves, but their behaviour).

6. *Service user self-determination* is the recognition of the right and need of service users to freedom in making their own choices and decisions in the casework process. Caseworkers have a duty to respect that need and help activate service users' potential for self-direction. Biestek stresses, however, that service users' rights to self-determination are limited by their capacity for positive and constructive decision-making, by civil and moral law and by the function of the agency.

7. *Confidentiality* is the preservation of secret information concerning the service user which is disclosed in the professional relationship. Biestek describes confidentiality as based upon a basic right of service users and as an ethical obligation for the social worker, as well as being essential for effective casework service. However, service users' rights are not absolute and may be limited by a higher duty to self, by rights of other individuals, the social worker, agency or community.

Source: Adapted from Biestek (1961).

During the 1960s and 1970s many other theorists adopted modified versions of Biestek's list of principles, often with the addition of the ultimate or basic principle of 'respect for persons' (see, for example, Butrym, 1976; CCETSW, 1976; Moffet, 1968; Plant, 1970; Ragg, 1977). A key theme running through all these principles could be identified as the Kantian theme of *respect for the individual person as a self-determining being*. It is significant that the first principle in the list, and one which was taken on board by all the other writers noted above, is 'individualisation' – the recognition of each service user's unique qualities based upon the right of human beings to be treated as individuals with personal differences. The other important principle that has also been adopted by all the other writers is 'service user self-determination' – recognition of service users' rights to freedom in making their own decisions and choices. Many of the subsequent writers did, in fact, include in their lists the basic or ultimate principle of 'respect for persons' and although Biestek himself did not include this, his principles are compatible with it. Some of Biestek's principles directly follow from this ultimate principle – not just service user self-determination, but also acceptance, non-judgementalism and confidentiality. Accepting a service user as she is, rather than stereotyping or categorising, is obviously part of respecting the innate worth and dignity of every human being. Similarly with non-judgementalism – the social worker should not judge the person as unworthy, evil or inadequate. Breaking confidence would violate the principle of respect for persons, because it would entail not respecting the service user's wishes, treating her, perhaps, as a means to an end.

Commentators on social work ethics and values in the 1980s, however, tended to be critical of the 'list approach' and the focus solely on the nature of the social worker–service user relationship. There are a number of reasons why the kind of list of principles suggested by Biestek and others have been regarded as unsatisfactory. First, such broad general principles can be interpreted variously and there are confusions both within and between writers using the same terminology. McDermott (1975) indicates, for example, that the term 'self-determination' has been defined persuasively in social work and that the favourable connotations of freedom from constraint are used to justify what amounts to a recommendation that the social worker should decide what service users' real interests are and may be justified in promoting them against their will, a tendency that can be seen in the Biestek formulation. In fact, self-determination can mean all things to all people, from maintaining that each individual should be completely free to do whatever they want (a version of negative freedom that might be associated with a libertarian interpretation of Kantian philosophy based on respect for persons), to justifying fairly large-scale intervention from the state to enable individuals to become more self-determining or self-realising (a version of positive freedom that might be associated with Hegelian or Marxist ethics). Within social work, interpretations at the negative end of the spectrum would tend to advocate freedom from restraint unless another's interests are threatened; whereas on a more positive view, a further clause is often added, 'and/or unless the person's own interests are threatened'. The concepts of principled and relational autonomy developed more recently by moral philosophers and feminist theorists (see Mackenzie and Stoljar, 2000; O'Neill, 2002) are attempts to reclaim 'autonomy' as a concept from the clutches of an extreme libertarian, individualistic and masculinist political philosophy.

Similar problems regarding meaning arise for the principles of non-judgementalism, acceptance and confidentiality. For example, Stalley (1978) argues that non-judgementalism appears to be about refraining from making moral judgements about a person's character, yet, at the same time, social workers have a responsibility to society to help service users and to maintain their own moral integrity by making moral judgements. This raises the question of where we draw the lines around these principles, which can only be answered in relation to other principles within a more systematic framework of moral beliefs and principles. This is complicated by the second difficulty arising from such lists of principles, namely, that very little indication is given of the status of the different principles. Some appear to be methods for effective practice (for example, purposeful expression of feelings), others might be regarded as professional standards (for example, confidentiality), others might be classified as general moral principles (such as self-determination) and one (respect for persons) has been characterised as the basic presupposition of any morality.

A third problem is caused by the fact that many writers do not rank the principles and no indication is given of what to do in cases of conflicting principles. We may well ask what criteria are to be used for judging whether to promote a service user's self-determination at the expense of revealing a confidential secret. Some theorists do state, following Downie and Telfer (1969), that their sets of principles follow directly from one ultimate principle, respect for persons. If this were the case, then respect for persons could be referred to in cases of conflict. However, apart from Plant (1970), and to some extent CCETSW (1976), little detail is given as to how respect for persons can actually be used to justify the other principles or how it can be used in actual moral decision-making to arbitrate between principles. While Downie and Telfer do articulate a moral system for social work based on respect for persons, they do not derive from it the kinds of principles suggested by Biestek as relevant to social work. This may not be surprising, since these principles, if regarded as moral principles, are certainly not complete for social work. Indeed, as Biestek envisaged them they were more a set of principles for effective casework, focusing on the *content of the relationship* – how the individual service user should be treated by the social worker. Insofar as moral matters were involved for Biestek, these centred around notions of individual rights/liberties, rather than the questions of social justice and responsibility, which attention to the *context of the agency* and society generally would raise for the social worker.

Promoting welfare and justice in society: utilitarian principles

More recent writers on social work ethics have been critical of the lists of principles focusing on the individual worker–service user relationship within a broadly Kantian ethical framework, pointing out that other types of moral principles also influence social work practice (Banks, 1990; Clark, 2000; Clark with Asquith, 1985; Horne, 1999; Rhodes, 1986). Social workers are not autonomous professionals whose guiding ethical principles are solely about respecting and promoting the self-determination of service users. They are employed by agencies, work within the constraints of legal and procedural rules and must also work to promote the public good or the well-being of society in general. Other types of ethical principles concerned with utility (promoting the greatest good) and justice (distributing the good(s) as widely and/or fairly as possible) are important. There may be conflicts between the rights or interests of different people – for example a parent and a child, a confused older man and his carer. Within a Kantian framework it is difficult to decide whose right to self-determination has priority. The Kantian approach also advocates always following one's duty no matter what the outcome. For example, lying is always wrong, because it would involve manipulating a person and failing to treat them with proper respect – even if by lying a life could be saved. Such an approach fails to take account of how social workers actually do behave. Very often they have to look to the consequences of their actions and weigh up which action would be least harmful/ most beneficial to a particular service user and which action would benefit most people or use resources most efficiently. This kind of ethical theory has been termed 'utilitarianism' (see Mill, 1972; Shaw, 1999).

The basic idea of utilitarianism is that the right action is that which produces the greatest balance of good over evil (the principle of utility). However, so many philosophers have added so many qualifications and modifications to enable this doctrine to capture more and more of our ordinary conceptions of morality that any discussion of what is known as utilitarianism becomes very complicated. First, Bentham and some recent philosophers equate the good with happiness (the sum of pleasures) and the bad with unhappiness (the sum of pains), espousing what has been called *hedonistic utilitarianism* (see Plamenatz, 1966; Smart and Williams, 1973), whereas others, notably Mill, claim that the good consists of other things besides happiness (for example, virtue, knowledge, truth, beauty), a view known as *ideal utilitarianism* (Mill, 1972). Second, some philosophers espouse what has been called *act utilitarianism*, which involves deciding the rightness of each action with reference directly to the principle of utility (Smart and Williams, 1973). Others advocate *rule utilitarianism*, claiming that we do in fact use rules to speed up the process of moral reasoning and decision-making and that the rules themselves are tested and justified with reference to the principle of utility (Downie, 1971). For example, we adhere to the rule of promise-keeping despite the fact that on some occasions it might produce a greater balance of evil over good, because promise-keeping as a whole generally produces good. This has often been regarded as the most plausible account of utilitarianism and not surprisingly tends to result in the articulation of rules and principles (such as promise-keeping, truth-telling, not stealing, respecting autonomy) that would also be prominent in a Kantian system. However, utilitarians would have less tendency to regard these rules as absolute in the way Kant did, they would test their efficacy against the consequences they tend to produce and they might be more willing to admit of exceptions if this resulted in greater utility.

However, the principle of utility on its own tells us nothing about whose good we should promote, that is, about the distribution of the good. If we could choose between an action that produced a large amount of good (let us assume we are talking about happiness) for two people and nothing for eight people and an action that produced slightly less total happiness, but distributed it equally between 10 people, would we choose the former? This led Bentham to introduce his proviso – everyone to count for one and no one for more than one – and to Mill's formulation of the principle of utility as the greatest good of the greatest number. Here we seem to have a principle against which conflicts between derived principles and rules (if we are rule utilitarians) or between particular actions (if we are act utilitarians) can be decided. However, as critics have pointed out, we now have two principles, in effect: utility (urging us to produce as much good as possible) and justice (as equality of treatment, urging us to distribute it as widely as possible), which themselves may conflict. As Raphael (1981) suggests, the most difficult conflicts in life are between these two principles: he gives the example of whether the government should give large grants to engineering students in the national interest (utility) or the same amount to each student for the sake of fairness (justice). This difficulty does not mean utilitarianism cannot be defended as a system of morality, but if we accept it, it does mean that it cannot be regarded as a system that is founded on one ultimate principle that can be used to decide all conflicts between other principles, rules or alternative courses of action.

Approaches to social work ethics that are explicitly and wholly utilitarian have not been well developed, partly because such approaches do not lend themselves to taking account of the personal relationship element of social work that has always been regarded as so crucial. Although Downie and Telfer (1980) attempt to develop a form of ideal rule utilitarianism for social work and medicine, insofar as they ground this in the principle of respect for persons, I would categorise it more as a combined Kantian–utilitarian approach, which will be considered later in this chapter.

Commitment to emancipation and social justice: the challenge of radical and anti-oppressive principles

Both Kantian and utilitarian theories of ethics are premised on the assumption of the human being as a freely acting individual. Individuals are the basic unit of analysis and they can make choices about how to act and hence can and should take moral responsibility for their actions for which they can be praised or blamed. These theories of ethics reflect the twin values of freedom and individualism that lie at the heart of western capitalist societies. During the 1970s a radical movement within social work developed based on a growing awareness that treating each service user as an individual, and seeing the problems faced by that person (such as poverty, homelessness, mental illness) as problems belonging to them was, in effect, 'blaming the victims' for the structural inequalities in society. Radical social work at this time tended to be based on Marxist theory (see Corrigan and Leonard, 1978), which regards humans as essentially social beings and the idea of human freedom as a myth.

The radical literature does not discuss ethics per se, and indeed Marx himself regarded morality as a 'bourgeois illusion' – part of the prevailing ideology promoted by the ruling classes to control and dominate (Lukes, 1987; Marx and Engels, 1969). Further, a key theme of radical social work (although not always expressed very clearly) is 'praxis' – the notion of 'committed action'. On this view, it makes no sense to regard values, theory and practice as separate. The radical social work approach acknowledged social workers' role as agents of social control on behalf of an oppressive state and called on them to raise the consciousness of the people they worked with, to encourage collective action for social change and build alliances with working-class and trade union organisations (Bailey and Brake, 1975; Brake and Bailey, 1980; Corrigan and Leonard, 1978; Galper 1980). Although the radical social work literature of the 1970s and early 1980s did not itself seem to influence the literature on social work values and ethics of the same period, the broadening of the understanding of oppression created by the feminist and anti-racist movements of the 1980s began to find its way into the lists of social work values in the mid-1980s. While the contributions from feminist and anti-racist theorists are often highly critical of the Marxist-inspired radical social work with its preoccupation with class at the expense of other social divisions (Ahmad, 1990; Day, 1992; Dominelli, 1997; Dominelli and McLeod, 1989; Shah, 1989), they can nevertheless be seen to have grown out of and alongside the radical social work movement of the 1970s, and the collections of articles on radical work in the 1980s included substantial contributions from feminist and black perspectives (Brake and Bailey, 1980; Langan and Lee, 1989).

While such approaches to social work have not been concerned with articulating ethical principles per se, a moral–political stance is embedded in the commitment to working for social change and the more recent literature on anti-oppressive, structural and critical social work identifies values such as equality, collectivism/community and social justice as central to emancipatory forms of social work (see, for example, Dominelli, 2002; Mullaly, 1997).

Social justice, in particular, has been stressed in social work and in its broadest interpretation also embraces equality in all its senses of equal treatment, access to services and equality of outcome or result. Social justice is based on the idea of distributing resources in society according to need (as opposed to desert or merit), challenging existing power structures and oppressive institutions and actions.

Insofar as anti-oppressive and emancipatory approaches to social work are based on structural analyses of society, we can see them as fitting into principle-based approaches to ethics, which articulate universal, abstract principles. Other versions of anti-oppressive practice may be more focused on issues of diversity and culture, including post-structuralist and discourse approaches (discussed in Chapter 3) or may balance structural and cultural approaches (critical postmodern approaches, also mentioned later in the book, see Fook, 2002; Leonard, 1997; Pease and Fook, 1999). I will continue to use the term 'radical' to refer to approaches premised on a commitment to structural social change, which includes certain versions of 'anti-oppressive', 'emancipatory', 'critical' and 'transformatory' social work.

From the point of view of traditional social work, radical approaches have been criticised for focusing less on the here and now, the immediate and pressing problems facing individuals, and more on the creation of a better society in the future. This might involve treating individual service users as a means to an end and not respecting their own current expressions of needs and wants. In the short term, Marxist and neo-Marxist approaches could be interpreted as recommending a utilitarian approach – using people as a means to an end, for the greater good of humanity as a whole. However, more recent versions of radical and transformatory social work do propose working on micro-changes at an individual and local level (Adams et al., 2005; Langan and Lee, 1989, p. 8).

'Common morality' approaches to ethics

Beauchamp and Childress (2001), in their work on bioethics, propose what they call a 'common morality' approach based on four principles. I will briefly outline how they develop this within what I identify as a 'Kantian–utilitarian' framework, before going on to consider how such an approach in social work might also include 'radical' principles based around social justice.

Kantian–utilitarian principles

The earlier discussion of Kantian and utilitarian theories of ethics suggests that neither of these can furnish us with one ultimate principle for determining the rightness and wrongness of actions. Both Kantianism and utilitarianism, being idealised theoretical systems of morality, inevitably fail to take account of certain aspects of our ordinary moral thinking. The Kantian system tends to emphasise the individual person and their rights and duties, particularly the principles of liberty and justice (as desert); utilitarianism stresses the notion of the public good, looking to the consequences of actions with respect to the principles of utility and justice (as equal treatment). Kantian ethical theory has a tendency to advocate rigidly following what is thought to be one's duty for its own sake, whereas utilitarianism focuses on amounts of good and evil in the abstract as opposed to the people who will experience the pleasure or whatever. Taken to its extreme, the Kantian doctrine might entail, for example, that in a particular case it was morally right to keep a promise even if this resulted in many people suffering (because the consequences or general utility would not be taken into account), whereas utilitarianism might entail that it was right to kill an innocent person for the good of society (because individual liberty would not be taken into account).

Insofar as Kantians and utilitarians have attempted to modify their views to account for such cases, they become less distinct, at least in practice, even though they may be unwilling to relinquish the basic emphasis of their outlook. Interestingly, in the field of professional ethics, several influential theorists have advocated an approach that combines Kantian and utilitarian principles – recognising that in our ordinary moral thinking we do, in fact, draw on both. Downie and Telfer, in their book *Caring and Curing* (1980) (which covers medicine and social work), advocate a form of ideal rule utilitarianism, based on the ultimate principle of respect for persons. They argue that the principle of utility presupposes the principle of respect for persons. This argument is elaborated in their earlier book, *Respect for Persons* (1969, pp. 38–9). Taking Mill's formulation of the principle of utility (that right actions promote happiness), they claim that the reason we organise action to maximise happiness is because happiness matters; and it is unintelligible to suppose that happiness matters unless the people whose happiness is in question matter; and to say that they matter in this way is to say that they are objects of respect. The logic of Downie and Telfer's argument may be questioned. For example, we might ask whether individual persons are the only beings capable of experiencing happiness (what about groups or animals?) and indeed whether this sense of people mattering (being valued in themselves) is equivalent to being worthy of respect (which Downie and Telfer interpret as an active sympathy towards others as rational and self-determining agents). However, the important point to note is that they develop a framework for moral thinking that combines Kantian and utilitarian principles, such as liberty, equality, utility and fraternity (Downie, 1971), although by retaining respect for persons as the ultimate principle they still seem to be propounding a foundationalist ethical theory (that is, an ethical theory grounded in one ultimate principle).

Beauchamp and Childress (2001), in contrast, in developing a principle-based approach for bioethics, explicitly eschew such foundationalist aspirations. They advocate what they call a 'common morality' theory that is both pluralistic (based on two or more non-absolute moral principles) and relies on 'ordinary shared moral beliefs' for its starting content (Beauchamp and Childress, 2001, p. 403). They advocate four principles that they claim are usually accepted by rival moral theories: autonomy, non-maleficence, beneficence, and justice. These principles have been very influential in medical and health care ethics and in other, related, fields, such as counselling (see Bond, 2000). Since a common morality approach has not been developed in any depth for social work, I will outline the four principles briefly and summarise Beauchamp and Childress's approach. The four principles are as shown in List 2.2.

List 2.2 Beauchamp and Childress's four principles of biomedical ethics

1. *Autonomy* – the obligation to respect the decision-making capacities of individual people.

2. *Non-maleficence* – the obligation to avoid causing harm to others.

3. *Beneficence* – the obligation to provide benefits and balance benefits against risks.

4. *Justice* – obligations of fairness in the distribution of benefits and risks.

Although common morality ethics relies on ordinary shared beliefs for its content, Beauchamp and Childress stress that their principles are universal standards. They make use of Rawls's (1973, pp. 46–50) notion of 'considered judgements' as a starting point for ethical theory. These are the moral convictions in which we have the highest confidence and that we believe to have the lowest level of bias. Beauchamp and Childress (2001, p. 398) give as examples judgements about the wrongness of racial discrimination, religious intolerance and political repression. However, such judgements are only provisional fixed points and are liable to revision – a process that Rawls terms 'reflective equilibrium'. This involves adjusting considered judgements so that they coincide and are rendered as coherent as possible. For example, there is a long-standing rule in medicine about putting the patient's interests first, and Beauchamp and Childress (2001, p. 398) state that this needs to be made as coherent as possible with other considered judgements about clinical teaching responsibilities and responsibilities to patients' families, for example.

Principles and rules will never be perfectly coherent and will certainly conflict. They also need to be interpreted (what meanings do they have?), specified (when and how do they apply?) and balanced (which should have priority in certain types of cases?). According to Beauchamp and Childress (2001, p. 399) 'moral thinking is analogous to hypotheses in science that we test, modify, or reject through experience and experimental thinking'. Following Ross's (1930) account of 'prima facie duties', they describe their four principles as prima facie principles – that is, we have a duty to uphold each of these principles unless it conflicts with or is overborne by another. When we face conflicts, between, say, respecting a person's request for confidentiality (autonomy) and saving that person's life (beneficence) then we have to make a judgement which involves interpreting the principles in the light of this situation, specifying how and why they apply and balancing them against each other. There is no ultimate principle or set of rules that can tell us how to do this in every possible type of case.

Kantian–utilitarian–radical principles in social work

A common morality approach as such has not been explicitly developed for social work ethics in the level of detail offered by Beauchamp and Childress for bioethics. However, in the lists of ethical principles put forward for social work in recent literature, we can detect a range of principles of Kantian, utilitarian and radical origin, which are based on different underlying assumptions about the nature of human beings and society, which have the potential for conflict and must be weighed against each other in making decisions

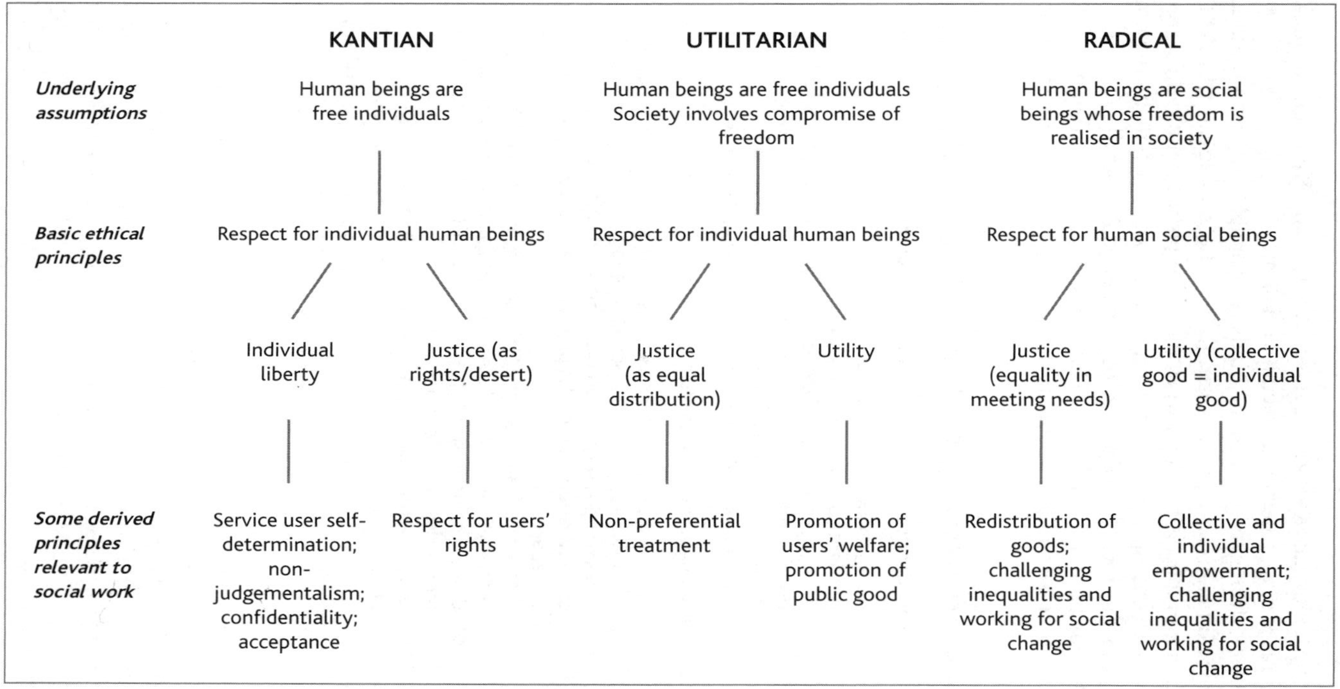

	KANTIAN	UTILITARIAN	RADICAL
Underlying assumptions	Human beings are free individuals	Human beings are free individuals Society involves compromise of freedom	Human beings are social beings whose freedom is realised in society
Basic ethical principles	Respect for individual human beings	Respect for individual human beings	Respect for human social beings
	Individual liberty — Justice (as rights/desert)	Justice (as equal distribution) — Utility	Justice (equality in meeting needs) — Utility (collective good = individual good)
Some derived principles relevant to social work	Service user self-determination; non-judgementalism; confidentiality; acceptance — Respect for users' rights	Non-preferential treatment — Promotion of users' welfare; promotion of public good	Redistribution of goods; challenging inequalities and working for social change — Collective and individual empowerment; challenging inequalities and working for social change

Figure 2.1 Kantian, utilitarian and radical approaches to social work ethics

in particular cases. Figure 2.1 summarises the Kantian, utilitarian and radical approaches to social work ethics.

One difference between the kinds of principle proposed for medicine and health care more generally and those of social work is the stronger emphasis in social work on social justice, with radical overtones. An example of such a list from the UK, drawn up by the body responsible for the validation of professional education in the late 1980s, is outlined in List 2.3. This list focuses on Kantian principles in the first part and radical/anti-oppressive principles in the second.

List 2.3 Values of social work, 1989

1. Qualifying social workers should have a commitment to:

   - the value and dignity of individuals;
   - the right to respect, privacy and confidentiality;
   - the right of individuals and families to choose;
   - the strengths and skills embodied in local communities;
   - the right to protection of those at risk of abuse and exploitation and violence to themselves and others.

2. Qualifying social workers must be able to:

   - develop an awareness of the inter-relationship of the processes of structural oppression, race, class and gender;
   - understand and counteract the impact of stigma and discrimination on grounds of poverty, age, disability and sectarianism;
   - demonstrate an awareness of both individual and institutional racism and ways to combat both through anti-racist practice;
   - develop an understanding of gender issues and demonstrate anti-sexism in social work practice;
   - recognise the need for and seek to promote policies and practices which are non-discriminatory and anti-oppressive.

   Source: CCETSW (1989, pp. 15–16)

The second part of this list contains a strong statement of radical/anti-oppressive principles, reflecting the concerns in the profession at the time. This list of values did, however, receive some criticism, both from the more traditional conservative elements in social work who questioned Part 2 of the list and from the more radical practitioners and theorists who felt that the principles outlined in Part 1 did not fit easily with Part 2. Jordan (1991), for example, points out the contradictions between the traditional or

Kantian values contained in the first part of the list (which includes variations on respect for persons, service user self-determination and confidentiality) and the statements about structural oppression in the second part of the list. The individual freedom that social workers have a commitment to promote is, he claims, dependent on the structural inequalities in society which they also have a duty to challenge. He argues that the liberal values on which the first set of principles is based (including property rights and traditional personal morality founded on notions of freedom of choice) are among the strongest intellectual defences of the privileges of wealth, whiteness, and maleness upon which structural oppression is based (Jordan, 1991, p. 8). This reasserts the point that social workers in the radical tradition had been making earlier: that the agenda of structural change conflicts with the individualist premises at the heart of social work.

This list was later superseded with a list of principles that spoke of the role of the social worker in 'counter[ing] discrimination' rather than 'anti-oppressive' practice (CCETSW, 1995). In this later list (see List 2.4) the ambiguities and tensions in the social worker's role are acknowledged and the utilitarian values of individual welfare and the public good ('assist people to increase control and improve the quality of their lives'; 'recognising that control of behaviour will be required at times') are much more evident.

List 2.4 Values of social work, 1995

In order to achieve the award of Diploma in Social Work, students must demonstrate that they:

- Identify and question their own values and prejudices, and their implications for practice;

- Respect and value uniqueness and diversity, and recognise and build on strengths;

- Promote people's rights to choice, privacy, confidentiality and protection, while recognising and addressing the complexities of competing rights and demands;

- Assist people to increase control of and improve the quality of their lives, while recognising that control of behaviour will be required at times in order to protect children and adults from harm;

- Identify, analyse and take action to counter discrimination, racism, disadvantage, inequality and injustice, using strategies appropriate to role and context; and,

---

List 2.4 cont'd

● Practise in a manner that does not stigmatise or disadvantage either individuals, groups or communities.

Source: CCETSW (1995, p. 4)

The list of values produced by CCETSW (1995) for qualifying social workers has now been replaced by the codes of practice for social care workers and employers adopted by the recently established regulatory bodies in the four countries of the UK, which also validate professional education and training (the General Social Care Council, the Northern Ireland Social Care Council, the Scottish Social Services Council and the Care Council for Wales). The codes were developed together by the four councils and take the form of codes of practice rather than simply lists of values (see GSCC, 2002). The main statements in these documents are characterised as 'standards of professional practice and conduct' and are therefore more action oriented and specific than the lists of values. List 2.5 summarises the standards for social care workers (an occupational category that includes but is broader than social work).

List 2.5 Standards of conduct for social care workers, 2002

Social care workers must:

● Protect the rights and promote the interests of service users and carers;
● Strive to establish and maintain the trust and confidence of service users and carers;
● Promote the independence of service users while protecting them as far as possible from danger or harm;
● Respect the rights of service users whilst seeking to ensure that their behaviour does not harm themselves or other people;
● Uphold public trust and confidence in social care services; and
● Be accountable for the quality of their work and take responsibility for maintaining and improving their knowledge and skills.

Source: GSCC (2002)

Clearly these statements take the form of prescriptions for action, commonly found in codes of ethics or professional practice, which will be the subject of further discussion in Chapter 4. Other configurations of principles, values and standards of varying levels of generality and specificity can be found in the literature. For example, Thompson (2000, pp. 106–23) presents an all-inclusive list of 'traditional values', which includes Biestek's complete list along with

'Rogerian' principles of respect for persons, congruence, empathy and unconditional positive regard, in addition to what he calls 'emancipatory values', namely: deindividualisation, equality, social justice, partnership, citizenship, empowerment and authenticity. Clark (2000, p. 143), identifies what he calls 'four stocks of ethical practice', also described as 'a set of definitive principles for ethically sound social work'. These are: respect (in the Kantian sense of respect for persons); justice (a comprehensive account including procedural, needs- and desert-based conceptions); citizenship (as rights to welfare); and discipline (as professional knowledge and expertise). His inclusion of 'discipline' marks his list out as different from some of the others in the academic literature, although it reflects preoccupations often found in professional codes of ethics.

Values and principles identifiable in codes of ethics vary in how they are expressed (see Chapter 4), but the recent codes of ethics produced by the professional associations in Australia (AASW, 1999) Britain (BASW, 2002) and the USA (NASW, 1999) all include as values variations on: human dignity and worth; service to humanity; and social justice, alongside values relating to qualities of character and professional standards.

It is clear from this discussion that there is not one commonly agreed and coherent set of principles for social work. However, an examination of recent literature suggests that variations on the first three broad values identified in the codes of ethics just listed could be a useful starting point for any ethical framework based on principles, as outlined in List 2.6. Although the codes use the phrase 'service to humanity' as the second value, I have reframed this as 'promotion of welfare', interpreting this broadly to include the concept of 'service'. The three codes mentioned earlier also include 'integrity' and 'professional competence' in their lists of values, but since these are of a different order to the first three values they have been excluded from List 2.6 and will be discussed later in Chapters 3 and 4, which cover qualities of character and professional standards. Although in these codes of ethics, the term 'value' is used to describe initial general statements about dignity, welfare and social justice, it is clear that these fall into the category of general principles as defined at the start of this chapter.

List 2.6 Principles of social work (drawn from recent ethical codes)

1. *Respect for the dignity and worth of all human beings.* In the context of social work, this applies particularly to service users and

List **2.6** cont'd
includes respecting and promoting individuals' and groups' rights to self-determination.
2. *Promotion of welfare or well-being* of service users and in society generally.
3. *Promotion of social justice*, including working to remove inequalities and promoting fair distribution of goods and services among people and groups.
Sources: Drawn from AASW (1999), BASW (2002), NASW (1999).

If we start to flesh out and interpret these principles then it soon becomes clear that each one contains a cluster of sub-principles and can be interpreted in many different ways. The analysis that follows is not drawn directly from the codes of ethics (which are full of repetition and inconsistencies, as is usually the case with such documents) but from a range of other literature.

Dignity and worth

This principle is reminiscent of Kant's ultimate principle of 'respect for persons', which entails treating people as ends in themselves and never as a means to an end. It stresses that every human being should be treated in this way, regardless of who they are or what they have done. In Kant's scheme the term 'person' is used rather than 'human being'. As discussed earlier, Kant regarded a 'person' as essentially a rational and self-determining being, hence parentalist or controlling treatment might be justified if someone is regarded as lacking the capacity for self-determination. The use of 'human being' rather than 'person' in this context emphases the dignity that belongs to each human regardless of their capacities.

In a social work context, 'self-determination' or autonomy is a crucial concept and has various meanings, which we have already identified, including:

- *negative* – allowing someone to do as they choose (that is, not interfering in someone's freely chosen course of action);
- *positive* – creating the conditions that enable someone to become more self-determining (that is, helping someone to reach a state where they have the capacity to see what choices might be available).

Recent emphasis on service user participation (allowing service users to have a say) and empowerment (developing service users' skills and self-confidence so they can participate more) are manifestations of negative and positive self-determination. Self-determination in both senses has been for a long time one of the fundamental principles stated for social work practice, often phrased as 'client self-determination'. Yet while the social worker may sometimes be able to focus largely on one individual service user and take on the role of advocate for the service user's rights, often the social worker has to take into account the rights of significant others in a situation. In the interests of justice, it may not always be morally right to promote the service user's rights at the expense of those of others. Furthermore, the focus of attention may not always be on individuals. The worker may be involved in working with groups of people to enable them to exert their collective rights (for example, Muslim young people in a particular neighbourhood). Implementing this broad principle relies on us interpreting the meaning of 'human being'.

Welfare or well-being

The concept of 'welfare' embraces both individual welfare (the well-being of individual people) and social welfare (which can be interpreted as the sum of all individuals' welfare or as some communal or collective well-being, not necessarily reducible to the sum of individuals' welfare). Promoting someone's 'good' or welfare is also open to interpretation depending upon what we think counts as human welfare (happiness, pleasure, wealth, satisfaction, as discussed earlier in the context of utilitiarianism) and whether we adopt our own view of what a person's welfare is or the person's own conception of their welfare. It is dependent on cultural views about what are the basic human needs and what is a good quality of life. Much of modern social work is explicitly about ensuring that the best interests of particular service user groups are served (for example, children in child protection work). Codes of ethics generally stress the social worker's duty to work in the interests of service users. Often it is the social worker's view of what service users' interests are that is regarded as important. However, as with self-determination, while in some cases it may be clear cut that it is service users' interests the social worker should be protecting, in other cases the social worker has to consider the interests of significant others and the 'public interest' (for example, through preventing re-offending in work with young offenders). These various interests may conflict.

Social justice

The principle of social justice links with both utilitarian and radical approaches to ethics. Social justice embraces the concepts of equality and justice – both of which are essentially contested and which themselves may frequently be in tension, depending on which versions are at stake. In earlier editions of *Ethics and Values in Social Work* (Banks, 1995, 2001), I separated equality and distributive justice. However, the tendency in the social welfare literature is to use 'social justice' to encompass both these principles. According to Spicker (1988, p. 125), equality means 'the removal of disadvantage'. This can be interpreted in many ways including:

- *Equal treatment* – preventing disadvantage in access to services, including treatment without prejudice or favour. For example, it should not be the case that a middle-class white man seeking resources for his elderly mother is dealt with more quickly than a black woman seeking similar support.
- *Equal opportunity* – the removal of disadvantage in competition with others, giving people the means to achieve socially desired ends. For example, a social worker may arrange for an interpreter for a Bengali-speaking woman so that she can express her needs in detail and have the same opportunity as an English-speaking service user to receive the services she requires.
- *Equality of result* – in which disadvantages are removed altogether. For example, the residential home that would provide the best-quality care for two older service users with similar needs is very expensive. The service user with a rich son who is prepared to pay is able to go to this home; the service user who is poor is not. To achieve equality of result might entail the state or some agency acting on its behalf paying the full fee for the poorer service user, or, to avoid stigmatisation, the state providing free high-quality care for all people with similar needs.

Social workers are concerned to promote all three forms of equality, although equality of treatment is much easier to achieve than equality of opportunity or result. Equality of treatment would follow logically from the principle of respect for persons. Equality of opportunity and of result require some more positive action to redress existing disadvantages and may require additional resources or changes in government policy. To aim for equality of result may require structural changes in society – challenging certain people's existing rights to wealth, property and power. It is this type of principle that underpins some of the more radical and anti-oppressive approaches to social work.

The other key concept embedded in the principle of social justice is 'distributive justice', which is about distributing goods according to certain rules and criteria. The criteria for distribution may be selected:

- according to people's already existing rights (for example, property rights);
- according to desert;
- according to need.

Although justice and equality are linked, and some commentators would argue that equality is subsumed within justice, this depends upon which concept of justice is being used. A concept of justice based on property rights or desert may result in inequality. Rawls's (1973) concept of justice, for example, is based on two principles: equality in the assignment of basic needs and resources; and social and economic inequalities only in so far as there are compensating benefits for everyone, especially the least advantaged. Distributive justice is a central focus in social work (especially for those working in the public sector) in that social workers are responsible for distributing public resources (whether they be counselling, care or money) according to certain criteria based variously on rights, desert and need. It is becoming more central in the present climate as resource allocation becomes an increasingly common role for social workers.

Conclusions

In this chapter we have explored some of the philosophical foundations of approaches to social work ethics. We have argued that principle-based approaches have tended to dominate professional ethics, that the traditional principles of the profession have been broadly 'Kantian', resting on the doctrine of respecting the individual as a rational and self-determining human being and focusing on the form and content of the social worker–service user relationship. However, the context in which social work is practised, as part of a welfare bureaucracy with a social control and resource-rationing function (based on more utilitarian values), also places ethical duties upon the social worker that may conflict with her duties to the service user as an individual. Issues relating to the fairness of the distribution of welfare and challenging existing inequalities and injustices are also very important in social work. It was argued that a combined Kantian–utilitarian–radical approach might better encapsulate our everyday moral thinking in social work and that a set of key principles might comprise respecting the dignity, worth and self-determination of human beings (particularly service users); promoting the welfare of service users and in society generally; and promoting social justice for service users and in society generally.

This is similar to the 'common morality' approach advocated by Beauchamp and Childress (2001) for biomedical ethics. However, in social work the emphasis on *social* justice is much greater. This feature of social work values distinguishes social work from other caring professions, such as medicine and nursing, with which social workers increasingly have to work in multi- and inter-disciplinary contexts. It is a source of strength and distinctiveness, while also potentially leading to conflict and misunderstanding as social workers are more committed to anti-oppressive approaches to practice and working for change in society (see Banks, 2004a, ch. 5 for a discussion of inter-professional ethics). Social workers require, therefore, not only a good understanding of the concepts and principles of social justice, autonomy and welfare, but also the confidence, commitment, motivation and skills to put these principles into practice in difficult and challenging contexts. Issues of motivation, commitment and qualities of character are the subject of the next chapter.

putting it into practice

Exercise 2

Aims of the exercise – to encourage readers to reflect critically on the stated ethical principles of social work in the light of their own value commitments.

1. List what you think are the important ethical principles *you* hold as a social worker.
2. How do they compare with those in Lists 2.1–2.6?
3. From what you have read in this chapter and elsewhere, can you suggest any modifications/additions to List 2.6?

Further reading

Boss, J. (1998) *Ethics for Life: An Interdisciplinary and Multi-Cultural Introduction*, Mountain View, CA, Mayfield. Useful background on various ethical theories, written in clear, practical style. Has photographs/drawings of key thinkers, biographical details and includes discussion of religion and cultural relativism.

Cooper, D. (1998) *Ethics: The Classic Readings*, Oxford, Blackwell. Extracts from works of key thinkers/texts, ranging from Mencius to the *Bhagavadgitá* and including Kant and Mill.

Singer, P. (ed.) (1993) *A Companion to Ethics*, Blackwell, Oxford. Edited collection of chapters covering the 'great ethical traditions' (from Indian ethics to Islamic ethics), the main ethical theories, aspects of applied ethics and debates about the nature of ethics.

3 | Character- and relationship-based approaches to social work ethics

There have been many critiques of 'principlism' in professional ethics, particularly the version developed by Beauchamp and Childress (2001), and indeed of Kantian and utilitarian approaches to morality and Marxist/neo-Marxist versions of radical social work. These critiques have come from several directions, arguing that a principle-based approach to ethics (including professional ethics) places too much stress on actions (as opposed to the person doing the action), the rational and impartial nature of ethical decision-making and the universality of principles. Principle-based approaches ignore important features of the moral life and moral judgements, including the character, motives and emotions of the moral agent, the particular contexts in which judgements are made and the particular relationships and commitments people have to each other. I will now consider three alternatives to the principle-based approach to ethics, namely: 'virtue ethics', the 'ethics of care' and 'postmodern ethics'. These have not been well developed for social work, but interest is now growing and I will discuss the extent to which they may be applicable. There are many other overlapping and inter-related ethical theories and theoretical approaches to ethics that could be covered (for example, existentialist ethics, situation ethics, ecological ethics, dialogical ethics, narrative ethics), but the purpose here is not to produce a complex 'map' – rather to explore the possibilities of a selection of approaches (for further discussion of ethical approaches relevant to social work see Banks, 2004a; Hugman, 2005).

Importance of character in the professional role: virtue-based approaches

In recent years in the field of philosophical ethics there has been a revival of virtue ethics (Crisp, 1996; Crisp and Slote, 1997; Hursthouse, 1999; MacIntyre, 1985; Slote, 1992; Statman, 1997; Swanton, 2003). While there are many versions, including that stemming from Aristotle and those contained within many religious traditions, what they have in common is a focus on the character or dispositions of moral agents as opposed to abstract obligations, duties or principles for action. One of the reasons suggested for the growing popularity of virtue ethics is the failure of the attempts of Kantians and utilitarians to articulate sets of principles for right action. As Statman (1997, p. 6) comments:

> principles are just too abstract to provide helpful guidance in the complicated situations met in everyday ethics. These situations typically involve conflicting considerations, to which principle-ethics either offers no solution, or formulates higher order principles of preference, which, again, are too abstract and vague to offer any real help.

Virtue ethics is an approach 'according to which the basic judgements in ethics are judgements about character' (Statman, 1997, p. 7). In Hursthouse's version of virtue ethics, an action is right if it is what a virtuous agent would do in the circumstances; a virtue is 'a character trait a human being needs to flourish or live well' (Hursthouse, 1997, p. 229). What counts as 'living well' or 'flourishing' then becomes an important question in deciding what characteristics count as virtues. Some virtue theorists argue that these vary according to different time periods and cultures (for example the kinds of characteristic cultivated as virtues in ancient Greece may not all be applicable in twenty-first-century Europe); others claim that there are universal virtues. Nevertheless, the kinds of disposition usually regarded as virtues include courage, integrity, honesty, truthfulness, loyalty, wisdom and kindness, for example. A virtuous person will tell the truth, it would be argued, not because of some abstract principle stating 'you shall not lie' or because on this occasion telling the truth will produce a good result, but because they do not want to be the sort of person who tells lies. Virtue ethics also tends to emphasise the particular relationships people have with each other. It could be argued that it makes more sense to see my kindness towards my best friend as arising out of the fact that I have a relationship of friendship with her, I like her and care about her, rather than from some abstract moral principle about promoting the welfare of others.

If we are to develop a virtue-based ethics for social work, we need to consider what are the virtues of the social worker. In one sense, they should reflect the virtues recognised in society at large. According to MacIntyre, the virtues are relative to culture and role; they are qualities 'the possession and exercise of which tends to enable us to achieve those goods which are internal to practices' (MacIntyre, 1985, p. 191). While not all virtue theorists adopt this kind of view, the importance of roles and the idea of virtues as relative to 'practices' or communities of practitioners are useful if we are to attempt to articulate a virtue-based theory for professional ethics. We would have to ask ourselves what it means to be a 'good social worker'. 'Good' would be internal to the role of social worker and would be defined by the community of practitioners who do social work.

There have been some recent attempts to develop a virtue-based approach in the context of professional ethics, for example, Solomon (1992, 1997) does so for business ethics and Oakley and Cocking (2001) for medical and legal ethics. There is also some interest in social work (see Houston, 2003; McBeath and Webb, 2002). As Rhodes (1986, p. 42) claims:

> a virtue-based ethics seems particularly appropriate to professions, because the ethical issues so often focus in the nature of the relationships and our responsibilities in those relationships – to the client, other colleagues, our supervisors, the agency itself. What sort of person ought a 'professional' social worker to be? What is human excellence in that context?

In her book on ethical dilemmas in social work, Rhodes (1986, p. 44) claims to have 'adopted the questions appropriate to a virtue-based ethics'. This involves, she says, considering what our relationships ought to be to our service users, the agency, the profession, colleagues and society; what sort of human excellence we are striving for; and in what social and political context. While Rhodes does give consideration to these questions, she does not explicitly or in any depth develop a virtue-based theory for social work ethics. She only briefly touches on the kinds of virtue that might be appropriate for social work, identifying from textbooks on social workers' responsibilities virtues such as compassion, detached caring, warmth and honesty. She also suggests some additional virtues that might seem appropriate: a certain kind of moral courage, hopefulness and humility (Rhodes, 1986, pp. 42–3). Beauchamp and Childress (2001, p. 30), when considering the virtues in bioethics (which they acknowledge are an important complement to principles), identify compassion, discernment, trustworthiness, integrity and conscientiousness as important, along with others that they think correspond to their key principles: respectfulness, non-malevolence, benevolence, justice, truthfulness and faithfulness.

Clark (2000, pp. 49ff.), while not mentioning virtue ethics or explicitly proposing a set of qualities or character traits, in expounding a set of eight rules of ethical practice for social work, nevertheless frames some of them in terms of the qualities of the social worker. Four of these 'rules' state that social workers should be: knowledgeable and skilful; careful and diligent; effective and helpful; legitimate and authorised. Others are framed as qualities of social work practice ('ethical practice is respectful'); social work services (services should be offered in a manner that is honest and truthful); and of professionals and agencies (as reputable and creditable). The final 'rule' is 'collaborative and accountable', which is referred to as a principle ('the principle of collaborative working') as well as a quality of professionals. Although not clearly elaborated as a set of virtues, this list demonstrates the way in which qualities or character traits are regarded as important components of social work ethics and are frequently undifferentiated conceptually from principles and rules of action.

There is no doubt, therefore, that developing certain traits of character, being a certain sort of person, is important in professional ethics, even if academic writing on professional ethics has tended to focus more attention on the articulation of general ethical principles and their use in rational moral decision-making. Indeed, many codes of ethics stress the kind of person a professional should be, as well as listing principles of ethical action, although interestingly few codes in the caring professions contain more than passing references to character traits (see Banks, 1999, pp. 15–16), which is probably a reflection of the current focus of attention towards principles and actions. Actions are more concrete and measurable than traits of character. However, the list of values of social work produced by CCETSW (1995) for the UK (see List 2.4 in Chapter 2), in addition to listing principles, also states that it is essential that social workers are honest, trustworthy, reliable, self-aware and critically reflective. Similarly the *Code of Practice for Social Care Workers*, published by the General Social Care Council (2002), which covers England, includes 'being honest and trustworthy' and 'being reliable and dependable' in its list of statements describing the standards of professional conduct and practice. In the same vein, the codes of ethics produced by the professional associations in Australia, Britain and the United States mentioned in the previous chapter include 'integrity' as a value (defined variously as comprising honesty, reliability and impartiality). In Aristotelian ethics, integrity was not regarded as a virtue per se, but as the holding together of all the virtues as a whole. In the context of professional practice, it is often used to mean holding true to the values of the profession (see Banks, 2004b for a more detailed discussion of professional integrity in social work).

These kinds of statement relate to certain views about what it means to be a professional. A virtue ethicist would argue that it is less important that professionals claim to abide by explicit sets of rules stating that they will not discriminate on grounds of religion and gender, for example, or that they will not exploit service users, than that they are particular types of people who have a disposition to act justly and in a trustworthy fashion. They are trustworthy, and therefore act in a trustworthy fashion, not because of a rule devised by their professional association, but because being trustworthy is part of what it means to be a good professional. However, this still leaves terms like 'trustworthy', 'just', 'honest', 'competent' to be explored.

Lists of virtues can be criticised in the same way as lists of values or ethical principles as being abstract and unhelpful in making everyday ethical decisions. It could also be argued that virtue ethics can be subsumed within principle-based ethics; that being a just person simply consists in a disposition to act justly. Therefore our moral judgements must be grounded in judgements about people's actions rather than their characters. This is an area that warrants much more discussion in the context of professional ethics. But it is interesting to note that even Beauchamp and Childress, often held up as the major exponents of principlism in professional ethics, introduced a whole chapter relating to virtues in professional life into the fourth edition of their textbook on biomedical ethics, acknowledging that:

> Principles require judgement, which in turn depends on character, moral discernment, and a person's sense of responsibility and accountability ... Often what counts most in the moral life is not consistent adherence to principles and rules, but reliable character, moral good sense, and emotional responsiveness. (Beauchamp and Childress, 1994, p. 462)

In their fifth edition, this chapter, renamed 'moral character' comes as a precursor to the coverage of principles.

The caring relationship between professional and service user: the 'ethics of care'

The theme of emotional responsiveness is a key element in what has been termed the 'ethics of care' or 'an ethic of care'. Okin (1994) points out that virtue ethicists, following Aristotle, have tended to focus on virtues such as justice, courage, honesty and generosity, while paying little attention to the kinds of virtue needed in order to help others. It is not surprising that the virtues put forward by Aristotle should be those appropriate to 'upper-status males', since in ancient Greece women and slaves were not regarded as citizens. Yet this tendency is also reflected in much recent work on virtue ethics where the kinds of virtue that might be displayed principally by women, for example in nurturing and caring for their families, are largely ignored. Okin suggests that such virtues might include the capacity to nurture, patience, the ability to listen carefully and to teach well and the readiness to give up one's own projects in order to pay attention to the needs or projects of others (Okin, 1994, p. 228). Since Okin wrote this article, MacIntyre (1999) has taken some account of the importance of the virtues in relation to human vulnerability and disability and dependence on others, but he does not focus on care as such.

Such qualities of caring and particular attention are the focus of the ethics of care, which has been particularly associated with feminist approaches to ethics. The majority of the proponents of care ethics have not located themselves within the virtue ethics tradition, although they do share the rejection of impartialist principle-based approaches to ethics and a concern with particularities and relationships. Although 'caring' is a quality of character, it is care as a relationship that is the main focus of attention of care ethicists. Noddings (2002, pp. 20–1) is very keen to make the distinction between care as a virtue and care as an attribute of relation. She points out that is it possible for someone to care sincerely (in the virtue sense) and yet not connect with the person receiving the care. It is this *connection* that is the focus of attention of the ethics of care.

Recent developments of care ethics owe much to the empirical work of the psychologist Gilligan (1982), who identified two 'moral voices' in her interviews with people about how they conceptualised and spoke about moral dilemmas. She contrasts what she calls the 'ethic of care' with the 'ethic of justice'. The ethic of justice refers to principle-based approaches to ethics, including Kantian and utilitarian moralities which are based on a system of individualised rights and duties, emphasising abstract moral principles, impartiality and rationality. Gilligan argues that this is a very male-oriented system of morality that does not take account of approaches to ethics that tend to be adopted by women. These would emphasise responsibility rather than duty and relationships rather than principles – an 'ethic of care'. Gilligan herself is equivocal about the extent to which an ethic of care should be regarded as a 'female' or 'feminine' ethics, although others in this tradition (such as Noddings, 1984) explicitly adopt this kind of view. It should be noted that Gilligan and some of those following her use the singular term 'ethic' both to refer to a distinctive moral voice and a more detailed philosophical approach to ethics. However, over time, with the more systematic development of these ideas, many writers are now using the term 'ethics of care'. I will use the term 'ethics of care' in this book to refer to a developed philosophical approach to ethics, retaining the term 'ethic' when referring to the work of Gilligan or others who use this term.

Many feminists have argued that it is both dangerous and misleading to attribute an 'ethic of care' (as a distinctive moral voice) simply to women (see Farley, 1993; Groenhout, 2004; Hekman, 1995; Koehn, 1998; Okin, 1994; Sevenhuisen, 1998; Tronto, 1993). It may tend to reinforce essentialist views of women as 'merely' carers and leave unquestioned whether the caring role itself can have a negative and damaging effect on carers. Furthermore, research has shown that African-Americans, for example, adopt a view of the self that stresses a sense of cooperation, interdependence and collective responsibility, as opposed to the ethic of justice (Tronto, 1993, p. 84). This is echoed in Graham's (1999; 2002) account of an African-centred paradigm for social work, which emphasises values relating to:

● the importance of interpersonal relationships;
● a holistic view of the interconnnectedness of all things;
● and the collective nature of identity.

Tronto argues that an ethic of justice represents the dominant mode of moral thinking that reflects the power structure in society and tends to marginalise and exclude the experience of women, black people and working-class and other oppressed groups. The distinction between the ethics of care and justice is summarised in Table 3.1, which is based on material from Farley (1993).

It may seem surprising, given social work's caring role, that relatively little detailed work has been done hitherto to develop a care ethics approach to social work, although articles and book chapters are now beginning to appear indicating its relevance to social work (see, for example, Banks, 2004a, ch. 3; Clifford, 2002; Hugman, 2005, pp. 67–85; Parton, 2003). Rauner (2000), who offers an empirically based account of the practice of youth development

Table 3.1 Ethics of justice and care

	Justice	Care
Key value	Justice – reinforces separation of persons	Care – represents connectedness
Appeal to	Principles	Relationships
Focus on	Social contracts, ranked order of values, duty, individual freedom	Cooperation, communication, caring, relationship between persons

workers in the USA, bases her study within a framework of care ethics, using three of Tronto's (1993, pp. 127–36) four elements of care, as follows (I have added Tronto's fourth element of 'responsibility' and also 'integrity', which Tronto argues holds all the elements together):

- *Attentiveness* – caring about, noticing the need for care in the first place – actively seeking awareness of others and their needs and points of view;
- *Responsibility* – taking care of, assuming responsibility for care – with responsibility being embedded in a set of implicit cultural practices (rather than a set of formal rules or series of promises);
- *Competence* – care-giving, the actual work of care that needs to be done – one's ability to do something about another's needs;
- *Responsiveness* – care-receiving, the response of that which is cared for to the care – remaining alert to the possibilities of abuse that arise with the vulnerability of the care-receiver;
- *Integrity of care* – according to Tronto, good care requires that the four phases fit together as a whole, which involves knowledge of the context of the care process and making judgements about conflicting needs and strategies.

There is also a growing literature in the field of nursing (for example, Allmark, 1995; Bowden, 1997; Bradshaw, 1996; Hanford, 1994; Kuhse, 1997) that may be instructive for social work. The philosophical work of Noddings (1984, 2002), who argues that the caring relationship is ethically basic, has been particularly influential in nursing where it has been used both as a basis for the nurse–patient relationship and to provide a theoretical basis for nursing ethics. According to Noddings (1984, p. 30), caring involves 'feeling with' the other, which she explicitly distinguishes from empathy (putting oneself in the other's shoes). She describes caring as 'receiving the other into myself' or what she calls 'engrossment' (p. 33). She talks of this as the 'subjective–receptive' mode in which we see clearly what we have received from the other. She distinguishes this from instrumental thinking – the use of reasoning to work out what to do once we have committed ourselves to doing something – but claims that rationality 'does not of necessity mark either the initial impulse or the action that is undertaken' (p. 36). Noddings develops her thinking in some depth to show how her approach applies to caring for strangers and for people for whom we do not naturally care; she also applies it particularly to the teacher–pupil relationship. Noddings is sceptical of the value of principles and rules per se and focuses on the concrete features of particular situations and our relationships to other people. She gives as an example Abraham's willingness to sacrifice his son Isaac: 'under the gaze of an abstract and untouchable God, he would destroy *this* touchable child whose real eyes were turned upon him in trust, love and fear' (p. 43).

While Noddings and other care ethicists have drawn our attention to important aspects of morality often lacking in traditional ethical theories, many critics question whether the ethic of care is sufficient to offer a complete account of either ethics in general or nursing ethics in particular. Kuhse (1997, p. 45) suggests that 'dispositional care' (an emotional response, a concern for the other, attentiveness and responsiveness to the needs of the other) is a necessary but not sufficient condition for nursing ethics, arguing that an adequate ethics needs impartiality or justice as well as care. It is very important that we are attentive to the nature of situations and sensitive to people's feelings, needs and the potential for hurt or harm. Kuhse gives an example taken from Blum (1988) where two adults are watching children playing in a park. One adult does not see that one of the children is being too rough and is in danger of harming the other child. The other adult, being more attentive and sensitive does, and hence sees the need to intervene. This enables the second adult to act on the principle 'protect children from harm'.

These arguments suggest that care alone is not sufficient for an adequate ethics. As Kuhse also points out, caring can sometimes be harmful (overbearing or stifling for the person on the receiving end), it can be narrow and parochial (as with the mother who only cares for her own child) and its focus only on the maintenance of the caring relationship means it can result in us failing to challenge racism or lying (if, as in an example given by Noddings, my father is racist and I put my care for him above all else). Care ethics, in focusing on the one-to-one relationship, does not help us in deciding how to allocate scarce resources between different patients or service users or in judging matters of policy. Issues of fairness, justice and equality are an equally important aspect of a professional's role – a feature that is perhaps even more evident in social work than in nursing. While Noddings has responses to these criticisms, particularly in her later work where she argues that 'caring-about' others may provide the link between caring and justice, she nevertheless regards the relationship of 'caring-for' another as the 'natural, desired state'. Caring-about is emotionally derived from caring-for and must serve caring-for to achieve its objectives (Noddings, 2002, pp. 22–3). As she herself acknowledges, she 'inverts Kantian priorities' in grounding justice in caring. This account, in effect, claims that justice is derivable from and reducible to care.

In the context of professional ethics, a reasonable conclusion to this debate might be that an ethics of care that can take into account the particularity of each situation, people's relationships with each other, cooperation, communication and caring is important and complementary to the ethics of justice, which stresses universal principles, individual freedom, social contracts and duty. An overemphasis in professional ethics on the latter may result in over-regulation, a damaging impartiality and neutrality and a mindless following of rules for their own sake. As Baier (1987) comments, justice is found to be too 'cold' and it is 'warmer', more communitarian virtues and social ideals that are being called in to supplement it. Yet, at the same time, in the delivery of publicly funded and organised services, universally applicable rules are an important part of what defines the work of the professional delivering these services. It is not expected that professional workers will give preferential treatment to their neighbour's daughter over and above a stranger, for example, although they might in everyday life. The ethics of care and justice are not mutually exclusive, but are, as Mendus (1993, p. 18) argues, 'complementary facets of any realistic account of morality'. As Hekman (1995) argues, following Gilligan's later work (Gilligan et al., 1990) justice and care are irreducible to each other. They are incommensurable (that is, cannot be measured against each other), but mutually intertwined (for further discussion see Banks, 2004a, ch. 3).

Diversity, narrative and constructionism: postmodern ethics?

This is a broad heading covering a number of recent trends in the ethics and social work literature that have been loosely labelled as 'postmodernist', but in fact cover a variety of overlapping and inter-connected themes, including, in some cases, an interest in virtue and care ethics. Postmodernism is often associated with what Lyotard (1984, p. xxiv) calls an 'incredulity toward metanarratives', that is, with a rejection of 'grand theories' designed to offer universal expla-nations or prescriptions for action. Instead, there is a focus on locally relevant 'theories' that work in specific fields or circumstances and a preoccupation with discrete and measurable competencies to perform particular tasks (Bauman, 1992, 1993, 1995, 1997; Harvey, 1990; Irving, 1994; Jameson, 1991; Leonard, 1997). In the context of ethical theories, this has led some commentators to speak of 'the end of ethics' (Caputo, 2000) – assuming ethics to be about founda-tionalist all-encompassing and universally applicable theories of right and wrong, good or bad. Others have developed a 'postmodern ethics'. Bauman (1993), for example, drawing on Levinas (1989), focuses on the particularity of the face-to-face encounter between self and other as the starting point of ethics. He speaks of the 'moral impulse' – the demand of the other person for our response.

In a social work context, a concern with fragmentation and post-modernism generally (Chambon, 1994; Chambon and Irving, 1994; Pardeck et al., 1994; Parton, 1994), diversity and difference (Briskman and Noble, 1999; Rossiter et al., 2000), small narratives (the service users' stories), constructionist accounts of knowledge and values (Milner, 2001; Parton and O'Byrne, 2000), empirical ethics, conversation and discourse analysis (see Hall et al., 1997; Taylor and White, 2000) are all evident in some recent writings.

While the approaches listed here are quite varied, and many are not explicitly about ethics, what they have in common (and this is shared with some versions of virtue and care ethics) is an 'anti-foundationalism', that is, they have abandoned the search for a secure and all-encompassing foundation for ethics (such as Kant's categor-ical imperative or utilitarian principles) and indeed for any know-ledge. All knowledges and values are particular, situated and subject to revision. The concern with diversity and difference was a reaction against not only liberal free choice approaches to ethics (such as Kantianism and utilitarianism), which failed to take full account of the power held and used by dominant groups in society to oppress and subjugate others, but also the totalising discourses of some of the universalist approaches of Marxism, feminism and anti-racist move-ments, which tended to focus on one type of oppression, such as class, ethnicity, gender, sexuality, age or ability, rather than see them as experienced together and in interaction, contributing to complex and shifting identities, particular to each individual and context. In social work, a concern with diversity (differences shared because of collective experiences) has led to a focus on the development of cultural competence, religious literacy and spiritual sensitivity, for example, as ways of ensuring that practitioners take account of diverse experiences and values and work alongside service users as co-producers of services and co-constructors of reality.

Constructionist approaches, which are becoming increasingly popular in some of the social work literature (for example, Hall et al., 1997, 2003; Parton, 2002; Parton and O'Byrne, 2000) are based on the notion that there is no objective 'reality' existing independently of the human subject, but rather humans construct reality through discourse – language and ways of thinking (see Velody and Williams, 1998). This leads to an interest in language, in particular to the examination of who has the power to define the dominant discourse and a concern with 'deconstruction' (that is showing how knowledge and values are made, changed, developed and challenged in the context of particular power relations, cultures and historical time periods). One implication of this for professional ethics is a shift from a concern with the development of abstract principles and their application to practice through a process of reasoning, towards the study of the actual practices that people perform (what social workers, service users, managers and policy-makers do on a day-to-day basis) and the interrogation of institutional frameworks, professional cultures and norms. It may lead to the empirical study of social work interactions using conversation and discourse analysis involving detailed study of turns in conversation, including examination of people's performances of moral blameworthiness, credibility, professional identity, trust and so on (see Hall et al., 1997; Taylor and White, 2000; White and Stancombe, 2003).

Parton and O'Byrne (2000) and Milner (2001) have developed 'solution-focused' approaches to social work, stressing the importance of the co-construction of selves and stories by service users and workers, advocating practice based on the role of narratives in empowering service users. One of the features of constructionist approaches in social work is a focus on the reflexivity of practitioners – developing a critical awareness of how they themselves are working within professional discourses that construct service users and social problems in certain kinds of way (as victims or as involving child abuse, for example).

At the same time, there is also a degree of wariness about some constructionist and postmodern perspectives. As Ife (1999, p. 215) comments:

> For the left to be spending its energies on analysing and deconstructing discourses of power, praising relativism and claiming that the era of unified visions of social justice is past, often in extremely inaccessible language, is very convenient for those who wish to pursue an ideology of greed, selfishness, increased inequality and a denial of human rights in the interests of free markets and private profit.

This kind of criticism applies particularly to postmodernists of the 'sceptical' variety (Rosenau, 1992, p. 15), who offer a 'pessimistic, negative, gloomy assessment' of the postmodern age as one of fragmentation, malaise and absence of moral parameters. In the social welfare field, however, the tendency has generally been to offer affirmative and critical postmodern perspectives that recognise the fragmentation and diversity of the postmodern condition, yet are open to positive political action (Leonard, 1997, is a good example).

Fragmentation of value: moral pluralism

Each of these different approaches to ethics, including the principle-based approaches discussed in the previous chapter, has something to offer, but none seems to be complete on its own. Regardless of whether we believe professional ethics is socially constructed as a discourse and a practice, there is no doubt that principles and rules play an important role and that one of the expectations of a professional is that she should act impartially, without favouritism, treating people in similar circumstances in similar ways and giving a reasoned account of why she acted as she did. Principles are frequently invoked in professional decision-making. Yet it seems equally important that professionals are educated to develop attitudes and dispositions that make them the kinds of people who are honest, trustworthy, caring, sensitive, discerning and critically reflexive and that they pay attention to the context of each situation and the special relationships they have with people. Surely all these are features of any comprehensive picture of what it is to be moral and to act morally?

Nagel (1979), noting the conflicts that often occur in moral decision-making, suggests that these arise because there are several fundamentally different types of value that cannot be ranked or weighed against each other on a single scale. Although he does not explicitly relate the types of value to particular theories of ethics, I think it is possible to make some connections, which I have included in brackets:

1. *General rights* that everyone has that function as constraints on action, such as rights to liberty or freedom from coercion (related to Kantian principles);
2. *Utility*, which takes into account the effects of what one does on everyone's welfare (a utilitarian focus on the ends of human action);
3. *Perfectionist ends* or values, that is, the intrinsic value of certain achievements or creations apart from their value to individuals (a non-utilitarian focus on the ends of human action, which may allow for religious values);
4. *Specific obligations* to other people or institutions which arise out of deliberate undertakings or special relationships (virtue and care approaches);
5. *Commitments to one's own projects* and undertakings (personal commitments which may link with the virtue ethicist's idea of desiring to be a certain sort of person or pursuing excellence. This is different from self-interest).

Nagel argues that sometimes there is only one significant factor in a moral decision – for example, personal obligation – and this makes things easier. On other occasions decision-making may be insulated against the influence of more than one type of factor – for example in the judicial system which tries to limit itself to claims of right. But on many occasions several different types of value are pertinent and according to Nagel (p. 134) there can be no system for ranking these values because they are fundamentally incommensurable:

> Human beings are subject to moral and other motivational claims of very different kinds. This is because they are complex creatures who can view the world from many perspectives – individual, relational, impersonal, ideal, etc. – and each perspective presents a different set of claims.

However, we nevertheless do have to make decisions when faced with conflicting and incommensurable claims. This requires good judgement – what Aristotle (1954) called practical wisdom, which Nagel (p. 135) claims reveals itself over time in individual decisions rather than in the enunciation of general principles. 'Good judgement' could be regarded as a characteristic of the professional. It can be linked with the notion of the reflective and reflexive practitioner, requiring, among other things, the ability to learn from and reflect on experience, a sensitivity to people's feelings and situations, attentiveness to features of situations and an ability to reason.

Nagel's argument for what Norman (1998, p. 200) calls 'moral pluralism' seems very plausible in relation to ethics in general. But how does it fit with professional ethics? Could professional ethics fall into a category like the judicial system, which, by its very nature, is artificially insulated from certain types of value? Although there has tended to be an emphasis on principles in the form of general rights based on Kantian principles, we have seen how utilitarian principles are also important and character traits and specific obligations, while underplayed, do not seem irrelevant considerations in professional ethics. Indeed, Beauchamp and Childress (2001, p. 408) while adopting 'principlism' in relation to bioethics, nevertheless reject the assumption that one must defend a single type of moral theory that is solely principle based, virtue based and so forth:

> In everyday moral reasoning, we effortlessly blend appeals to
> principles, rules, rights, virtues, passions, analogies, paradigms,
> narratives and parables ... To assign priority to one of these moral
> categories as the key ingredient in the moral life is a dubious
> project of certain writers in ethics who wish to refashion in their
> own image what is most central in the moral life.

So why do Beauchamp and Childress pay such a lot of attention to principles in their book? The answer may be because principles provide a useful framework for discussing and analysing ethical issues in professional practice. When a professional actually makes a decision in real life, a whole range of factors will influence the decision-making process (see O'Sullivan, 1999), including the emotional response of the practitioner, the quality of the relationships she has with people involved, her appraisal of the particular circumstances of the situation (including the feelings and attitudes of others involved) as well as consideration of her general obligations as a professional, the rights of the service users involved and many other aspects. However, in writing and teaching about ethical decision-making, we are not in the real life situation and cannot actually see the people concerned or feel the emotions generated. So the focus inevitably tends to be on the general principles involved in cases like this – on the rights and duties that pertain and how they might apply in such a case (a principle-based common morality approach). To examine the principle of respect for the self-determination of the service user, for example, to look at what it means or how it might apply in practice and what exceptions there might be is one way of developing critical thinking about ethical decision-making. What is important is to acknowledge that ethical principles are only one aspect of what is involved in decision-making.

What if we wanted to adopt a virtue-based approach to teaching professional ethics? If we want social workers in training to develop the virtues of honesty, respectfulness, trustworthiness or compassion, how is this to be done? It might involve examination of these characteristics and asking questions like what does it mean to say someone is honest or how would an honest person act in this situation? We might ask whether this would be very different from exploring what is meant by the principle of honesty and how we can implement it in practice. The difference would be in the focus on the character and motivation of the moral agent, which might encourage the social worker to question issues about her own identity and dispositions. But looking to what principles she espouses and when she might make exceptions to them might have a similar effect.

Surely there is something more to a virtue ethics approach than this? Virtue ethics is about developing good character and good judgement in professionals – what we might call moral education. An important part of this is having role models – teachers in both academic institutions and practice settings. According to Statman (1997, p. 13):

> Becoming a good person is not a matter of learning or 'applying' principles, but of imitating some models. We learn to be virtuous in the same way we learn to dance, to cook, and to play football – by watching people who are competent in these areas and trying to do the same.

This probably helps to explain why textbooks on practical ethics tend not to adopt a virtue-based approach, that is, because the virtues are largely developed in other ways. But I think it is possible to acknowledge the importance of developing the virtues through moral exemplars and imitating role models, while at the same time acknowledging the role of ethical principles and rules. Following Statman's analogy, if we want to improve our skills in football, apart from being coached and watching people playing, we may also read books on the principles of good football and indeed we certainly need to study the rules of the game. The two approaches are surely complementary.

The real danger of the principle-based approach would be if it degenerated into a focus on rules, which are more specific and determined than principles. And this then turns professional ethics into a matter of learning the rules and how to implement them, rather than a process of critical and responsible reflection. But principles are not the same as rules and it requires a lot of work to examine what they mean and how and when they apply. It also requires the development of the faculty of good judgement. In this sense both virtue-based approaches and principle-based approaches require the development of skilled, critical and reflective practitioners. A virtue-based approach is a good corrective to the tendency to adopt a rule-based approach to professional ethics. For we do want professionals to become more than simply rule-following automata. We do want to develop people who respect confidentiality because they are the kind of people who are trustworthy and respectful in all aspects of life, not just because their agency or professional association has laid down a rule to this effect. Yet not everyone is virtuous and it is not as easy to change or develop people's characters as it is for people to be required to follow a rule. Rules are action oriented and take account of the fact that people in professional roles should behave in certain kinds of way, even if they do this out of duty rather than because they have a disposition to act in such ways. Specific rules are needed precisely because people are *not* always virtuous and because they may *not* always have the capacity (or be trusted) to make good judgements. But the growth of more and more rules and the emphasis on the specific competencies of social workers to act in certain ways should not lure us away from the need to develop workers of integrity and trustworthiness. This is why consideration of virtue ethics is important, because it emphasises the moral education and development of the professional, as opposed to simply training in competencies for work.

Further exploration of the ethics of care and the role of emotions, such as empathy and compassion, is also important in a social work context (see Hugman 2005, pp. 48–84 for a useful discussion). Hugman (1998a, p. 95) distinguishes between caring as work (concerned with doing and action) and caring as commitment (to do with being and attitude). He argues that the tendency to focus on quantifiable aspects of welfare practice precludes caring as attitude/commitment, because caring comes to be seen solely in terms of 'the tasks performed'. The ethics of care offers a challenge to this tendency to separate attitude and action. Edwards (1996, p. 155), for example, while arguing for the primacy of principle-based ethics in nursing, nevertheless acknowledges an important role for the kinds of consideration that are of concern to care-based theorists. He points out that there is a difference between a cool detached application of principles and the implementation of principles 'in a manner which is infused with care'. These arguments do not necessarily distinguish between care as a virtue and care as a relation, as the two are inevitably intertwined. However, the emphasis on care as a relation in the ethics of care is what makes it highly relevant in the context of social work.

Recent care theorists have made connections between the ethics of care and versions of both virtue ethics and Levinas's ethics of proximity (see Groenhout, 2004). Here the focus on moral perception or sensitivity is important, generated initially in the face-to-face encounter with another person.

Conclusions

Although not well developed as yet for social work, we have discussed the merits and importance of character, relationship-based and postmodern approaches as a counterbalance to the detached rationality and impartiality of principle-based ethics. The development of good character, good judgement, reflexivity, the capacity to care and to be morally sensitive to the particularities of situations are equally important aspects of ethical being and acting. Social workers are often working with people who are very vulnerable and who enter into relationships of trust with them. It is therefore important that they take account of the unique circumstances of each person's life, recognise and respect diversity, express care and compassion, exhibit empathy and act in ways that honour the trust placed in them by the people with whom they work. In this sense, social work has a lot in common with other 'caring' professions, particularly those in the health and education field with whom social workers are increasingly working in inter-professional contexts. However, the qualities of character and nature of professional relationships appropriate for other professionals with whom social workers collaborate (such as the police) are quite different, which means that it is important to be clear in inter-professional contexts about professional values so that social workers can play a distinctive role that complements and sometimes challenges that of other professionals (this is illustrated in the analysis of the team manager's case in Chapter 7 of this book; see also Banks, 2004a, ch. 5).

putting it into practice

Exercise 3

Aims of the exercise – to consider the role of emotion, qualities of character, caring relationships and professional power in a social work encounter.

1. *Scenario* – Take as a starting point a scenario where a 15-year-old young man meets a female social worker for the first time in a local social work office. He has come to ask for help with looking after his mother, who is severely depressed. The young man is an only child and has been giving quite a lot of support to his mother since his father left home a year ago. He says he is now very worried about his mother as during the last few weeks she has been spending most of the time in bed, she is eating very little and cries a lot. He has been missing school in order to stay with her and has been advised by his neighbour to come to the social work agency for support. He bursts into tears during the meeting with the social worker.

2. (a) *Role play (in a group situation)* – Act out this scenario with two people taking the roles of social worker and the young man. The rest of the group should act as observers. The 'actors' should imagine themselves in these roles and act out a first encounter between the two people lasting about five to 10 minutes. The teacher/facilitator or another group member should take responsibility for stopping the role play at a suitable point and debriefing the two participants (asking how it felt for them in the roles and being prepared to talk them through any disturbing emotions it may have raised for them). Other group members should observe the encounter carefully, noting what the participants said, their tones of voice, body language and non-verbal communication. Questions to consider might include:

   - Did the social worker convey, perform and/or develop various qualities of character, emotions, relationships, positions or statuses (for example, trustworthiness, compassion, empathy, moral sensitivity, a caring relationship, professional distance, professional expertise)? Different observers could be asked to look for different features of the conversation.
   - How was this accomplished?
   - What emotions, positions, claims did the young man convey or perform (for example, despair, victim, hero)?
   - How was power manifested in the relationship?

   (b) *Reflection (on an individual basis, or for a group instead of role play)* – imagine yourself first as the social worker, then as the young man in the scenario described. Consider what emotions, relationships and performances might be generated by the meeting in the social work office and how you would recognise these. How might these be constrained or influenced by the agency context in which the encounter takes place and the professional role of the social worker?

3. *Discussion* – What do you think were the specifically ethical dimensions of this encounter? Does it help us to separate out the ethical aspects of a situation? Can we view this encounter both from the perspective of an ethics of care and an ethics of principles/justice? How do the two perspectives inter-relate?

Further reading

There are useful chapters on virtue and care ethics in the books listed at the end of Chapter 2, Boss (1998) and Singer (1993) and extracts from Aristotle, Mencius and St Thomas Aquinas in Cooper (1998).

Hugman, R. (2005) *New Approaches in Ethics for the Caring Professions*, Basingstoke and New York, Palgrave Macmillan. This book has useful chapters that critically evaluate the ethics of compassion, care, postmodernity and constructionism in relation to caring professions.

Taylor, C. and White, S. (2000) *Practising Reflexivity in Health and Welfare*, Buckingham, Open University Press. This book takes a social constructionist approach to analysing the discourses of professional practice in health and social care. It uses transcripts of professional conversations and documents and includes consideration of how professionals bring off and negotiate professional identity and authority.

4 | Professionalism and codes of ethics

Earlier chapters have taken for granted that social work is a recognisable occupation and that people who belong to this occupation share certain sets of common values. I have occasionally used the term 'profession' to describe social work, but not critically examined what this means. 'Professionalism' is, however, a contested and contestable concept, both in its own right and as applied to social work. So I will briefly discuss various approaches to the study of professions as a precursor to examining an important source of statements of occupational values – namely, professional codes of ethics. The discussion is illustrated through examination of codes of ethics collected from professional associations of social workers from different countries.

Professionalism, professions and power

In most western and many other countries across the world, the occupation of social work has a code of ethics, generally produced by a professional association. This is often said to be one of the defining features of a profession. In the 1960s and 1970s there was much debate about whether social work was a profession (Etzioni, 1969; Toren, 1972). The 'trait' theory of professionalism tended to be used, which maintained that, to be a profession, an occupation must possess certain characteristics. A commonly quoted list of ideal attributes of a profession was that of Greenwood (1957), which is outlined in List 4.1.

List 4.1 Ideal attributes of a profession

1. A basis of systematic theory;
2. Authority recognised by the clientele of the professional group;
3. Broader community sanction and approval of this authority;
4. A code of ethics regulating relationships of professionals with service users and colleagues;

> **List 4.1** cont'd
>
> 5. A professional culture sustained by formal professional associations.

Social work has often been termed a 'semi-profession' because while it meets some of these criteria (it has codes of ethics and professional associations), it does not meet them all fully. First, it does not rest on a firm theoretical knowledge base. It draws on theories from other disciplines and these are plural and contested (for an overview of various theories see Healy, 2005; Payne, 2005). Second, members cannot claim a monopoly of exclusive skills – many people not qualified as social workers may be performing the same or comparable tasks and the authority of social workers is often contested. In some countries, the title of 'social worker' is not protected by law and unqualified people or volunteers may be called 'social workers'. This was until recently the case in the UK, before general councils were established in 2001 in each of the four countries of the UK to register social care workers and the title 'social worker' became legally protected from 2005. Third, as was suggested in Chapter 1, there is a public ambivalence regarding the authority of social workers. Fourth, social workers' special area of competence (their function) is less well defined compared with the so-called 'fully fledged' professions and their period of training is relatively short (Toren, 1972, p. 52).

There has, however, been considerable criticism of the 'trait theory' of professionalism (see, for example, Abbott and Meerabeau, 1998; Freidson, 1994, 2001; Hugman, 1991; Johnson, 1972; Koehn, 1994; Larson, 1977). First, there is disagreement over what the essential characteristics of a profession are. Some commentators speak of 'state licensing' rather than 'community sanction'; 'esoteric knowledge' rather than 'systematic theory'; and a 'public pledge' as opposed to a 'code of ethics' (see Koehn, 1994, p. 40). Others add additional criteria such as professional education and qualification (Millerson, 1964). According to Koehn (1994), the most defensible trait of professionalism is the public pledge that professionals make to render assistance to those in need. This often takes the form of a code of ethics that new entrants to a profession pledge to uphold. Koehn argues that the other traits are neither necessary nor sufficient to define a professional.

Another criticism of the trait theory is that it is modelled on the old-established professions, such as medicine and the law, defining any occupation that does not share the same characteristics as less than a profession (Abbott and Meerabeau, 1998; Hugman, 1991).

Commentators have pointed out how the 'caring professions' such as social work, nursing and occupational therapy have tended traditionally to be women's occupations and have been denied full professional status partly for this reason. Caring work (meaning caring for others) is thought to be women's work; it has less status and prestige and does not require special knowledge and skills. Medicine is not a 'caring profession' in the same way. Although medicine is based on a commitment to serve patients, this entails caring about them, not for them. It is the nurses who care for patients in performing the everyday tasks of bathing or feeding (Hugman, 1991, p. 17).

Some have argued that an alternative set of traits is needed for the 'people work' professionals, which takes account of their location in bureaucratic settings (as 'bureau professionals') and 'their affective knowledge based on intuitive interpersonal understanding' (Holmes, 1981, p. 27). However, this would perpetuate the trait model of professionalism, which has not been very useful in developing our understanding of the nature and role of professions in society. As Johnson (1972, p. 29) points out, professions have developed in different ways depending on historical and cultural factors and variations in the role of governments and academic institutions. There is no one set of traits that uniquely characterises a profession or one set of stages that an occupational group passes through to reach this end point of 'professionalism'. There are big differences in these respects in the development of professions between countries, as well as between professions in the same country (see Burrage and Torstendahl, 1990; Siegrist, 1994).

Johnson and others following him (Hugman, 1991; Wilding, 1982) focus instead on power as a factor in the success of an occupation in achieving status in society and see professionalism as a peculiar type of occupational control whereby a community of practitioners defines the relationship between professional and service user. Hugman argues that the language of professionalism often obscures the issue of power. Talk of the service ideal, trust, expertise, colleague control and public accountability appeal to the sentiments embodied in the trait approach, but can be interpreted as 'occupational bids for status and privilege' (Hugman, 1991, p. 6). On this analysis, it would be more useful to explore the reasons behind and the process of the professionalisation of social work than to debate whether it could be regarded as a profession in the terms delineated by the trait theory. Nevertheless, although discredited, trait theory is still influential in that occupations continue to make claims to certain attributes in order to affirm their professional status. As Johnson (1984, p. 19) comments:

> professionalism has become an occupational ideal in a society in which its attainment becomes less and less likely as more and more work is routinized through technological advances and occupational practice increasingly finds its typical setting within bureaucratic organizations of various kinds.

While 'caring professionals' may not be regarded as full professionals in many people's eyes, and are given less status and recognition than, for example, doctors, they do wield considerable power, particularly over service users. And this aspect of professionalism – the claim to expert knowledge, the control not just of resources, but also the power to define the terms of the professional–service user relationship – has been strongly attacked from many quarters, ranging from right to left. Illich speaks of the 'disabling professions', arguing that power and control over individuals' lives has been taken away by so-called 'experts' such as doctors, teachers or social workers (Illich et al., 1977). Professions can be seen as protective and exclusive groups, seeking to retain power over their own occupations and hence over service users (Wilding, 1982). These criticisms may be levelled at social work, regardless of whether one regards it as an aspirant profession, a semi-profession or a profession.

Within social work in the UK, from the 1980s, there began to be talk of 'the new professionalism' entailing an increasing focus on partnership with service users and with viewing service users as experts on their own lives and issues (for further discussion of the 'new professionalism', see Chapter 5). In defending professionalism from the critiques of recent decades, Freidson (1994, pp. 9–10) talks of a professionalism reborn, 'stripped of the compromising institutions that assure workers a living, a professionalism expressed purely as dedication to the committed practice of a complex craft that is of value to others'. While this may seem an unrealistic aspiration, this notion relates to Koehn's highlighting of the importance of the 'public pledge' or service ideal of the professional, which is quite commonly expressed through a code of professional ethics.

Professional codes of ethics

It is partly an acknowledgement of the power that professionals have – particularly related to their possession of specialist knowledge and skills, which may not be fully (or even partially) understood by the service users – that professions are said to need codes of ethics. The first code of ethics produced by the British Association of Social Workers (BASW, 1975) states:

> Social work is a professional activity. Implicit in its practice are ethical principles, which prescribe the professional responsibility of the social worker. The primary objective of the Code of Ethics is to make these implicit principles explicit *for the protection of clients* and other members of society. (BASW, 1975, para. 1; emphasis added)

The term 'code of ethics' is used to cover quite a broad range of different types of code of conduct or behaviour. Millerson regards professional ethics as a part of what is entailed by 'professional conduct', dividing professional conduct into professional practice and professional ethics. This is a useful distinction, which links to a distinction that will be developed later between codes of practice and codes of ethics. Thus, according to Millerson (1964, p. 149), professional conduct consists of:

1. *Professional practice*, which relates to the adoption of schedules of uniform professional fees and charges, standard forms of contract, regulation of competition for projects;
2. *Professional ethics*, which are concerned with moral directives guiding the relationship between the professional and others; they are designed to distinguish right from wrong action. A professional ethic may be a formal code, or an informal understanding.

It is professional ethics, in the form of written codes of ethics, that concern us at present. In social work, the codes produced by national professional associations generally include a statement of the fundamental values of the profession – usually recognisable variations on the themes of respect for persons and service user self-determination and frequently some statement of commitment to the promotion of social justice and to professional integrity. This is usually followed by short statements of ethical principles, often with a brief commentary attached. Some codes are quite detailed and offer guidance about how to act in certain types of situation. Others offer general statements of principle with little commentary or specific guidance. They range in size from one to over 20 pages. Whatever the level of detail, however, probably none would claim that it aims to provide detailed guidance to social workers about how to act in particular situations. The United States' code, which is also the longest, states quite clearly in its preamble:

The *Code* offers a set of values, principles, and standards to guide decision making and conduct when ethical issues arise. It does not provide a set of rules that prescribe how social workers should act in all situations. (National Association of Social Workers (NASW), 1999, p. 2)

In attempting to counter criticisms of the first code of ethics proposed for the British Association of Social Workers, Rice argues that a code of ethics should not attempt detailed guidance and those who expect this misunderstand the nature of such a code. Those critics who say that the code of ethics will be of no use to a social worker 'confronted by conflicts about Mrs X, with agency Y' are, he claims, seeking a particularity of rules and of guidance 'that would become a substitute for ethical reflection, not a stimulation and illumination of it' (Rice, 1975, p. 381). He continues:

A code of ethics creates the spirit and standard of ethical reflection in that community [of social workers] of ideals, skills and practical concern. A code, over-precise and detailed, would undervalue the professional community. (ibid.)

This point is also echoed by Watson (1985) in his reflection on the purpose of the BASW code of ethics 10 years after its introduction and by other commentators on codes of ethics (Banks, 1998a, 1998b, 2004a; Clark, 1999; Harris, 1994; Jackson, 1994).

Why have a code of ethics?

Although it is often assumed that a code of ethics is a key hallmark of a profession (if one follows the 'trait theory'), Millerson argues that the presence or absence of a code of conduct does not signify professional or non-professional status:

Some occupations require greater control than others, due to the nature of the work involved. Some need a severe, comprehensive code, others do not. Need for a code depends upon the professional situation. (Millerson, 1964, p. 9)

Millerson (pp. 151–3) identifies the factors determining the need for introducing a code of ethics as follows:

1. *Type of practice* – a professional working alone in a non-institutional practice would need the guidance of an ethical code much more than an individual in an institutional setting.
2. *Nature of the practice* – if it is based on a so-called 'fiduciary' rela-

tionship between the professional and the service user, especially trust involving life and property, there is more need for a code.

3. *Technique involved* – if the technique is complex, a code may be necessary to remind the professional to provide the best possible service to the user.

4. *Technical comprehension by service users* – where the service user cannot be expected to understand the professional's work, a code is required for the protection of the service user.

5. *Contact with the service user* – if contact is distinct, direct and personal, then it is open to possible abuse, owing to its intimacy. A code therefore protects both professionals and service users.

6. *Duty towards the service user* – when there is a single service user, the duty needs to be clearly defined by a code. With multiple service users there is less chance of hiding responsibility (for example, as with the teacher's responsibility to the child, parents, school authorities, the community, in different ways and for different reasons all at once).

Factors that particularly apply in the case of social work relate to its fiduciary nature (2); the level of comprehension of the service user (4) – although this may be less to do with the complexities of the techniques than service users' lack of knowledge of social workers' powers and legal duties; and the fact that it involves direct, personal contact with the service user, often involving the service user giving confidential information (5). The other factors – a non-institutional setting, working with single service users and using complex techniques – may apply in social work practice, particularly in non-statutory work in private practice or in specialisms such as family therapy. However, in public sector, generic social work, they tend not to apply.

Millerson then goes on to look at the elements that determine the possibility of actually introducing an ethical code. He concludes that it is easier to introduce a code where there is a single form of training leading to qualification, where the professionals concerned are mainly involved in one type of work and where they work for many employers in a strongly organised and registered profession. Given these factors, it may seem surprising that there are codes of ethics for social work, particularly in countries where social work is not a registered profession and social workers are involved in many different types of activity. However, apart from the factors mentioned here in connection with determining the need for a code of ethics, there are perhaps several other reasons why social work has developed codes of ethics that relate to our earlier discussion of professional status and power:

1. Social work is aspiring to be a 'full profession' with comparable status to, say, medicine and the law. Therefore, it is felt to be important to have this feature of professionalism to demonstrate professional status and integrity to the public. It can be seen as part of a move towards becoming recognised as a profession. As Wilding (1982, p. 77) suggests: 'Codes of ethics are political counters constructed as much to serve as public evidence of professional intentions and ideals as to provide actual behavioural guidelines for practitioners.'
2. Equally important, a code of ethics may help to generate a sense of common identity and shared values among the occupational group. It may be as much about internal recognition as external. Given that social workers are quite fragmented in terms of the variety of types of work they do and the settings in which they operate, the code of ethics and the values upon which it is based may be the one feature that is held in common.

Form and content of codes of ethics

In order to study in more depth the nature of codes of ethics in social work, the codes of ethics that were lodged on the website of the International Federation of Social Workers (www.ifsw.org) were consulted in January 2005. The professional associations in membership of IFSW without codes on the site were contacted requesting a copy of their codes of ethics, if they had them. At this time 88 associations were in membership of IFSW.

Copies of codes of ethics have been obtained from 31 associations in the countries listed in Table 4.1. When no reply was received from an association contacted in 2005 and I had a copy of their code that was sent in 1999 (the date of my survey for the previous edition of the book), this code has been used. It is possible that a significant proportion of those associations not responding did not reply because they did not possess a code of ethics. However, the request for information was written in English and a much higher proportion of English-speaking countries and those where English is a common second language replied. So the information from the codes that were obtained cannot be said to be representative of social work worldwide. It simply serves to illustrate our discussion of the nature and purpose of codes of ethics. It is also important to note that these codes of ethics are those produced by *professional associations* for social workers. In some countries where social work is regulated by law, a statutory regulatory body may issue a code of ethics or its equivalent, (for example, Conselho Federal de Serviço Social (1993) in Brazil or the General Social Care Council (2002) in England), which may be the only code in existence or may be additional to the code produced by a professional association. In other countries, the current or previous statement of ethical principles produced by the IFSW, designed as a generic document to promote ethical awareness and reflection in the national member organisations, may be in use (IFSW, 1994; IFSW/IASSW, 2004), as is the case in Finland, where the professional association, Talentia, refers its members to IFSW (1994).

Table 4.1 List of codes of ethics of national professional associations

Country	Name of association	Date of code	Date received/ downloaded
Australia	Australian Association of Social Workers (AASW)	1999	2005
Austria	Österreichischer Berufsverband Diplomierter Sozialarbeiterinnen (OBDS)	2004	2005
Britain	British Association of Social Workers (BASW)	2002	2005
Bulgaria	Bulgarian Association of Social Workers	1999	2005
Canada	Canadian Association of Social Workers (CASW)	1994	2005
Croatia	Croatia Association of Social Workers	2004	2005
Czech Rep.	Sociálních Pracovníku České Republiky	1995	1999
Denmark	Dansk Socialrådgiverforening	1997	2005
France	Association Nationale des Assistantes de Service Social (ANAS)	1994	2005
Germany	Deutscher Berufsverband für Soziale Arbeit e. V. (DBSH)	1997	2005
Greece	Hellenic Association of Social Workers	n.d.	2005
Hong Kong	Hong Kong Social Workers Association (1998)	1998	1999
Iceland	Stéttarfélag íslenskra félagsráðgjafa	n.d.	2005
Ireland	Irish Association of Social Workers (IASW)	1995	2005
Italy	Ordine Nazionale Assistenti Sociali (ONAS)	1998	2005
Japan	Japanese Association of Social Workers, et al.	2004	2005
Luxembourg	Association Nationale des Assistantes d'Hygiène Sociale, Assistantes Sociales et Infirmières Graduées du Luxembourg	1995	2005
Netherlands	Nederlandse Vereniging van Maatschappelijk Werkers (NVMW)	1999	2005
New Zealand	New Zealand Association of Social Workers (NZASW)	1993	2005

→

Table 4.1 cont'd

Norway	Fellesorganisasjonen for Barnevernpedagoger, Socionomer og Vernepleiere (FO)	1998	2005
Portugal	Associação dos Profissionais de Serviço Social (APSS)	1994	2005
Romania	National Federation of Social Workers in Romania	2004	2005
Russia	Russian Union of Social Educators and Social Workers	2003	2005
Singapore	Singapore Association of Social Workers	n.d	2005
Slovakia	Asociácia Sociálnych Pracovníkov na Slovensku (ASPS)	1997	1999
S. Africa	South African Black Social Workers' Association (SABSWA)	n.d.	1999
Spain	Consejo General de Colegios Officiales de Diplomados en Trabajo Social y Asistentes Sociales, España	n.d	2005
Sweden	Akademikerförbundet SSR	1997	2005
Switzerland	Association suisse des professionnels de l'action sociale (ASPAS)	1999	2005
Turkey	Association of Social Workers in Turkey	n.d.	2005
USA	National Association of Social Workers (NASW)	1999	2005

Taken as a whole, the codes of ethics show a great deal of variation. This is immediately obvious in terms of their length, which ranges from the one-page document produced by the South African Black Social Workers' Association (SABSWA, n.d.) to 27 pages from the USA (NASW, 1999). They also vary in the level of detail included, especially the extent to which they discuss professional practice issues such as guidance or rules on advertising, charging fees, service user access to records and service user participation in research. However, the majority of codes, not surprisingly, have many similarities. The SABSWA code is the only one that takes the form of an oath ('I swear ...'). Most others start with a list of values and/or principles, which generally include variations on: respect for the unique value of the individual person; service user self-determination; social justice and professional integrity. There is a growing trend for the codes to become longer over time and many now have sections discussing the responsibilities of the social worker under several headings – those to service users, agency, colleagues, society and profession.

One of the reasons for the similarities between the codes of ethics is that the professional associations exchange their codes and may adapt or adopt aspects of another code if they are judged to be

appropriate. For example, the British code of 2002 is heavily deriv-
ative of the Australian code of 1999 and the Luxembourg code is
very similar to the 1981 version of the French code. Many countries
have, in fact, adopted codes of ethics that are versions of the current
or past statement on ethics of the International Federation of Social
Workers, modified slightly to refer to their own countries, for
example Portugal (Associação dos Profissionais de Serviço Social
(APSS), 1994) and Spain (Consejo General de Colegios Officiales
de Diplomados en Trabajo Social y Asistentes Socialies, España,
n.d) or included the IFSW principles and standards as part of their
own code, for example, Norway (Fellesorganisasjonen for
Barnevernpedagoger, Socionomer og Vernepleiere (FO), 1998) and
New Zealand (New Zealand Association of Social Workers
(NZASW), 1993). Many codes have been recently revised or created
in the mid- to late 1990s and early 2000s. The Russian code (Russian
Union of Social Educators and Social Workers, 2003) explicitly
acknowledges a debt to the ethical guidelines of associations in
Australia, Denmark, Finland, Great Britain, Lithuania, Poland and
the USA. The code produced by the National Federation of Social
Workers in Romania (2004) draws heavily on the US code, as does
that of the Association of Social Workers in Turkey (n.d.). These two
factors – that some countries have used codes developed elsewhere
and slightly modified or adapted them and that some versions of
codes are much more recent than others – means that differences in
the form and content of the codes do not necessarily reflect current
differences in social work practice, its legal basis or cultural norms
in the various countries. Even the code produced by the Bulgarian
Association of Social Workers (1999), which explicitly states that it
has been 'worked out with a view to the traditional Bulgarian
values', follows a fairly standard format covering the various professional responsibilities of the social worker.

In some cases, the codes of ethics have remained virtually the
same with minor revisions and slight changes of wording and format
over several decades. Others have changed significantly in style and
content. For example, the Akademikerförbundet SSR (1997) code
for Sweden is a completely different document from that of 1991.
The majority of the document now comprises a background discussion of ethical issues and potential conflicts, with a very short set of
ethical guidelines at the end. The Irish code (Irish Association of
Social Workers (IASW), 1995) has also changed its style and is more
succinct and general (a double-sided A5 sheet) than its earlier
version. These, however, are exceptional, with the overall trend

being for codes to become gradually longer and more detailed over the years (the NASW code for the USA is a very good example of this, having expanded from a nine-page booklet in 1990 to a 27-page booklet in the 1999 version). As the codes become longer, they try to take account of the complexity of the ethical issues in social work. The code of the British Association of Social Workers (BASW), when first introduced in 1975 and in subsequent editions, stated in its preface (quoted earlier) the importance of the code for the protection of clients. In the latest version of the code (BASW, 2002), the preamble includes reference also to obligations to employers, colleagues and society and to the rights of social workers.

The codes are predominantly principle based as opposed to character based, with a greater emphasis on Kantian-type rights and duties than on utilitarian principles. However, many codes do make some reference to characteristics or qualities of workers ('virtues' in the ethical terminology). For example, the US code states that the principles and standards must be applied by 'individuals of good character' (NASW, 1999, p. 4) and the Slovakian code mentions 'honesty' as important (Asociácia Sociálnych Pracovníkov na Slovensku (ASPS), 1997, para. 1.D). The Hong Kong code has one statement referring to the characteristics of workers as follows: 'The social worker should maintain honesty, integrity and responsibility in professional practice' (Hong Kong Social Workers Association, 1998, p. 6); while the Russian ethical guidelines speak of the importance of the 'unselfishness' of the social worker (Russian Union of Social Educators and Social Workers, 2003, para. 4.6). Many codes list 'integrity' as a core value of social work – a consistent feature of the Australian and US codes from the late 1980s. The South African Black Social Workers' code talks of serving the profession with 'dignity, honour, diligence and faith' and being 'conscientious, sincere and unselfish' (SABSWA, n.d.). However, this code is very different in style, format and tone to all the others, explicitly taking the form of a one-page oath, rather like the Hippocratic oath in medicine. The Swedish document, in its discussion of ethics in social work (not in its brief 'guidelines in professional ethics'), refers on occasion to character traits. For example, a meeting between people in a public setting is described in terms of 'empathy, respect, responsibility, commitment, trust, prudence, equality, modesty and sincerity' (Akademikerförbundet SSR, 1997, p. 4) and later 'moral maturity' is defined in terms of 'compassion, respect, veracity, attention to detail, humility, bravery and generosity' (p. 5). As noted earlier, the Swedish document is unusual in that it largely comprises discussion about ethical issues with only a very short set of guide-lines, in the form of principles, at the end. It makes the only refer-ence in any of the codes to 'love' as a 'central theme within ethics' (p. 2):

> Morals lack a deeper personal basis without experience of values and love. Ethics purely under subjects such as rational egoism, obedience, group pressure or care of one's own conscience is not sufficient, as they have not been touched by love and seriously discovered the other individual and the value of one's own life.

As this brief discussion indicates, there are some interesting differences between codes, which may arise for many reasons, including national law, culture and attitudes towards the welfare state and the role of social work, as well as the composition of the committees responsible for drafting the codes. Yet there are also some very striking similarities. The majority of codes start with an initial statement of 'ethical principles' (Romania), 'general princi-ples' (Netherlands), 'basic values and beliefs' (Hong Kong), 'guiding principles' (Singapore), values and principles (Australia, Japan) or 'philosophy' (Canada) that tend to include statements about respecting the unique value and dignity of every human being, promoting service user self-determination, working for social justice and maintaining professional integrity. We will now discuss some of these values and principles in turn, before looking at the extent to which codes separate out the duties or responsibilities of social workers to various parties (such as service users, employers, colleagues) and whether they cover professional practice issues such as advertising and setting fees.

Service user self-determination

Most codes make reference to the promotion of service user self-determination in their statements of general principles (although the term 'client' rather than 'service user' is found in many codes). The codes vary, however, in the extent to which this principle is devel-oped in the further guidance or principles of practice through, for example, talking of social workers promoting 'full involvement and participation of people using their services' (IFSW/IASSW, 2004) or making efforts to build cooperation and mutual understanding with service users (Akademikerförbundet SSR, 1997, para. 7). In some codes, most notably the very lengthy code for the United States Association, explicit statements about service user participation and control are not included over and above the general statement about social workers fostering maximum self-determination on the part of service users. There is little evidence of positive commitment to empower service users, more a concern that their rights should be protected (negative freedom). However, at the end of the code, under the heading of 'social and political action', a statement is made about the social worker acting to expand choice and opportunity for all persons (NASW, 1999, para. 6.04(b)).

While the general emphasis of most codes is, as Briskman and Noble (1999, p. 57) point out, on 'individual choice, minimising structural disadvantage and diversity', there is nevertheless some subtle variation in the way 'self-determination' is presented. Many talk simply in terms of respecting and promoting service users' rights to make their own choices (negative and positive self-determination, as discussed in Chapter 2). However, the Dutch code speaks in terms of recognising 'clients' responsibility to decide on their own actions' (NVMW 1999, p. 10) and the code of the Association of Social Workers in the Czech Republic states: 'The social worker leads his [sic] clients to the consciousness of self-responsibility' (Sociálních Pracovníku České Republiky, 1995, para. 2.1.1). The use of the term 'responsibility' moves the emphasis away from enabling people to exercise their rights and more towards encouraging them to recognise their responsibilities, for themselves and for others in society. The South African Black Social Workers' Association code has another interesting twist in talking about people's rights to 'make their own decisions in conducting their lives within the framework of the standards of behaviour accepted by society' (SABSWA, n.d., para. 4). Although this probably reflects the reality of social work practice in most countries, it is generally not stated in this explicit way in most codes, which tend to be idealistic and dwell little on the constraints of the social and economic context within which social work is practised.

Social justice

Since the late 1990s, emphasis on social justice is becoming more apparent in codes of ethics. The 1994 version of the Australian Association's code stood out at the time with its emphasis on the social worker's proactive commitment to social justice, which was said to be 'co-equal with the attainment of fulfilment for the individual' (Australian Association of Social Workers (AASW), 1994, p. 1). The most recent version of the code (AASW, 1999, para. 3.2) states:

The social work profession holds that each society has an obligation to pursue social justice, to provide maximum benefit for all its members and to afford them protection from harm.

Even if 'social justice' is not mentioned explicitly, many codes include statements such as that found in the Swiss code about 'denouncing and reducing injustices' (Association suisse des professionnels de l'action sociale (ASPAS), 1999, p. 5) or as in the Norwegian code, that social workers are expected to:

reveal structures and systems which contribute to inequalities, social injustice and oppression and to work to modify and change such structures and systems. (Fellesorganisasjonen for Barnevernpedagoger, Socionomer og Vernpleiere (FO), 1998, p. 17, para. 2.2)

This statement from the Norwegian code, which featured in previous versions of the International Federation of Social Workers code, is found in many codes that either adopt with minor modifications or are loosely based on the IFSW code.

The New Zealand Code discusses the 'dual focus' of social work and affirms that its members are fully committed to both enabling service users to find solutions to their problems and changing the structures of society (NZASW, 1993, p. 1). This may well be the intention in some of the other codes, but it is certainly not stated as clearly in any of the others, where statements such as 'a social worker shall maintain the best interest of the client as the primary obligation' (Canadian Association of Social Workers, 1994, p. 9) imply that the social worker's first responsibility is to the welfare of the individual service users.

The New Zealand code is also distinctive in that it contains a separate 'Bicultural Code of Practice', which affirms the right of the Maori people to independence. The code of ethics is in three parts: 'Principles' (based on the IFSW principles current at the time, with minor modifications); 'The Social Worker's Ethical Responsibilities' (which give more detail about specific responsibilities to clients, agencies, society and so on); and the 'Bicultural Code of Practice' (which is based on the same IFSW principles as the first part of the code, but with significant changes). The bicultural code calls on social work organisations and workers to 'acknowledge and support the whanau [the extended family] as the primary source of care and nurturing of its members' and 'recognises the rights of Maori clients to have a Maori worker' (NZASW, 1993, p. 17). Social workers are called upon 'actively and constructively [to] promote change in those organisations that operate from a monocultural base' and it is suggested that 'monocultural control over power and resources needs to be relinquished so that Maori can achieve liberation' (p. 18). Briskman and Noble (1999) regard the New Zealand code as a good example of a code that attempts to accommodate difference and diversity and offers some direction for change. They see this as a possible model for reformulating codes in the light of diversity and otherness, unlike most other codes with their 'global assumptions' and tendency to discuss all social workers and service users as having the same concerns and occupying the same political positions in society.

There is no doubt that the Maori people have a very significant position in New Zealand society, recognised in the Treaty of Waitangi, which explains why the New Zealand Association felt concerned to acknowledge this in its code of ethics. Yet this does not fully explain the decision to have a separate 'bicultural code' relating specifically to Maori people, rather than integrating those principles into the first part of the code. If we pursue the recognition of 'diversity and otherness' as suggested by Briskman and Noble, there seems no reason why there should not be a proliferation of separate codes for social work with different groups. Their starting point, a 'critical postmodernist' approach, would more logically lead to the abandonment of codes of ethics as such, since, however specifically they are targeted, their format is inevitably prescriptive and general (relating to 'all Maori people', for example).

Professional integrity

Most codes also lay great stress on what is often termed 'professional integrity'. Indeed, this could be said to be the whole purpose of a code of ethics – to affirm publicly the commitment of members of the profession to a set of values and to act consistently in a manner befitting their knowledge and status in society (see Banks, 2004b for a more detailed discussion of professional integrity). In those codes that identify 'integrity' as a core professional value (for example, AASW, 1999; BASW, 2002; NASW, 1999), this is associated with qualities of character such as honesty, trustworthiness, reliability and impartiality. In many other codes, integrity is framed in terms of actions, which include professionals taking responsibility for their actions and ensuring they are in line with the code, a commitment to the continuing development of their knowledge and skills, not using their special knowledge and skills for inhuman purposes, not abusing the relative powerlessness of the service user through having sexual relationships, not bringing into disrepute the good name of the profession through malpractice and monitoring and challenging agency policies and practices that may be contrary to the ethical code.

However, the codes vary in the extent to which they clearly and unequivocally state that the professional code must take priority over agency rules and procedures. For example, the Canadian code states: 'If a conflict arises in professional practice, the standards declared in this code take precedence' (CASW, 1994, p. 7), whereas the other codes simply call upon social workers to work for the creation in employing agencies of conditions that will support and facilitate social workers' acceptance of the obligations of the code.

Range of duties

Some codes are also much clearer than others about the potential for conflict between different principles and duties (for example, duties to the agency or to society as opposed to the promotion of the service user's interests). The 1994 version of the International Federation of Social Workers code, which was very influential in that many countries adopted or adapted it, includes a separate section entitled 'problem areas', which itemises areas of potential conflicting interests and also mentions the problems of the dual function of social worker as carer and controller. This is perhaps the clearest statement about the potential for conflict of all the codes. However, the 1994 version of the IFSW code, partly no doubt because it is intended to apply universally, does not give any guidance regarding how to solve such conflicts. An increasing number of codes, although not that produced by IFSW, probably for the reasons just mentioned, are actually laid out in a format that itemises in turn the social worker's responsibility to service users, colleagues, employers and employing organisations, the profession and society. The US code is a good example of this and many others are also laid out in this way, although some do not separately itemise responsibility to society. This does seem a very helpful format, because it acknowledges that the social worker has a range of duties to a variety of interest groups.

Professional practice issues

Fewer codes cover professional practice issues such as advertising or the participation of service users in research. However, recent revisions of some codes are moving in this direction – for example, the British code was completely revised in 2002 (BASW, 2002) and is now a much longer and more detailed document and includes a special section on ethics in research. Some codes are very lengthy and go into a lot of detail on issues such as advertising, fees or the use of videos. The most detailed is the US code, where in the section on 'Ethical Standards' statements of the following specificity can be found:

> Social workers should not discuss confidential information in public or semipublic areas such as hallways, waiting rooms, elevators, and restaurants. (NASW, 1999, para. 1.07(i))

As was noted earlier, the US code has gradually grown over the years. For example, the section on confidentiality and privacy consists of five relatively short statements in the 1990 version of the code. In the 1999 version, the equivalent section comprises 18 statements, some of which are of paragraph length. The Netherlands code of 1999 explicitly itemises the revisions made since the first 1990 code, which include new rules relating to confidentiality, in particular dealing with service users' records and providing information about service users to other organisations. In explaining these additions, comments are made that: 'Society is becoming ever more complex' and 'The privacy of clients has been placed under increasing pressure'. A separate chapter is also included in the latest version of the Netherlands code to take into account 'partnership agreements, where all participants contribute their own objectives, codes of conduct and methodologies' (NVMW, 1999, p. 7).

The Canadian code is also relatively detailed, giving some very specific guidance including, for example, a detailed specification of the knowledge and skills it is the social worker's duty to possess, when educational degrees can be cited, what to do when disclosure of confidential information is required by order of a court and how the self-employed social worker should disclose charges at the beginning of a relationship. It is at this point that codes of ethics, or statements of general principles and general guidance, begin to merge into what we earlier called 'codes of practice'. Some codes state nothing about matters such as advertising of qualifications or setting reasonable levels of fees; others make some general statements, but not at the level of detail of the some of the items in the Canadian and US codes.

Obviously issues about fees and advertising are pertinent in countries where private practice is commonplace. Elsewhere, it may not be thought necessary to include these matters in a code of ethics, although it is noteworthy that the most recent British code (BASW, 2002, para. 6.3.3) features a small section on 'independent practice'. The extent to which such detailed codes of practice are appropriate and enforceable will also depend upon whether the profession of social work is legally recognised in a country and whether the professional association (or some other regulatory body) has established committees and procedures for hearing complaints, making investigations into breaches of the code and disciplining members through fines, suspension or termination of membership. For example, the Swiss code includes a section on the 'application of the code', outlining procedures in cases of infringements of the code and the measures and sanctions that can be taken by the Association's commission on professional ethics. Attached in a pocket at the back of the Netherlands Association's code is an eight-page booklet of 'Regulations for Disciplinary Procedures'. It is reported that the Netherlands Association set up a professional register of social workers in 1990 'as part of the professionalisation of social work' (NVMW, 1999, p. 4). This suggests that the disciplinary procedures can be used to strike people off the register. This appears to be the role of the professional associations in many countries where the title of qualified social worker is legally protected. However, in the UK, separate regulatory bodies (general councils that are funded by the state) have been established to take on the function of registration and regulation of social care workers (which is broader than social work) and have developed 'codes of practice' for both employees and employers that can be used for disciplinary purposes (see, for example, GSCC, 2002).

'Professional autonomy' and codes of ethics in bureaucracies

'Professional autonomy', that is, the power of professionals to make their own considered decisions and judgements based on their expertise and ethical values, is a feature traditionally associated with professionalism. Several codes of ethics explicitly refer to this, including the Netherlands code, which stresses that 'social workers have to shape and guard their own professional autonomy' (NVMW 1999, p. 8). This point is also made in the Italian code:

The profession is based on ethical and scientific foundations, on technical–professional autonomy, on independent judgement, on personal knowledge of the profession and on personal consciousness of the social worker. The social worker has the duty to defend his/her autonomy from pressure and conditioning. (Ordine Nazionale Assistenti Sociali, 2002, para 1.6)

Similar sentiments are expressed in the codes from Luxembourg (Association Nationale des Assistantes d'Hygiène Sociale, 1995, art. 24) and France, with a specific stress on the fact that social workers should not agree to practise in 'conditions that compromise the quality of their interventions' (Association Nationale des Assistantes de Service Social, 1994, art. 7) and should assume 'responsibility for the choice and application of techniques concerning their professional relationships with people' (ibid., art. 22). However, the majority of codes are not so explicit, perhaps because it has long been acknowledged that professional autonomy for social workers is less than that of some other professions and is declining, as is the case for all professions.

Social work is frequently practised in bureaucratic organisations, and there is a tension between the ideal of professional autonomy and the reality of a rule-governed, hierarchical structure. As Toren states:

One of the main features of a bureaucratic organisation is that the work of its members is directed by a set of universalistic rules and procedures. These can be maintained only if the work done is specific and routine; the helping professions, and in particular social work, are neither. (Toren, 1972, p. 57)

She argues that the approach of social workers to service users (which would be in accordance with the codes of ethics as well as their education and training) is to treat them as whole people, taking account of all of their needs; and also to see them as unique – in which case there will always be special circumstances or exceptions to the rule. So the primacy of the ethical code, which professionals are supposed to apply according to their own judgement, is challenged by the clearly defined organisational rules and supervision or line management of a bureaucracy.

While there is obviously some truth in this, it may be questioned whether the distinction is as clear and straightforward as has been made out. We might question whether doctors working in a state-funded hospital or a lawyer employed by a large law firm are really completely autonomous or free of control from their superiors

(Toren, 1972, p. 53). Talcott Parsons (1959) outlined a system of dual authority that could be applied to a hospital: the administrative system that is concerned with the organisation as a whole – patient numbers, financial matters, recruitment of staff; and the operative system that is concerned with implementing the organisation's goals, that is, treating patients. A hospital could be characterised as what Mintzberg calls a 'professional bureaucracy'. Mintzberg makes quite a useful distinction between what he calls 'machine bureaucracies', which rely on authority of a hierarchical nature, and 'professional bureaucracies', which allow for participative decision-making by the 'frontline' staff with less hierarchy imposed over them (Mintzberg, 1979). In professional bureaucracies standardisation or quality of output is not controlled by direct supervision, but by 'professional' standards, learnt through training and experience and regulated by professional bodies and peer pressure from outside any one organisation. Individual staff work largely autonomously with little need for direct supervision. Examples might be universities, hospitals, social work and other human service agencies (Bloxham, 1993).

However, while it may be appropriate to describe many of the organisational settings in which social work is practised as professional bureaucracies, arguably social workers do not have as much control over their own work or as much professional respect and status as doctors or university lecturers; also the structures in which many state social workers still work are traditionally quite hierarchical and rule bound. While it may be argued that the concept and practice of 'supervision' in social work is as much about personal development and support in an emotionally demanding job as it is about management, close supervision is nevertheless enshrined in social work and it is largely carried out by people in a managerial role (although usually qualified social workers). It could still be argued that there is less scope for social workers employed in bureaucratic organisations to retain as large a degree of professional autonomy as other professionals such as doctors who also work in bureaucracies or as social workers working in less bureaucratic structures in small independent or private agencies. This would seem to imply that there might be less scope for retaining professional identity and upholding the code of ethics as a primary obligation to the profession. There are changes taking place in the management and structure of social work in Britain and in other countries that are resulting not only in more responsibility being devolved to social workers (for example by managing budgets) but also in the centralising and proceduralising of more of the tasks undertaken by social workers (see Banks, 2004a; Exworthy and Halford, 1999; Harris, 2003; Hugman, 1998b; Langan, 2000; Malin, 2000). The implications of this will be discussed later.

It may be more useful to explore those aspects of a professional's practice that are controlled, by whom and how, than to try to categorise professions in terms of which are autonomous and which are not. Toren argues that the encounter between the social worker and service user is usually not observable and is therefore not directly controllable, which allows the social worker a great degree of autonomy in relation to contacts with service users. Yet many other aspects of the job are much more controlled, such as the distribution of resources and services to users. It is these aspects of the job that are subject to bureaucratic procedures as opposed to professional standards. This is reflected in the fact that most codes of ethics are more concerned with how the social worker should treat the individual service user than they are with prescribing how resources should be allocated between service users, which might seem to be an agency or governmental matter.

Yet, while, in theory, it may be possible to separate the pure encounter with the service user from the bureaucratic controls and procedures of the agency, in practice, it is the rules of the agency that define who is to be regarded as a service user and provide the context in which the social worker operates. They already define the *person* who approaches the social work agency for help or who is approached by the agency offering help, surveillance or control, as *a service user* and the kind of help that can be given or control required. Within this context, the social worker has some freedom to treat the service user in the way she thinks fit. Yet this is limited, and is being even further limited in many countries as governments and social work agencies develop many more sets of procedures and rules regarding how to carry out the work. This trend is happening not only in social work, but also in the older established professions of medicine and the law, as part of a challenge to the autonomy and power of professionals and a de-professionalising process. There is also a trend towards the fragmentation of social work into specialisms and multidisciplinary work, which again tends to result in a loss of professional identity. This was noted by Thérèse Rossel at a European seminar in 1990 when she commented on:

> the movement towards the administrative decentralisation of social
> services on the one hand; and the introduction into work and to

projects or programmes of notions such as multidisciplinary and community development. (IFSW, 1990, p. 27)

She suggested that these changes were responsible for 'the fragmentation of the profession, and the dangers of a loss of identity'. The International Federation of Social Workers recommended therefore:

> that to develop, at an European level, the values on which social work depends in our respective countries constitutes a professional obligation, articulated in the International Code of Ethics. This code is the proper expression of values which must, here and now, guide social work and social action. (IFSW, 1990, p. 29)

The code of ethics is seen to be a unifying factor that may help to hold together the profession at a time of fragmentation. Yet, equally, it could be argued that professional codes of ethics may become increasingly irrelevant if this trend continues and the occupational identity of 'social worker' begins to crumble. We noted earlier Millerson's view that it is difficult to introduce a code of ethics if there is not one main dominating kind of work. If there are many different specialisms (child protection, community care, mental health, family therapy, welfare rights, case management) in different agency settings (public, private, independent, not-for-profit), this may mean there is an even greater need for a code of ethics to hold the profession together, while at the same time it becomes more difficult to maintain the code as important, relevant and a primary source of moral guidance. Certainly there will be very different codes of practice and arguably the agency rules and procedures will be more influential than a set of general moral principles published by the professional association.

How useful are codes of ethics?

Some commentators are sceptical about the value of codes of ethics. This is not just because of their link with the evolution of an occupation towards professional exclusivity and elitism (Wilding, 1982). Downie and Calman (1994), when examining codes of ethics in health care, identify a number of limitations:

1. The codes tend to imply that professionals are given their ethics, whereas it is at least as true that professionals bring with them their own individual values.
2. Many aspects of welfare and caring work are not expressible in

terms of rules or duties – for example, the cultivation of certain attitudes such as compassion.
3. Codes tend to be exclusive to one profession, whereas welfare and caring work are now increasingly provided by multidisciplinary teams.
4. Codes assume an exclusive professional–service user relationship, with the professionals doing the best they can for the individual service users; this ignores the pressing economic considerations in welfare and caring work.
5. Codes assume a consensus on values both within the professions and their public. But it is doubtful whether this still exists, as professions are fragmented and service users are increasingly demanding that services are delivered in terms of their own values rather than those of the professions.

As Downie and Calman (1994, p. 268) comment:

> To the extent, then, that professions are now expected to work *through* the community rather than *on* it, the position of codes of ethics has shifted from the centre of professional life to the margins.

Indeed, many social workers are also rather sceptical about the value of a code of ethics. How useful a code of ethics is depends upon what one wants to use it for. While many of Downie and Calman's criticisms are very valid, we need to recognise that a professional code performs a number of different functions, one of which may be an attempt to maintain professional power and identity at a time when these are threatened. We have already noted that there are a number of reasons why a profession may have a code of ethics, including:

1. to contribute to the 'professional status' of an occupation;
2. to establish and maintain professional identity;
3. to guide practitioners about how to act;
4. to protect service users from malpractice or abuse;
5. to discipline and regulate the profession.

The first two reasons relate to the occupation of social work as a whole and are about perceptions and identity rather than directly about practice. They are about how the outside world sees social work and how social workers view themselves. Of course, if it is effectively to fulfil the first two aims, the code must relate to social work practice and be known about by members of the profession. But such a code can be quite general in nature; indeed, it is probably helpful if it is general – consisting of statements of values or general moral principles that can be accepted by all members of the occupation. It is this kind of function that the International Federation of Social Workers sees for its code at a time of change and fragmentation within the occupation. Arguably, this is also the main role played by many of the more general codes, such as those produced by the Irish or Swedish Associations, discussed earlier. In some countries where social work and professional associations have recently been established, with new codes (for example Croatia, the Czech Republic, Slovakia), these codes may also be short and general – more akin to mission statements. Nevertheless, there are also some more recently written codes that are moderately long and include some detailed matters of professional practice, for example those produced by the professional associations in Bulgaria, Romania and Russia.

However, most of the codes include other aims or purposes, particularly (3) guiding social workers and (4) protecting service users. How effectively can they do this? If social workers are looking for detailed guidance on how to act in particular situations, then they will usually be disappointed. As was stated earlier, this would both be impossible, given the complexity of social work practice, and would also contradict a key feature of what it means to be a professional – namely that education and a commitment to a set of values enable professionals to make their own (autonomous) informed and considered judgements on professional matters. If the code of ethics were to be turned into a detailed rulebook, then the social worker would merely have to follow it unthinkingly and there would be no room for discretion and judgement.

By the same token, while recognising that ethical codes cannot and should not be detailed rulebooks, it could be argued that they frequently consist of a set of principles of such a general nature as to be open to wide interpretation and are therefore useless in guiding practice. It was suggested in Chapter 2 that service user self-determination, for example, could be interpreted as meaning anything from leaving the service user completely alone to justifying parentalist intervention to increase the service user's capacities for self-determined action. To be successful in their aims of guiding practitioners even in a general way, the codes probably need to be related more clearly to practice than many in fact are. One way of doing this is to ensure that the general value statements are discussed and analysed during the course of social work education and training and related to the daily practice of social work. Otherwise, the codes of ethics are left hanging in a vacuum or sitting in a drawer unused and unusable. Another way in which they can be related to practice is by including codes of practice alongside the codes of ethics (as is the case with the Canadian code). The problem with the development of more detailed codes of practice at a national level by the professional association alongside the codes of ethics is that they can be over-prescriptive and do not allow for variations in work contexts and service user groups in which some of the 'rules' or guidance may not apply. While it may be appropriate for the Law Society in Britain to devise detailed codes of conduct relating to the minutiae of fees or advertising, in social work such a project seems much more problematic.

What is happening, however, is that most agencies are developing their own codes of practice for dealing with specific issues, especially relating to the service user's rights – such as confidentiality, access to records or making complaints. These vary from agency to agency, but such codes of practice seem much more clearly designed to protect and clarify service users' rights and to clarify the roles of the social worker and the agency. What is important is that these codes of practice are related clearly to the more general value statements in the codes of ethics and can be seen to be a development from them. The most appropriate statement that might be made about confidentiality, for example in a national code of ethics, might be that social workers should ensure that their agencies have policies and codes of practice clearly stating the extent to which information given by the service user to a social worker will and will not be kept confidential. Obviously the extent to which information can be kept confidential may be very different in an independent counselling agency, compared with a statutory child protection agency. Therefore the role of the code of ethics in guiding practice seems to be to outline the broad principles of the profession and the potential areas where ethical issues will arise.

Regarding the role of a code of ethics in protecting the service user, this can only be fulfilled in a very general way in laying down broad principles relating to respect, non-exploitation or abuse. Yet these should be obvious anyway and it is the more subtle and detailed use of power and knowledge from which the service user may need some protection. Perhaps this can also be better served (although still very imperfectly) through well-publicised and clear agency codes of practice regarding such issues as making contracts with service users, procedures for access to records or rights to complaint. It also requires emphasis in professional education, continuing professional development and supervision on the development of professional qualities of trustworthiness, respectfulness, care, moral sensitivity and, above all, commitment to challenge inhumane and unjust practices and to understand and promote anti-oppressive practice.

Conclusions

In this chapter, we have examined the nature and function of codes of ethics in social work. We noted that the existence of codes of ethics for social work is intimately related to the notion of professionalism and one of their main functions is to maintain professional status and identity. In looking at codes of ethics developed by professional associations in different countries, many common features were noted, particularly a congruence around the stated values or principles underpinning social work including: respect for the individual person, promotion of service user self-determination, promotion of social justice and working for the interests of service users. The extent to which the codes acknowledge that the societal and agency contexts in which social work is practised may also place demands on social workers varies, as does the level of detail regarding practical guidance on matters such as charging fees, advertising qualifications or service user access to records.

The extent to which social workers regard such codes as useful will depend upon what they want to use them for. For practical guidance on how to act in certain types of situation and as a means of safeguarding service users' rights, agency codes of practice may be more useful. However, as a means of defending the profession from outside attack, of maintaining professional identity and of setting some general benchmarks against which to judge agency policies and practice, they do most certainly have a role to play. The codes emphasise that social workers have a responsibility over and above just doing the job and following the agency's rules. This may be useful at a time when resources for social work are being reduced and standards of work and the quality of service to users may be threatened. The codes of ethics remind social workers that, because they possess particular knowledge and skills and work on a daily basis with people living in poverty and suffering crises and problems, they have a duty to inform governments and agencies of inequities, lack of resources or the need for policy changes. Yet, because of the changes in the management and delivery of social work, codes of ethics are also becoming increasingly irrelevant, with their emphasis on professionally defined values (as opposed to those defined by the service users), their assumption of a professional consensus (when much work is specialised and multidisciplinary) and their focus on service to service users (in a climate where economy and efficiency are also of prime importance). In such a climate, codes of practice developed by social work agencies are more important ways of safeguarding service user rights. Social workers still need to be prepared to challenge agency policies and practices and to view themselves as more than just employees doing a job. Professional codes of ethics, along with education and training, obviously have a role to play in this.

putting it into practice

Exercise 4

Aims of the exercise – to encourage reflection on the nature and purpose of codes of ethics and to link this to developing awareness of the nature of professionalism.

1. Consult the website of the International Federation of Social Workers, http://www.ifsw.org.
2. Read the latest version of the IFSW ethical statement and the national codes of ethics from at least three different professional associations.
3. Consider their main similarities and differences.
4. What is the balance between general statements of principle and more practical guidance or rules?
5. What is the balance of emphasis between promoting individual service users' rights; protecting service users and the public; and challenging inequality and promoting social justice? Can you link any of the statements to ethical theories or approaches discussed in Chapters 2 and 3?
6. Are there any references to qualities of character?
7. How useful do you think these codes are in protecting service users and in guiding practitioners?
8. What is said about what happens if social workers breach the principles or rules of the code? How is the disciplinary process linked to the code, if at all?

Further reading

Banks, S. (2004a) *Ethics, Accountability and the Social Professions*, Basingstoke, Palgrave Macmillan. Chapter 4 in this book has a more detailed discussion of codes of ethics, comparing those produced by the South African Black Social Workers' Association, the US National Association of Social Workers and the National Youth Agency in the UK.

Chadwick, R. (ed.) (1994) *Ethics and the Professions*, Avebury, Aldershot. This is a useful edited collection, which has several chapters on codes of ethics.

IFSW website: http://www.ifsw.org. This website has a selection of codes of ethics from different national professional associations in membership of IFSW. It also has statements and discussion about the nature of social work and human rights issues in social work.

5 | Service users' rights: clienthood, citizenship and consumerism

The last chapter argued that the main role of codes of ethics is to establish and maintain professional identity. Although they do play a role in protecting the interests and rights of users and in guiding social workers, this is an indirect role. The general principles in the codes of ethics cannot immediately and obviously be put into practice. They must be interpreted and translated into some more specific principles and implemented in practice. In this chapter we will look at what is meant by 'rights' in relation to service users, considering the difference between regarding the user as a person, a citizen or a consumer and the approaches that need to be adopted by social workers to enable service users to exercise these rights.

Rights

The idea of rights is generally associated with the principle-based ethics or the 'ethics of justice', although rights-based approaches to ethics have also been developed independently of ethical theories based on foundational principles (see Dworkin, 1977; Gewirth, 1996; Rawls, 1973). There are many different political and philosophical theories about rights (see Edmundson, 2004) that cover questions concerning:

- the nature of rights – for example, are they best understood as claims, benefits, choices or entitlements?
- where do rights come from – are they derived from God, nature or a social contract, for example?
- what kinds of entity hold rights – is it all or some of: humans, potential humans, future generations, animals, plants or other features of the environment?

While these questions are all important and do have an impact on social work as part of society, in this chapter I will confine myself to a brief discussion of the nature of human rights as a precursor to exploring the rights of social work service users.

Rights are an important part of the western liberal tradition in politics and moral philosophy, which we have already linked to the Kantian notion of respect for persons. If respect for persons is regarded as the ultimate principle of morality or indeed a precondition for any morality whatsoever, then it follows that persons have certain rights that should be respected. In western philosophy, human rights have generally been regarded as belonging to individuals. However, as noted in previous chapters, this view does not necessarily make sense in societies or cultures where the individual person is not the prime focus of cultural norms and ways of life. In the next section, I will discuss one view of individual human rights and how this relates to social work. I will then discuss the concept of 'relational rights' as a possible conception of rights that goes beyond the focus on the isolated individual.

Individual rights as valid claims

The term 'rights' is a very broad one and is used to refer to a range of claims, liberties, powers and relationships. According to Feinberg (1973, p. 64) a right is a valid claim. By 'valid' he means justified according to a system of rules. If someone has a right, then at least one other person must have duties towards that person. He elucidates the concept of a right with reference to a claim, arguing that a right is more than just a claim. Whereas claims may differ in degree (some may be stronger than others), rights do not. Whereas claims may be invalid, rights cannot be. He gives the example of young orphans throughout the world needing a good upbringing, including a balanced diet. He argues that this is a claim, not a right, because in many places resources are not available and therefore no particular person has a duty to provide goods.

This definition of rights obviously has implications for how we regard some of the 'rights' included in the United Nations Universal Declaration of the Rights of the Child: for example, the right of all children to 'adequate nutrition, housing, recreation and medical services' (1959, principle 4). Feinberg regards the use of the term 'human rights' in the UN and other similar declarations as a 'special manifesto sense of right' that identifies basic needs with rights. He argues that such statements should more properly be described as urging on the world community the moral principle that all basic human needs ought to be recognised as 'claims worthy of sympathy and serious consideration now, even though they cannot yet plausibly be treated as valid claims' (Feinberg, 1973, p. 67). Whether or not we agree with Feinberg's characterisation of rights in the strict sense as 'valid claims', he is making an important distinction between different types of 'right' as the concept is used in our ordinary language – including those that have co-relative duties on other people and those that do not.

Classifications of individual rights

We will now explore further classifications of different types of right. The distinction is often made between claim rights (often termed 'positive rights') and liberties ('negative rights') as follows:

- *Positive rights* (claim rights) claim against someone else to do something (for example medical treatment).
- *Negative rights* (or liberties) relate to the freedom to do something without interference (for example free speech).

Another distinction is that between legal rights and moral rights and both of these can be either positive or negative:

- *Legal rights* are valid claims by virtue of the legal code or customary practice (for example the right to vote).
- *Moral rights* are valid claims bestowed by a moral code (for example the right to be treated with honesty).

These two categories are not mutually exclusive, as many moral rights are also legal rights (for example the right to free speech). There are two further important distinctions between types of right: absolute (or unqualified) rights and conditional (or qualified) rights; and universal rights (applying to everybody without exception) and particular rights (applying to a limited class of people). Clark with Asquith (1985, p. 24) draw up a useful table relating to the four possible combinations of rights in these categories, from which the following list is derived:

1. *Absolute universal rights* – apply unconditionally to everybody. Clark with Asquith argue that there is probably only one right in this category and that would be the right to be treated as an end and not simply as a means (which logically follows from the concept of respect for persons).
2. *Qualified universal rights* – apply to everybody, except they may be withdrawn from anybody on the basis of the application of criteria that apply to all. This category would include those rights that have often been put forward as 'natural rights' (that is, rights

simply deducible from the nature of humankind) and some of what are included as 'human rights', such as the right to liberty, which can be withheld on certain grounds. For example the right to liberty is suspended for the imprisoned criminal.

3. *Absolute particular rights* – apply without qualification to every-body in a certain category. For example, all parents who are British citizens have an absolute right to claim child benefit.
4. *Qualified particular rights* – apply to certain persons under certain conditions. For example, a British citizen has a right to a state pension if over the prescribed retirement age and having satisfied the necessary contribution conditions.

There is an on-going debate as to whether the concept of universal human rights – based, perhaps, on some basic human needs applying to everyone across the world – makes sense (see Doyal and Gough, 1991; Outka and Reeder, 1993). In relation to social work, it is important to note that the International Federation of Social Workers certainly believes in the existence of universal moral rights and endorses as part of its code of ethics the UN Declarations of Human Rights and the Rights of the Child.

Clark with Asquith (1985, p. 27) argue that social workers mainly deal with qualified particular rights on a day-to-day basis and that the 'application of universal rights cannot, without absurdity, be essentially different in social work from any other context'. However, the statements of values and ethics made by the social work profession invariably focus on what appear to be regarded as either absolute or qualified *universal rights*.

Clark with Asquith produce a typical list of service users' rights drawn from the social work literature as follows:

1. to be treated as an end;
2. to self-determination;
3. to be accepted for what one is;
4. to be treated as a unique individual;
5. to non-discrimination on irrelevant grounds;
6. to treatment on the principles of honesty, openness and non-deception;
7. to have information given to the worker in the course of social work treatment treated as confidential;
8. to a professionally competent service;
9. to access to resources for which there exists an entitlement ('welfare rights').

The first six rights on this list could be said to be derived from the principle of respect for persons and are very similar to Biestek's list discussed in Chapter 2. The first right is an absolute universal right, and (2) to (5) could be regarded as qualified universal rights. The right to welfare (9) relates to service users as citizens of a specific country; the welfare rights may be universal in that country (the right to health care) or, more usually in the UK, particular (the right of parents to child benefit). The right to confidentiality (7) and a professionally competent service (8) refer specifically to someone in the role of a social work service user and therefore are particular. Confidentiality is qualified, as there are rules regarding when one is allowed to break confidentiality (for example, when someone else's rights or interests are seriously threatened or if it is in the service user's interests). The right to a professionally competent service is, arguably, an unqualified right. It may be the case that a professionally competent service is not delivered due to lack of qualified staff as a result of resource constraints. However, this should not negate the service user's right to that standard of service.

Relational rights and responsibilities

The list of service users' rights discussed earlier is a useful starting point for social work in individualist cultures, but it seems less relevant to practice in more collectivist societies or indeed in many of the multi-cultural contexts where social work is practised in most western countries. Responsibilities and relationships rather than rights may be the primary focus of attention, as described by Graham (2002) in her account of the African-centred worldview and Ejaz's (1991) discussion of social work in India, for example. If rights are talked about at all, then it may make more sense to talk of the rights of groups of people. Certainly in the context of social work in western countries, this would be the case in relation to indigenous peoples, ethnic and religious groupings. For example, we noted in the previous chapter the concern with the rights of Maori people, as Maori, in New Zealand. Nevertheless, there remains a question as to whether we should impose what is essentially a western concept of rights on societies where this concept is alien to their ways of thinking and acting. Internationally, through the United Nations, the concept of human rights as the rights of peoples (that is, territorial, ethnic, religious groups) to self-determination has been an important way of attempting to protect minority groups from persecution, ethnic cleansing and other forms of oppression and abuse. The concept of individual human rights has also been important as part of a worldwide movement (exemplified through organisations such as Amnesty International) to challenge regimes and individual cases of unjust treatment, torture, imprisonment and murder. Such abuses are frequently perpetrated upon individuals because of their membership of particular religious or ethnic groupings, but equally they may be perpetrated on people for other reasons and a concept of individual human rights (absolute and universal) may be an important one to draw upon to mobilise support to challenge such treatment as inhuman and degrading.

However, some commentators speak of 'relational rights' as a more useful concept. Boss (1998, p. 341), for example, argues that even where rights have not been explicitly discussed in traditional writings, such as Buddhist philosophy, 'the assumption of rights is embedded in the concepts of duty and respect for the dignity of people'. Buddhist ethics, for example (see de Silva, 1993; McFarlane, 1994), is based on the notion of human inter-dependence and can be interpreted as both affirming the worth of the individual being and regarding the individual as subservient to the good of many. A similar interpretation could be made of Graham's (2002) African-centred worldview. Whether we wish to interpret Buddhism or other religious or cultural worldviews as having a concept of relational rights embedded within them or as placing a primary focus on responsibility and the inter-connectedness of all things (humans and the whole of the natural world) may seem like an academic question. What is important is the use of the term 'relational', which stresses the importance of people and things in connection, rather than 'individual', which implies abstraction and isolation.

The individualistic conception of rights in use in western society at present is also questioned by the care ethicists discussed in Chapter 3, and by communitarian philosophers, from a variety of perspectives that can be viewed as both progressive and reactionary (see Etzioni, 1995, 1997; MacIntyre, 1985; Sandel, 1998; Taylor, C., 1989). The relatively conservative ideas of Etzioni, for example, have been quite influential in the social policy thinking in the UK and USA. Etzioni (1995) argues that a rights-focused culture is developing in the western world (he focuses particularly on the USA), which generates individual demands without balancing these with a more developed commitment to responsibilities to other individuals, groups and communities. Not only needs, but desires and wants may be given the status of rights. He calls for a moratorium on the creation of rights, alongside the development of communal responsibility, with a focus on family and community life. However, his particular brand of communitarianism could be regarded as quite authoritarian and dangerous. If communities police themselves, for example, how do we guard against exclusion of minority interests, racism, sexism and so on? As was pointed out in the discussion of the concept of international human rights, so in a national context, rights have been important in the struggles of oppressed groups for recognition and redistribution of power and resources. The social rights of women to state support for childcare, for example, have been a vital element in women shaking off their traditional responsibility for home and family caring roles in their fight for equality and justice. There is no doubt that it is important to guard against the excessive 'manufacture' of social rights, as this undervalues important and fundamental human rights to life and freedom of expression as well as creating a culture of complaint and unfulfilled expectations. But in social work we are often working with people whose voices are not heard, whose basic needs are not being met, who are being treated with disrespect – so a concept of individual and group rights is important, alongside a balancing of rights with responsibilities. In this context, 'relational rights' may be a useful idea to hold on to.

The service user as a person (in a relationship of clienthood)

The lists of principles such as those of Biestek and the others discussed in Chapter 2 focus on individual rights, with more emphasis on the universal rights that should apply to all people than on the particular rights applying to the service user qua service user. The emphasis on the social work service user as a *person* with the basic moral rights derived from the principle of respect for persons was the dominant one in the social work literature until perhaps the 1980s, although the term 'client' was used to refer to the person in a relationship with a social worker. This meant that the kinds of moral principle stated for social work were no different to the kinds of moral principle that would be stated for morality in general, although the context in which they were applied (social worker–client relationship) obviously presented specific issues and difficulties for workers. This type of view based on Kantian philosophy and Biestek's list of casework principles has already been discussed in the section on the principles of the social worker–service user relationship in Chapter 2.

However, the traditional notion of 'personhood' presented problems for social work, in that it entailed a focus on the abstract individual in isolation and a particular view of persons as rational individuals with a capacity for self-determined choice and action. This seemed to downplay features of the social context in which any relationship took place and to legitimate parentalist ('paternalistic') treatment of those judged to be less than fully rational (children, people with mental health problems or learning disabilities, for example). So although 'respect for persons' might appear to entail an equal relationship between social worker and service user, the very narrow and undifferentiated view of 'personhood' (which took no account of relationships of power and control, differentiated and diverse cultural and religious identities or contextual features of the professional relationship with the 'client') also contained within it the seeds of parentalism and professional control.

The service user as fellow citizen, equal and ally

In the late 1970s and early 1980s the notion of 'clients as fellow citizens' began to be stressed (BASW, 1980; Jordan, 1975) as part of the reaction against the view of the social worker as expert giving psychological explanations of service users' problems and as a move towards regarding social workers as allies of service users (Payne, 1989, p. 121). In the UK, studies had been published (for example Mayer and Timms, 1970) relating to service users' views of social work, which contributed to the pressure to alter the power balance between service users and social workers. As Phelan commented: 'As social workers we have a responsibility to bear constantly in mind that our clients are equal with us. They have complete citizenship' (BASW, 1980). This led to a redefinition of professionalism, often termed the 'new' or 'democratic' professionalism concerned with shifting the balance of power between workers and service users (BASW, 1989).

This kind of view entails that the rights of service users should be seen as rights of citizens not to be treated arbitrarily by state officials, and therefore as having rights of access to information about the purpose of social work, to see personal information held by social work agencies on file and to participate in planning and decision-making, for example. The principle of respecting the service user as a fellow citizen could be regarded as a development of the idea of respect for persons. However, the term 'citizen' is narrower than 'person', in that it focuses on the rights of the person in the role of citizen, rather than respect for the person as a person.

Citizenship entails more specific rights, including social rights to the benefits and services of the welfare state, as well as political and civil rights. The 'service user as fellow citizen' approach therefore increases the accountability of social workers, although it is reductive in its view of the service user.

The term 'citizen' is as contested as many of the others we have been using. The notion of the service user as a fellow citizen will be interpreted differently depending on how citizenship is construed – whether in terms of the liberal tradition of individual rights, social citizenship with a stress on reciprocity and common interests (Jordan, 1989) or citizenship based on meeting people's needs (Taylor, D. 1989). The idea of service users as fellow citizens suggests that both social workers and service users are members of a common community or society and as such possess certain rights. If we follow T. H. Marshall, these could be described as political (for example the right to vote), civil (for example the right to freedom of speech) and social (for example the right to education). According to Marshall, citizenship is: 'a status bestowed on those who are full members of a community. All those who possess the status are equal with respect to the rights and duties with which the status is endowed' (Marshall, 1963, p. 87).

This implies that these rights and duties apply equally to everyone. Yet as D. Taylor (1989) has argued, citizenship, with its notions of membership of a community (particularly a nation) is based on a set of practices that exclude certain people from full membership. He gives as an example the UK Immigration Act 1988, which ruled that the wives of British and Commonwealth men settled in Britain could only be brought into the country if they could be supported and would have no recourse to public funds. Similar examples can be given of the way asylum seekers and refugees are currently treated in the UK and many countries around the world. Hayes (2005, p. 189) graphically describes the separate and inferior welfare benefits, housing and dispersal schemes operating in the UK for asylum seekers, which social workers are involved in implementing (see also Humphries, 2004).

There are many other ways in which some people are denied full citizenship rights, particularly women, black people, people with disabilities, people who are lesbian, gay or bisexual and children (Lister, 1991; Taylor, D., 1989). It is likely that a significant number of the people who become users of social work services may not have or may not be able to exercise full citizenship rights. While social workers may believe that everyone in society ought to have equal status and it may be a good principle for the social worker to regard service users as fellow citizens, we cannot pretend that this is the case in our present society. Service users are often people who have been excluded from the political process (for example with no address they cannot vote) and who do not share in the rights and benefits associated with employment. Social workers alone do not have the power to make people fellow citizens, but it is important that they are not complicit in implementing inhumane and degrading systems of welfare and control, that they do advocate on behalf of people who are denied basic citizenship rights and that they engage in campaigns to change practices and policies that they regard as unjust (for example in the case of asylum seekers and refugees). Furthermore, at the micro-level, the services and contact offered by social workers can treat people in a way fellow citizens ought to be treated – that is, service users should not be stigmatised or treated as undeserving.

Social work, as part of a welfare state or system, is one of the institutions responsible for delivering what Marshall called 'the right to welfare' or social rights. Social rights include the right to education, a state pension, and many other rights, some of which social workers may be regarded as contributing to, ranging from: 'a modicum of economic welfare and security to the right to share to the full in the social heritage and to live the life of a civilised being according to the standards prevailing in society' (Marshall, 1963, p. 74). Some of these rights are enshrined in law (such as education), others are what might be described as moral rights (such as the right to live the life of a civilised human being). The fact that these are all described as rights of citizenship means that those who receive benefits or services through a state welfare system should regard them as theirs of right, that is, they should not be regarded as dependent or stigmatised and should not be treated arbitrarily by state officials (Campbell, 1978). This obviously poses a challenge for social work. Many of the people seeking social work help or required to have contact with social workers may have already been denied full citizenship rights and/or may find it difficult to exercise their rights due to poverty, lack of confidence or competence, for example. They may feel they do not have a genuine right to services or they do not have the power or confidence to complain if the services are inadequate. In the past, except in areas of social work that are subject to the law, such as child protection, mental health or work with offenders, there were few clear rules or guidelines about who should be offered social work help and what the nature of the help should be. This made it doubly difficult for service users to complain or appeal about the service received from social workers. If social workers have discretionary powers over service users based on their professional judgement of what is in the service users' best interests, this makes it very difficult to appeal against the treatment or service received. One of the ways in which service users' rights as citizens can be made more real is if they are given more information about the service offered and the right to appeal and treated more as equals and partners than as needy recipients of welfare handouts and social work advice. As Marshall said: 'the right of appeal helps keep alive the idea that the granting of assistance is not a fact of grace, but the satisfaction of a right' (Marshall, 1963, p. 89).

It should also be noted that there was a growing trend towards the end of the twentieth century to emphasise not just citizenship rights, but also the duties and responsibilities of citizens to each other. As Lund (1999, p. 447) comments in relation to the welfare reforms of 'New Labour' in Britain, there is a 'fastening of duties to rights' and a stress on the importance of mutual obligations. These kinds of idea are part of the 'new communitarian' thinking, mentioned earlier in the section of this chapter on relational rights and also link to ideas of active citizenship, democratic renewal and citizenship as a practice (Banks, 2004a, pp. 87–9; Shaw and Martin, 2000).

The service user as a consumer

The notion of the service user as a 'consumer' possessing quite specific rights to be treated in a certain kind of way and to receive a certain standard of service is an even further narrowing down, or arguably a move away from, the concept of a person with universal rights. This developed in the 1980s and 1990s as part of the growth of charterised standards and quality assurance indicators and the development of markets, private provision and business principles in welfare services (see Harris, 2003). One of the aims of adopting the terminology of consumers (sometimes used interchangeably with 'customers') was to emphasise the notion of *choice*. Although customers are people who receive services, they are able to choose between the services on offer. If they do not like a particular service, they are free to go elsewhere (the power of 'exit'). They exert some power in exercising this choice and are therefore not merely passive recipients. This model is obviously based on the traditional idea of the marketplace, with sellers of goods and services competing with each other to find buyers. The buyers will be looking for services that meet their particular needs, offering the level of quality desired, at the right price. Such a notion has not traditionally been applied to the services provided by the welfare state – largely because there has usually been a monopoly supplier, the state, and although it would make sense to say that people's welfare rights entitled them to a certain standard of service, it was usually difficult for them to 'take their custom elsewhere'. This is probably why the term 'consumer' is more commonly used than 'customer' in a social work context.

With the introduction of 'quasi-markets' into many of the key services of the welfare state (Adams, 1999; Le Grand and Bartlett, 1993) some might argue that this notion of the service user as consumer is becoming more meaningful. However, the 'consumers' of health and social services are still in a very different position from consumers in the marketplace and therefore the notion of consumer choice is misleading (Banks, 1998a; Payne, 1995, p. 181). Despite the introduction of internal markets, it is still not the service user as such who is the 'purchaser', it is usually the doctor or the social worker (or 'care manager') who actually buys the services on behalf of the patient or service user and it is not just the interests and needs of that service user that are taken into account, but also the level of resources available in the budget and the agreements the purchaser may have to contract with certain providers. Indeed, Rea (1998, pp. 203–4) argues that the market in health and social care is best understood as a 'metaphorical device' and comments that 'markets have not been extended to permit consumers to determine expenditure levels, nor to determine any particular type of provision'. Although service users may have more choice than previously, it is still restricted. This is one of the reasons why Hugman (1998a, p. 149) prefers to use the term 'quasi-consumer'. Of course, the notion that consumers in a marketplace can exercise free choice is also a myth. The extent to which choice can be exercised depends upon the wealth and the power of the consumers. Berry argued in the 1980s that the perspective that sees consumerism as about offering choice is interpreted as letting market forces have a controlling influence:

This moves away from the idea of universal entitlement to benefit or service towards a perception of the tenant or client as customer. It is a short step from here to introducing charges for services and basing choice on ability to pay. Since the ability to be perceived as a consumer is limited to those who can pay for the privilege, this analysis can also lead to the targeting of specific (second-class) programmes at those who are too poor to exercise that choice, too poor to be customers, or even to pay indirectly as tax- or ratepayers. (Berry, 1988, pp. 268–9)

This prediction has been confirmed in the UK in the early part of the twenty-first century. Choice for many social service users may, in fact, mean the right of exit from declining services that have been starved of resources. In fact, many users of social work services cannot be regarded as consumers even in the very tenuous sense we have discussed earlier. Some people, such as those on a compulsory court order or a parent whose child is suspected of having been abused, do not have the right of exit from the 'service' – or if they do exit, their choice may be imprisonment, a fine, or removal of a child. This does not mean that many of the service users' rights promoted under the auspices of the new consumerism do not apply in the case of compulsory statutory social work involvement (such as rights to access to files or to information about legal rights). Rather, the idea of consumer *choice* makes even less sense in this context.

Calling the service user a consumer also serves to hide the fact of social worker as controller. It implies an active role and the possibility to exercise choice. It covers up the role of welfare as control – what Foucault (1999, p. 93) called 'surveillance-correction' and others have termed the 'new authoritarianism', which is based on the notion of the service user as dangerous, as a risk to be assessed, as deviant and as outsider (Jeffs and Smith, 1994; Parton, 1999). This is another feature that can be identified in the policies and ideologies of both what have been termed 'the new right' and 'the new left' that is contrary to the traditional social work values of respect for persons – the re-emergence of the distinction between the deserving and undeserving poor; the determination to punish and control those on the margins of society, the 'outcasts' or the 'underclass'. Some of these trends are exemplified in the implementation of legislation in the UK in the 1990s relating to child protection, community care and criminal justice. While aspects of this legislation could be regarded as progressive in the promotion of children's rights and service user participation in service delivery, other aspects are about treatment and control – the service user as a problem to be technically assessed, clinically managed and processed through a proceduralised system. These policies and procedures are now based much more explicitly than in the past on the utilitarian values of procedural justice and the promotion of public welfare.

Nevertheless, there are also ways in which the notion of the service user as a consumer is quite helpful, provided it is not linked with the idea of consumer choice. It is more honest about the nature of the social work relationship, which is not a relationship between two free individual persons, or even two fellow citizens, but between representatives of an agency that provides services or purchases services on behalf of the state and someone who enters into a relationship with that agency or its representatives for a specific purpose. While this may not be how social workers wish to see the relationship, this may, in effect, be an important aspect of how it is, especially in the context of state-sponsored social work.

Democratic professionalism or consumerism?

The increasing concern with service users' rights has been characterised as both a move towards a 'new' or 'democratic' professionalism and as consumerism.

Democratic professionalism entails giving more power to service users in the context of the professional relationship, but the focus is on the professional as the one giving the power. So although the service user may be given more rights and be referred to as a 'partner' or even a 'co-producer' (Øvretveit, 1997, pp. 83–4), it could be argued that it is still the professional that is in control. A consumerist approach, by way of contrast, is moving away from the idea of the social worker as a professional who exercises professional judgement on the basis of expertise towards the idea of social workers as officials – as distributors of resources according to certain prescribed standards and procedures. Consumerism has strong strands of anti-professionalism embedded in it, exemplifying a desire on the part of the government as well as the consumer rights movement to challenge the power and exclusiveness of professional groups (in medicine, law and education, as well as social work). Democratic professionalism, contrariwise, may be trying to retain some of the status and power, or at least the identity, of the professional, while also becoming more responsive to service users' rights – developing a new model of professionalism that does not have to be elitist and exclusive. As Bamford says: 'The new professionalism does not deny the existence of that [professional] knowledge and skill but seeks to bridge the gap between worker and client, and to widen the range of choices open to the client' (Bamford, 1990, p. 57).

The new professionalism, or 'democratic' professionalism, seeks to retain the notion of the social worker as a professional requiring special education and adhering to a professional code of ethics while trying to regard the service user as more of an active participant. The traditional values still apply, although the way they are put into practice has changed. For example, promoting service user self-determination has been extended to include service user participation in decision-making. In practice it is sometimes difficult to distinguish democratic professionalism from a consumerist approach. Developments that began as part of the new professionalism (for example, complaints procedures, advocacy and contracts between worker and service user) have become absorbed into the broader changes brought about by government legislation and a focus on consumerism. A consumerist approach tends to see the social worker more as a 'producer' of services (Hugman, 1998a, pp. 109–34), which would include assessment and care planning, according to certain standards and criteria. Some of the traditional values still seem relevant. For example, service user self-determination means service users having the choice whether to accept the service or not or whether to complain. The social worker has to tailor the service (which relates to treating each person as a unique individual) to take account of individual needs. However, this must be according to the criteria laid down and the type of needs prioritised by the agency, so the social worker becomes more of a rule-follower and the principles of fairness and consistency in allocating resources will be important. Rules, procedures and consistency are all vital in enhancing consumer rights.

Yet, while laws, policies and procedures can lay the ground rules for service users' rights, they are meaningless if not developed alongside the commitment of agencies and workers to give support and resources for service users to exercise their rights. For example, the records about service users are still kept by the social work agencies and although service users have a right to see them, this is often treated as a concession. Similar blocks also occur for service users wishing to make complaints. Systems for complaints and appeals have been criticised as inadequate and lacking independence (Amphlett, 1998). Even if leaflets are produced outlining the range of services available, the standards of treatment to be expected and how to make complaints, social work service users are very often reluctant to complain. In the next part of this chapter we will look at various ways of working alongside service users positively to enhance their ability to recognise and exercise their rights, including the promotion of participation in decision-making and empowerment to take action for change.

Involvement and participation of service users in decision-making

The degree of service users' involvement or participation in decisions about their own cases obviously varies not just according to the policies of particular agencies and the commitment of individual social workers, but also according to the social worker's judgement regarding service users' abilities to understand the situation and to make an informed statement of their own needs and choice of services or courses of action. However, as Lansdown (1995, p. 29) points out, it is important to distinguish between a service user's capacity for self-determination (the right to make their own decisions), which will be limited by judgements of their competence and their need for protection, and their rights to participate in the process of making decisions about their case. In the context of work with children, he argues that the right to participate and have their views listened to is not contingent on adults' judgements about children's competence or their best interests. However, this depends on what we mean by 'participation'. The term can be used in a number of senses and is often regarded as a continuum or 'ladder' (Arnstein, 1969) or more usefully a sphere (which suggests a circular process, see Abrioux, 1998), which may include:

1. informing, listening to or consulting service users;
2. giving service users some involvement in decision-making;
3. joint decision-making with professionals, or service users having full decision-making powers (see Øvretveit, 1997, pp. 85–8).

The terms 'consultation' 'involvement' and 'participation' are often used rather loosely and interchangeably. While the consultation (1) and involvement (2) of service users should no doubt be a right, 'participation' in the strong sense of joint or full decision-making powers (3) will usually depend on the capacity of the service user to make a decision.

The question of how to judge whether someone is capable of understanding what is going on and making a decision has been more discussed in the context of medicine and the principle of 'informed consent' to treatment. According to Wicclair (1991), decision-making capacity is judged according to whether people have a capacity to understand and communicate, to reason and deliberate and whether they possess a set of values and goals. Not surprisingly, there is no single, universally accepted standard of decision-making capacity. This is not only because medical professionals' judgements about what constitutes a capacity to understand

and reason will vary, but also because the levels of competence required will vary according to the type of decision being made. Buchanan and Brock (1989) suggest that the relevant criteria should vary according to the risk to the person's well-being. If the treatment is relatively low risk, then a weaker standard of decision-making capacity is appropriate. These are debated issues (see Brock, 1991; Veatch, 1999; Wicclair, 1991), but are of relevance to the issue of service user choice in social work, particularly in relation to work with children, people with learning disabilities or mental health problems.

This is why it may be appropriate for some service users to have independent advocates to support them in speaking for themselves or to speak on their behalf. This is especially important where the social worker's role is to act on behalf of the agency in distributing resources or exercising control. In relation to community-based care for older people, for example, the social worker (or care manager) who assesses the service user and purchases and manages the care package may be separate from the person or organisation providing the care. It might therefore be assumed that the care manager would advocate on behalf of the service user to gain the best possible package. However, since the resources for purchasing are limited and the social work agency may have set some limits on certain types of service and prioritised the meeting of certain kinds of need, the care manager will be constrained. The care manager may be working on behalf of the service user, but he or she is also working for an agency. The rights and needs of the individual service user will often conflict with agency policies for distributing available resources between service users; and needs that cannot be met may not be taken into account. Brandon (1991, p. 118) argues that it is always preferable to have an independent advocate working on behalf of psychiatric patients:

> The advocate nurse, social worker or doctor has an inherent and critical conflict of interest. The alleged oppressor pays their salaries.

Laws, policies and procedures can lay the ground rules for service users' rights, but are meaningless if not developed alongside the commitment of agencies and workers to give support and resources for service users to exercise their rights. In the next section we will briefly look at the concept of 'empowerment' as going a stage beyond 'participation'.

Empowerment

'Empowerment' is also a contested concept. Rather like 'participation', it has a range of meanings from giving service users some limited choices (the consumerist approach) to power-sharing (the citizenship approach) to supporting and encouraging people or groups to realise their own power and take action for themselves (a 'radical' approach). A 'radical' approach is often advocated through linking empowerment to oppression, and seeing empowerment as part of anti-oppressive practice (see, for example, Ahmad, 1990; Mullender and Ward, 1991; Thompson, 1993). Thompson defines oppression as:

> Inhuman or degrading treatment of individuals or groups; hardship and injustice brought about by the dominance of one group over another; the negative and demeaning exercise of power. Oppression often involves disregarding the rights of an individual or group and thus is a denial of citizenship. (Thompson, 1993, p. 31)

Discussion of anti-oppressive practice is often couched in terms of challenging structural oppression – that is, challenging the systems of beliefs, policies, institutions and culture that systematically discriminate against and demean women, black people, people with disabilities, lesbian, gay and bisexual people, working-class people and other oppressed groups. Yet as this rhetoric has been incorporated into mainstream practice, it is questionable sometimes whether 'empowerment' and 'anti-oppressive practice' consist of anything more than enabling individual service users to gain confidence and offering 'individually sensitive practice' that takes account of, for example, a service user's dietary and religious needs and their personal experience of oppression. This is not to undermine some of the radical and challenging work that has happened and is taking place, but rather to suggest that this still does not necessarily represent the mainstream of social work practice. As we commented in Chapter 2, the values relating to challenging structural oppression are in fundamental opposition to the individualistic values underpinning traditional social work.

Mullender and Ward, in their book *Self-Directed Groupwork: Service Users Take Action for Empowerment* (1991), produced a statement of values or practice principles for empowering practice. This is a good example of some of the principles being promoted by the new, or democratic, professionalism regarding non-elitism and the participation of service users in defining the agenda to be worked on.

Yet it adds to these by adopting a structural approach to the cause of social problems and advocates challenging structural oppression while at the same time maintaining the traditional individualistic values of respect for persons and the right to self-determination. While the examples given in the book are very varied and include some that involve campaigning for change, the title of the book might suggest the focus is on empowerment as an end in itself ('service users take action for empowerment') rather than as means to an end (which might be 'service users become empowered to take action for change'). Obviously the process is circular and it is impossible to distinguish empowerment from action (as encapsulated in the concept of 'praxis', mentioned in the discussion in Chapter 2 in relation to radical approaches to social work). But in social work generally the emphasis is more on individual service users becoming more confident and personally powerful than on achieving societal change. Thompson's definition tends to reflect this when he states that empowerment 'involves seeking to maximise the power of clients and to give them as much control as possible over their circumstances. It is the opposite of creating dependency and subjecting clients to agency power' (Thompson, 1993, p. 80). Similarly, Adams et al. (2005, p. 2) describe social work as 'transformational' 'when it addresses people's lives in such a way that enhances their social relationships and well-being both now and in the future'. They give examples of helping someone overcome relationship difficulties with their parents (p. xxi).

In talking of service users gaining control over, rather than changing, their circumstances, this suggests that the aim is to empower people to live a better quality of life in the world as it is. Of course, other parts of Thompson's book on anti-discriminatory practice and Adams et al. (2005) do embrace societal change, but the focus in social work generally is on the individual service user or family and therefore inevitably the stress is on personal change, even if the broader societal context is acknowledged. This is particularly evident in the literature related to the development of community care and the promotion of the rights of people with disabilities (see Ramon, 1991). While the existence of structural oppression is frequently acknowledged and the role of social workers in challenging it is emphasised, in practice much of the work they do is about helping people with disabilities 'conform' to what is accepted as 'normal' behaviour (for a critique of normalisation theory see Brown and Smith, 1992; Dalley, 1992).

Conclusions

In this chapter we have examined the gradual shift from seeing the service user as a person in a relationship of clienthood to seeing the service user as a fellow citizen and/or as a consumer. In one sense, the move towards a consumer rights approach can be regarded as a development of the principle of respect for persons, in that it is actualising the rights of a person in the specific situation of being a social work service user – in particular, rights to information, certain standards of service and to choice. We noted the development of procedures for gaining access to records, shared record-making, shared decision-making and making complaints. Within the predefined boundaries of the social work relationship and the agency context, these procedures aim to give service users more power. But the procedures in themselves do not guarantee respect for the service user as an equal citizen or a consumer with real choice. The social worker inevitably tends to be more powerful and articulate than the service user and there may be constraints in terms of agency resources. Procedures need to be developed alongside a systematic and long-term approach that promotes the participation of service users in service delivery, works towards empowerment and offers advocacy for those service users who find it difficult to articulate their needs and rights. This is not an easy task, as it is time consuming and involves social workers and agencies being prepared to give up some of their power and change their ways of working. It also brings into focus the contradictions between individual and structural approaches to change. While social workers may work towards empowering individuals to take control over parts of their personal lives, unless the policies and practices in the state welfare system and in society generally that oppress certain individuals and groups are changed, then social work can only go so far towards putting these principles into action.

putting it into practice

Exercise 5

Aims of the exercise – to encourage the reader to think practically about what rights are possible and desirable in relation to a context of which he/she has experience.

1. Think of an agency that you are currently working for/have worked for.

> 2. Draw up a list of what you think should be the service users' rights in relation to their contact with this agency.
> 3. Why do you think these particular rights are important?
> 4. How would you ensure that they are put into practice?

Further reading

Edmundson, W. (2004) *An Introduction to Rights*, Cambridge, Cambridge University Press. A clearly written introduction to the subject, offering a historical overview of the development of the idea of rights and discussion of the nature and future of rights.

Ife, J. (2001) *Human Rights and Social Work: Towards Rights-based Practice*, Cambridge, Cambridge University Press. Offers a well-developed rights-based framework for social work practice.

Reamer, F. (1999) *Social Work Values and Ethics*, 2nd edn, New York, Columbia University Press. Reamer takes a rights-based approach to social work ethics, covering a range of ethical dilemmas and professional misconduct issues.

6 | Social workers' responsibilities: policies, procedures and managerialism

The last chapter focused on service users' rights. According to the narrow definition of a right (as a valid claim belonging to an individual or group of individuals), if service users have certain rights, then some person or some institution has a corresponding duty to fulfil those rights. In many cases, it may be the social worker directly (for example, the duty to treat the service user with respect) or it may be the social worker indirectly acting on behalf of an agency (the duty to provide services for children in need). The direct duties could be said to be inherent in the role of professional social worker and the indirect ones inherent in the particular job the social worker has. If we take a broader conception of rights (what we called the 'manifesto' sense of rights or relational rights, which might include the fulfilment of certain basic human needs across the world) then this may require a more expansive kind of duty – what has been characterised as 'relational responsibility'.

In this chapter we will explore the nature of social workers' duties to service users in relation to their other duties and broader responsibilities, including those to the employing agency, the profession and society. The professional codes say more about duties to service users and to the profession and tend to argue that these have primacy. Employing agencies, by way of contrast, tend to require that employees put agency policies and procedures first. This chapter will explore the conflicts that arise between different sets of duties and responsibilities, particularly in the context of the increasing proceduralisation and bureaucratisation of social work (managerialism). The term 'responsibility' is broader than 'duty' and has been used in the heading of this chapter to encompass abstract duties in a Kantian sense and specific procedural duties defined by the employing agency as well as the more situated relational responsibilities that are prominent in care ethics, for example.

Duties

The concept of 'duty' is central to Kantian ethics, which has often been categorised as 'duty ethics' or deontology. Many of the religious ethical systems also have 'duty' as a central concept, although focused around duty to a god. In the context of professional ethics, the types of duties we tend to talk about are those owed to the profession and to the employing agency; those duties that people commit themselves to when they take on the job of social worker. In this sense, a duty is a consequence of a contract or undertaking, either implicit or explicit:

> My duty is that which I am engaged or committed to do, and which other people can therefore expect and require me to do. I have a duty to keep a promise, because I have bound myself thereto.
> (Whitley, 1969, p. 54)

However, we may have conflicting duties, because different commitments may have been undertaken that are incompatible with each other in a particular situation. Therefore we may have to choose between different duties. For example, I have a duty to keep the information service users give me confidential; but I also have a duty to protect service users from serious danger. Therefore I might decide to break the confidence of a young person who has said she is planning to commit suicide. The duty of confidentiality may be said to be a prima facie duty – that is, it is what I ought to do, other things being equal. This notion of duty is connected also with accountability. If I have made a contract or undertaking to do something (duty) then I am also expected to be able to explain or justify my performance or non-performance of that duty (accountability). In social work, this latter aspect of a duty is regarded as important, as social workers must be publicly accountable for what they do (see Banks, 2002).

It is important to distinguish this sense of duty – an obligation or commitment as a consequence of a contract or undertaking – from how the term is sometimes used, particularly in moral philosophy, to mean 'the right action': 'what I ought to do'. We might say in relation to the case of the girl threatening to commit suicide that I decided it was my duty to tell her parents. 'Duty' in this sense is a definitive recommendation regarding what ought to be done taking all the circumstances into account. 'Duty' here means *the* right action and there is only one action. Therefore it would not make sense to talk of a conflict of duties. I am going to use the term 'duty' in the first sense, where duties are regarded as commitments or obligations that may be in conflict with each other. Therefore a duty is what I am committed to do, other things being equal. Very often, other things are not equal. It may be morally right for me to neglect one particular duty in favour of another. When talking about duty in the sense of the right action or what I ought to do having taken all circumstances into account, I will use terms such as 'making a moral judgement about how to act' or 'deciding on the morally right course of action'.

'Relational duties' or responsibilities

The concept of duty as proposed in Kantian ethics and some forms of religious ethics (but by no means all) is often associated with a set of commitments that have been externally defined (for example, by God, by a set of socially given norms, by a professional association). Nevertheless, it is the moral agent who has the task of interpreting and carrying out these duties and deciding how to act in cases of conflicting duties. The notion of 'responsibility' encapsulates this sense of engagement by moral agents with their commitments or obligations. The term 'responsibility' is frequently found in codes of ethics and literature on professional ethics and encompasses both the rather narrowly conceived professional duties (such as obligations to respect confidentiality or to protect children) and a broader sense of a network of commitments and ties that are created together with and shared with service users, other professionals, other people and groups. The term 'responsibility' is rooted in the notion of 'response', that is, responding to the perceived needs of other people, to demands or calls from others. This is a central focus of what has been called 'the ethics of proximity' found in the work of Buber (1937) and Levinas (1989, 1997), for example, and drawn upon by Bauman (1993), where ethics arises in response to the call of the other person. The starting point is not abstract principles outlining duties, leading to a process of moral reasoning, but a pre-rational face-to-face encounter with another person who evokes my response. Responsibility is also one of the concepts at the heart of the ethics of care, as discussed in Chapter 3, based around the relationship of caring for others and is the focus of much attention in feminist ethics (Noddings, 2002; Tronto, 1993). It is also at the heart of many non-western ethical traditions, which take a holistic starting point to ethics based on inter-connections and inter-relatedness (such as the African-centred worldview articulated by Graham (1999, 2002), also mentioned in Chapter 3).

This links with the discussion of 'relational rights' in the previous chapter. In broadening the concept of duty from an individualistic to a relational focus, this brings it closer to the notion of responsibility. We discussed a similar re-focusing of the concept of rights, which also leads us towards responsibility. Some theorists have developed the notion of 'relational responsibility' (McNamee et al., 1999), which may seem somewhat superfluous (if we see responsibility as centred around response to another/others), but it does serve to emphasise the dialogical and dynamic nature of responsibility and shifts the centre of concern from the individual. The starting point of the philosophy of Levinas and Buber, for example, is the I–Thou relation – the dyad, or twosome. For Gergen and colleagues, writing from a (social) constructionist perspective, it is the social. As Burkitt (1999, p. 79) comments:

> To supplement Levinas's (1989) notion of responsibility located in the recognition of the other's face, we can say that this is not just the bare face of human physiognomy but a face superimposed with social identity taken from the way the person to whom it belongs is situated in social relations.

Social work as a 'role-job' with specific duties

Social work takes place within an institutional framework of rights and duties defined by the law, the employing agency and the professional code. Chapter 4 discussed the duties of the social worker as laid down in professional codes of ethics. There are other rights and duties that make up the job, such as the legal right (or power) and/or the duty to intervene in people's lives in cases where a child is thought to be at risk or the procedural duty to follow agency guidelines in assessing risk in child protection cases. For this reason, Downie and Loudfoot (1978) describe social work as a 'role-job' – meaning that the job of social work is defined by a set of institutional rights and duties. They argue that it is important for social work to have an institutional framework because social workers intervene in the lives of others and it is in the interests of service users that they have a right to intervene. Second, social workers discover many intimate details of people's lives and it is important that there are rules, such as confidentiality, that provide security for the service user. Third, social workers themselves can find security from working in an institutional framework – for example, they can fall back on their official position to give guidance on proper procedures with a service user in case of legal action.

Downie and Loudfoot list four different types of right and duty that attach to the role of social worker, to which I have added a fifth:

1. *Legal rights and duties* to service users, employers and others.
2. *Professional rights and duties* arising from membership of a profession with its own standards of conduct.
3. *Moral duties* arising from the fact that the social worker is dealing with specific individuals in specific situations.
4. *Social duties* arising from the fact that the social worker is also a citizen who has the opportunity to do more civil good than many; for example, through working towards reforming or changing social policies.
5. *Procedural rights and duties* arising from the fact that the social worker is employed by an agency that has its own rules concerning how the work should be done and how social workers should behave.

When someone takes on the job of a social worker, they are in effect agreeing to work within this framework of rights, duties and rules. In particular, the employing agency will expect them to work within its rules and procedures, since it is this agency that is paying their wages. Usually an employing agency will also expect the worker to work within the framework of the law and indeed if it is a statutory agency many of its policies and procedures will be based on interpretations of acts of parliament and statutory guidance.

Conflicting responsibilities

In an ideal world, it might be assumed that legal, professional, social, moral and procedural rights, duties and broader responsibilities would complement or coincide with each other. However, this is not always the case. A social worker may judge that the employing agency's procedures regarding confidentiality are too lax compared with the standards laid down in the professional code, for example, or that the methods it uses entail treating service users as objects rather than respecting them as persons. The professional associations usually state that it is the principles laid down in the professional codes that should come first as these codes are designed with the protection of service users in mind, whereas the law or agency rules may be designed for the convenience of the majority.

In taking on the role of social worker, a person takes on several different layers of responsibilities that may conflict with one another. We can summarise these duties and the main sources of guidance as follows:

1. *Responsibilities to service users* – for example, to respect service users' rights to make their own decisions, to respect their rights to confidentiality, to safeguard and promote the welfare of children (acting on behalf of the state). Sources of guidance include: professional codes of ethics; agency policies and codes of practice; the law; public opinion; charters for service users' rights.
2. *Responsibilities to the profession* – for example, to uphold the good name of social work by maintaining effective and ethical practice. Sources of guidance include: professional codes of ethics; guidance from the professional association and/or regulatory body.
3. *Responsibilities to the agency* – for example, following the prescribed rules and procedures, safeguarding the reputation of the agency. Sources of guidance include: the worker's job description and contract; agency policies and procedures.
4. *Responsibilities to society* – for example, maintaining social order, executing the responsibilities of state social work agencies as laid down by statute, challenging inhumane practices. Sources of guidance include: the law; government guidance; public opinion.

How does the social worker judge between these different responsibilities when they conflict? It might be with reference to values and principles outlined in professional codes, statements of values and professional literature. But what if professional codes are not explicit enough or if there is a conflict between the principles of the code and what seems to be required by the agency or the law? There is an on-going debate about whether and how it makes sense to distinguish values that social workers hold or should hold as professionals from the prevailing values of their employing agencies, the wider society in which they live and personal values that a social worker has a commitment to as a private individual (this may include secular or religious values about what is morally good/bad, right/wrong and political beliefs or commitments about how these values should be implemented in society). We will now consider some of these debates briefly. (For more detailed discussion of the relationship between professional ethics and the ethics of everyday life, see Banks, 2004a, ch. 2.)

Unity of personal and professional values and life

There is a school of thought in social work (and other caring professions) that maintains that social work is a vocation, which suggests a blurring of the distinction between personal and professional life, values and responsibilities. This may be argued from a number of perspectives, including religious. Eastham (2002, p. 71) claims that the term 'vocation' is Jewish in origin, meaning, in this context, a direct invitation from God to lead a certain kind of life. On this view, becoming a social worker might be akin to someone taking on a religious calling – becoming a priest – whose whole life should be lived according to the moral duties of the religion, not just parts of it when he or she is performing the role of a priest. The idea of vocation has resonances with the origins of social work in the religious movements of the mid- to late nineteenth century, where the early inhabitants of the settlement houses and 'friendly visitors' were committed to their work as part of a religious calling, whether to convert or educate people or simply to alleviate poverty and suffering (Banks, 2004a, pp. 26–35; Younghusband, 1981). They did not regard their personal and professional lives as separate. As Picht (1914, p. 2) comments in relation to the early settlers in Toynbee Hall in East London: 'Not as an official but as a friend does he approach the poor.'

Other commentators on social work propose a 'humanistic ethics', as opposed to an ethics derived from a particular religious commitment. For example, the view taken by Ronnby (1993) seems to imply that someone becomes a social worker as part of their personal identity and the duties attaching to being a social worker are the same as, or become the same as, personal or private rights and duties. This is the kind of view taken by Wilkes (1985, p. 54) who notes Lewis and Maude's three views of professionals: as tradespeople with special skills; as officials using their techniques to modify people's conduct; or as:

> guardians of a tradition, humane and Christian, of study and service
> to their fellows, whether this is based on a confidential and
> fiduciary relationship with individual clients or on voluntary
> sacrifice of extra monetary gain in the interests of the community.
> (Lewis and Maude, quoted in Wilkes, 1985, p. 54)

Wilkes argues for this latter view of the professional social worker. This may seem a strange attitude to have towards state-sponsored social work. However, it may be easier to understand if we look more carefully at the professional codes of ethics and note that the kinds of duties they espouse are those of the liberal individualist ethics that are current in western society generally. The International Code of Ethics and some of the national codes explicitly acknowledge that they are based on the United Nations Declaration of Human Rights and the Rights of the Child. They are advocating the kind of moral behaviour that it is thought any morally upright decent human being should follow. This is why Ronnby (1993) asks why social workers feel the need to add in writing to their professional codes that one shall respect every human being's unique worth and integrity: 'Social worker's ethics do not differ from those that characterise others' humanistic ideals.' In effect, he is saying that there should be no need for a code of ethics for social work, because the person who is a social worker should have their own personal ethical code that involves treating others with respect as fellow human beings. According to Ronnby (1993, pp. 5–6):

> The prerequisite of ethically proper actions in social work would be that the social worker cares about, even cares for, the help seeker. The social worker must dare, and be able, to open herself for the client, she must be capable of being herself with open senses, feelings and empathy. Techniques and routines as well as professional self-interest can prevent the social worker from acting humanely.

This seems to amount to an argument against the separation of the personal and the professional. It may not amount to an argument against the notion that social work is a role-job with specific rights and duties attached to it; but it does imply that the specific rights and duties should not be fundamentally different from or in opposition to the general moral principles by which the social worker leads her life (see Banks, 2004a, ch. 2, for a more extensive discussion of the relationship between professional ethics and the ethics of everyday life).

Ronnby notes the tendency for the welfare state (of which social work is a part) to reinforce existing inequalities in society and to treat those who are the poorest and least powerful as objects to be pitied or changed. His solution is for social workers to adhere to their personal humanistic ethics and to come closer to their service users as fellow human beings. Halmos (1978) and Wilkes (1981, 1985) argue for a similar view. This has resonances with the references to 'love' in the 1997 version of the Swedish code of ethics (Akademikerförbundet SSR, 1997) and to the 'ethics of proximity' of Levinas (1989) and some Nordic ethicists such as Løgstrup (1997). Bauman (1993), in his discussion of postmodern ethics, is also influenced by

Levinas, talking of the 'moral impulse' – a personal capacity to act morally, which is the property of an individual as opposed to external ethical frameworks (such as professional ethics). Bauman (1993, p. 19) emphasises the moral responsibility of the individual over and above the various roles people play (one of which might be 'social worker'), each with their ethical rules. Husband (1995, p. 99) applies this to social work, arguing that the moral impulse is a necessary basis for responsible social work intervention: 'By its untrammelled innocence and generosity it is the creative core of caring.' This sort of view seems to entail that the relationship between social worker and service user might be one of unconditional caring, in the same way as a mother cares for her child, for example. It would involve removing the distinction between private and public morality. It has resonances with (although it is distinct from) the ethics of care discussed in Chapter 3, based on relationships of caring between connected individuals as opposed to the externally imposed ethics of justice based on duty, universal principles and the notion of separate individuals.

However, the view that the social worker should genuinely care about service users and treat them as she would friends or strangers in her ordinary life seems problematic in the context of much current social work practice, especially in the state sector. While an ethics of proximity based on the responsibility I feel in the face-to-face encounter between myself and the 'other' may be a foundation, a precondition or starting point of ethics, there is a need to go beyond 'the moral party of two' to reach justice – 'the realm of choice, proportion, judgement – and comparison' as Bauman (1997, p. 222) acknowledges. Bringing the discussion back to concrete realities, when out shopping on a Saturday I might give some cash to a man in the street who asked for some money for food and take him home for a cup of coffee. But surely I should not give money out of my own pocket to a service user in the social work office who asked for money for food and take him home for a cup of coffee while on duty as a social worker on Monday? First, this might leave me open to accusations of favouritism, as I cannot do this with all service users. Second, if I did give this level of personal care to all service users I would be impoverished and exhausted. Third, this would involve developing a personal relationship with a service user that might leave him and me open to abuse. These reasons echo those given by Downie and Loudfoot as to why it is important that social work operates within an institutional framework of rights and duties, to protect both the social worker and the service user.

It is doubtful if Halmos, Wilkes, Ronnby or Husband are actually arguing that social workers should treat service users as friends, rather that we should treat them as fellow human beings for whom we feel empathy and respect and that we should regard ourselves as people first and foremost, applying the same fundamental ethical principles to the situations we encounter in social work as we would to other situations in other parts of our lives. A more moderate version of this view would be to acknowledge that social workers are employed by organisations that operate by certain rules and procedures and are constrained by professional norms, societal mores and the legal system. Within this framework they should treat service users with as much honesty and respect as possible, but it is not usually regarded as part of the job to care for service users unconditionally. It is arguably more important that the social worker holds on to her own personal values not in order to give unconditional love to service users, but in order to challenge laws, policies and practices regarded as unjust and oppressive, including 'blowing the whistle' on institutionalised malpractice. This requires not just a commitment to a set of ethical principles, but also characteristics of moral perception, sensitivity and courage – qualities discussed in Chapter 3 in relation to virtue ethics.

The professional is political: challenging injustices and 'blowing the whistle'

Machin (1998) gives an account of her experience as a social worker in a secure hospital for mentally disordered offenders in the UK, her decision to give evidence to a public inquiry investigating allegations of patient abuse and her subsequent dismissal from her job. She speaks of her own beliefs as being important:

> My social work practice was born within the radical model. My formal training confirmed my belief that the traditional social work models need to be challenged in the light of human experience and emotion, and that workers need to get alongside their clients in order to foster empowerment and counteract the effects of their disabling conditions of life. My efforts to understand the context of the social and economic conditions in which my clients existed did not distance me from feelings of warmth and compassion, or from painful emotions born from understanding the effects of poverty and deprivation. (Machin, 1998, p. 118)

Machin specifically locates herself within the 'radical model' –

working for change in social conditions – while also retaining compassion for the people she is working with. One of the slogans of the early feminist movement was: 'The personal is political.' Machin's comments are a reminder that the professional is also political – that is, as a person in a professional role we have a duty publicly to challenge inhuman, degrading, unjust and oppressive practices committed by fellow professionals. Briskman (2005), writing from an Australian perspective on the abusive and inhumane treatment of indigenous people and asylum seekers by services that are delivered by social workers, exemplifies a similar commitment to expose and challenge unjust policies and practices with which social workers are often complicit. This was achieved through undertaking research, writing newspaper articles and campaigning with others within and outside the university where she worked.

Separation of personal, professional and agency values and life

At the other extreme, Leighton (1985) argues for the separation of personal, professional and agency values. He suggests that social work aims to manipulate and change people; social workers act not as ordinary human beings as they would in their personal lives, but take on a separate role, which requires them to appear to care, but not in the genuine way in which one would care for a friend. He gives the example of a social worker who needs to get certain intimate information from a young person in residential care (presumably for a report):

> The social worker is therefore obliged to try to draw the child into a relationship for no other purpose than to satisfy the social worker's job requirements. It is exceptional if the worker offers important parts of himself or herself to the child's personal social world. The relationship is part of a statutory and financial transaction from which only the social worker benefits financially. (Leighton, 1985, p. 78)

He argues that we must separate the personal and the professional, so that we do not feel guilty about manipulating people and using relationships as we would if we treated someone in the same way in ordinary life. According to Leighton, the social worker is required to:

> manipulate people and their relationships, and must learn the art of appearing to care when his natural feeling is not to care. To survive as a private person and to do his work well he must sometimes

operate within a mode of 'bad faith', a lack of absolute honesty in the relationship. (Leighton, 1985, p. 79)

Leighton's view seems rather extreme. It could ultimately lead to the social worker simply taking on a job and following all the norms, procedures and practices required by the agency regardless of whether they appeared to be morally wrong or to be allowing morally wrong actions to occur, according to the ethical principles of the profession or her own personal moral code. Taken to its limit, such a view could imply that a social worker working in a secure hospital where systematic abuse of residents is taking place (as described by Machin, 1998) could justify her actions by saying 'I was only doing my duty in accordance with the agency procedures' as if it was nothing to do with her if the agency norms were immoral or cruel. It would leave little room for whistleblowing as a moral duty in cases of institutionalised malpractice.

This type of view seems to entail that there is no person over and above a series of social roles of which the private/personal is just one. Leighton gives an example of a social worker, Mr Anthony, and argues that certain values from his personal life, such as converting people to Catholicism and believing abortion to be morally wrong, conflict with professional values such as service user self-determination and non-judgementalism, both of which conflict with the employer's values such as assisting with birth control techniques and encouraging conformity to social norms. His conclusion seems to be that being a social worker is a totally different and separate thing from being a private individual. But is it? Surely the private individual or person decided to accept the job of social worker with its particular values and duties. If he was the kind of person who was such a strong Catholic that he went around trying to convert neighbours, friends and people in the street and he strongly opposed birth control, then arguably he would not have chosen to become a social worker with this particular agency. Most Catholics do not try to convert people in the street or to dissuade strangers from having abortions. Surely moral standards similar to those Mr Anthony has for relating in his private life to strangers and acquaintances may apply also in social work. When Mr Anthony goes to a concert or visits the bank, certain rules of behaviour apply that do not usually involve trying to convert the bank clerk or handing out anti-abortion leaflets in the concert hall. Similarly, social work may be regarded as a particular setting in which certain ways of behaving are appropriate and to which particular duties apply. As Koehn (1994, p. 153)

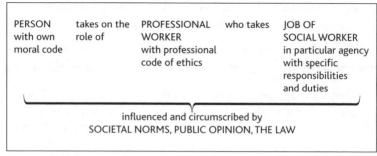

Figure 6.1 Relationship between personal, agency, professional and societal moral codes

argues, professionals do have special duties towards their clients and service users, but these are based in ordinary morality and represent an intensification of the relationship of trust in everyday life.

Most people would probably agree with Leighton that, as a general rule, social workers should refrain from trying to persuade service users not to have abortions and that social workers do not and cannot treat service users as friends. However, it does not follow that personal, professional and agency values should be treated as totally separate. Where they conflict, the social worker as a person has a moral responsibility to decide those that have primacy and to justify this decision. He may decide that he cannot work in an agency that involves so much work promoting birth control or that he will request not to deal with certain cases where he would feel compromised. Indeed, someone who has a strong commitment to the Catholic faith may actively choose to work for a Catholic charity that provides support to pregnant young women. Figure 6.1 illustrates the relationship between the personal, agency, professional and societal moral codes.

Committed/radical, professional and technical–bureaucratic models of practice

The two positions just outlined (that there should be no separation between personal and professional values and that they should be kept completely separate) represent very divergent views at a theoretical level. In practice, individual social workers may give more priority to personal, professional or agency values, depending upon what kind of work they do, how they view their jobs and lives, the conflicts and pressures arising in their work at particular times and the professional and societal norms operating in the country where they work. Table 6.1 outlines three ideal typical models of social work practice that I have called the committed/radical, the professional and the technical–bureaucratic. These are 'ideal types' as they are artificial categories and it would not be expected to find the practice of workers and agencies conforming neatly to these models. However, they are presented to help us explore the different emphases that social workers may adopt in their practice according to their ethical stance and their particular work settings. The committed/radical practitioner model sees the social worker as a person who has chosen to take on the job out of a personal or ideological commitment to work for change and who puts this first. This model encompasses many different types of approach ranging from the individual 'ministration in love' model to the more collectivist approaches espoused by Marxists, feminists and anti-racists. Although the same heading has been used to encompass all these approaches, there are obvious differences in focus ranging from individual empowerment to societal change.

Table 6.1 Models of social work practice

	Committed/radical	Professional	Technical–bureaucratic
Social work as	Vocation/social movement	Profession	Job
Social worker as	Equal/ally	Professional	Technician/official
Power from	Competence to deal with situation	Professional expertise	Organisational role
Service user as	Equal/ally	Client	Consumer
Focus on	Individual or group empowerment/ societal change	Individual worker– user relationship	Service provision
Guidance from	Personal commitment/ ideology	Professional code of ethics	Agency rules and procedures
Key principles	Empathy, genuineness/ raising consciousness, collective action	Users' rights to self-determination, acceptance, confidentiality, and so on	Agency duties to distribute resources fairly and to promote public good
Organisational setting that would best facilitate this	Independent voluntary agency or campaigning group	Private practice or large degree of autonomy in agency	Bureaucratic agency in voluntary, statutory or private sector

The professional model focuses on the social worker as an autonomous professional with expertise gained through education and guidance coming from the professional code of ethics. Her first priority would be the rights and interests of service users and her identity as a social worker would be as a member of the profession first and as a private individual or worker in an agency second. The technical–bureaucratic model regards the social worker first and foremost as a worker in an agency with a duty to carry out the prescribed tasks and roles of that agency. Guidance comes from agency rules and procedures.

All three strands are evident in the social work literature and social work practice. The professional codes contain elements of all three, but the emphasis is more on the professional model, tempered with duties to the employing agency (technical–bureaucratic) and personal commitment to work for societal change (committed/ radical). Social work has never comfortably fitted into the role of 'professional expert' for reasons that include its ideological tendency to identify with oppressed users and its location in state-sponsored agencies. As Howe (1991, p. 204) comments: 'I remain impressed with analyses which reveal social work to be largely a state-sponsored, agency-based, organisationally-tethered activity. It is not wise to tackle any examination of social work without taking note of this formidable context.' This is why attempts to make social work fit into either the professional or the committed models are very difficult, given the organisational context.

Arguably, the technical–bureaucratic model is becoming more dominant, at least in the state sector and large not-for-profit organisations. Many commentators have expressed concern about the 'de-professionalisation' of social work, which relates to the increasing specification of tasks and procedures, attempts to reduce indeterminacy in decision-making and to reduce reliance on or trust in autonomous professional judgement and the adoption of competency-based approaches to education and training (Dominelli, 1996; Hugman, 1998b). The growth of interest in 'evidence-based practice' could be seen to be part of this trend. Although a focus on evidence-based practice is relatively recent in social work (see Gibbs and Gambrill, 2002; Smith, 2004), in medicine it is already well developed and has been described as a 'process of systematically finding, appraising and using contemporaneous research findings as a basis for clinical decisions' (Long and Harrison, 1996, p. 11, quoted in Malin, 2000, p. 21). This has led to the development of an increasing number of clinical guidelines as a way of 'ensuring the avoidance of mistakes and/or sub-optimal treatments' (Dent, 1999, p. 161). This tends to result in a standardisation of practice and a reduction in the individual autonomy of professional practitioners. In a social work context, it has been criticised for focusing on measurable therapeutic interventions within a managerial and social control framework while neglecting reflexivity, flexibility and creativity in the social work role (for a useful summary of arguments for and against see Payne, 2005, p. 64; also Gibbs and Gambrill, 2002; Webb, 2001, 2002). However, Malin (2000, p. 21) sees the evidence-based approach as offering opportunities for greater professionalisation in the social care field and a way of advancing claims to professionalism. The reasons for this, of course, are that it is an approach based on scientific rationality that appears to give more credibility to the effectiveness of professional interventions, hence enhancing the notion of professional expertise in dealing with increasingly technical and complex tasks. In the context of medicine, Dent (1999, p. 161) argues quite categorically that these practices 'cannot be seen as the start of any process of deprofessionalisation, McDonaldisation, de-skilling or proletarianisation'. However, they do amount to a process of rationalisation that the organised profession is willing to countenance as a way of practitioners enhancing their collective autonomy (in defining the clinical guidelines) while giving up some of their individual autonomy (in each practitioner having leeway to make different judgements in similar cases). This could be seen as another feature of the 'new professionalism', whereby professions and professionals have absorbed aspects of the managerialist, technical–bureaucratic approaches, while still retaining the notion of professional expertise.

With the increasing fragmentation of social work in many countries, and with services previously provided by the local state being shifted to the private and not-for-profit sector, there is also an increasing opportunity in some areas of work for workers to operate within more traditional professional or committed models of practice. For example, specialist advocacy or counselling projects can be established with an unequivocal focus on the individual service user–worker relationship, where it is very clear that the advocate or counsellor is primarily concerned with the rights or interests of the service user. As it is increasingly recognised that people in powerless positions or who find it difficult to speak for themselves should have independent advocates to support them, then this is separating out the advocacy role from the general social work role. This means that the state-sponsored social worker may be concerned with allocating and rationing resources between many service users, whereas the advocate will push for the wishes, needs and rights of this particular service user. Similarly, there is a growth of a range of 'detached', outreach or street-work posts with specific service user groups (often defined as 'hard to reach') that recognises the importance of workers having personal and life experiences close to the experiences of those with whom they are working. Deverell's research in the UK with HIV prevention outreach workers demonstrates that many workers do the job because, as gay men, they have 'a keen interest in seeing HIV prevention done amongst gay men ... and because politically I wanted to be involved in a job that had something to say to me personally' (worker quoted in Deverell and Sharma, 2000, p. 29). Deverell found that at times they felt 'more like a peer than a professional' (p. 30), with workers using the terms 'vocation' (p. 35) and 'way of life' (p. 31). Yet, while recounting many instances when they were 'off duty' but still responded to requests for advice, many workers were also very aware of the importance of setting certain professional boundaries and standards in the work, which could otherwise be very fluid and open ended, with potential for exploitation (of service users by workers and vice versa). Much community and social development work may also have this character, particularly in countries where social work is less organised as a profession. For example, Herscovitch (in Healy, 2001, pp. 174–5) describes the practice of a social worker, herself a Cambodian refugee, working on mental health issues in a large refugee camp in Thailand through training 'natural helpers' (Buddhist nuns).

So while it may often be the case that a social worker will find herself working within all three models (and hence experience conflicts of duties), the emphasis will vary not only according to the individual worker's view of her role, but also according to the particular piece of work being undertaken and the type of work setting. A social worker employed as a counsellor by an independent voluntary organisation to work in complete confidence with people with HIV/AIDS will find the organisational and work setting much more conducive to operating within a professional model of practice than a practitioner employed by the local state, working in team, a large part of whose job is to assess and plan care packages for older service users. A community development worker employed by a neighbourhood residents' association with a campaigning brief will find it easier to work within a radical model. A youth development worker, herself a committed Muslim employed by a local mosque to undertake informal educational work with Muslim young people, will readily be able to see her work in promoting young people's spiritual development in terms of her own faith commitment. Exactly how these practitioners work and put these values, principles and commitments into practice will also depend upon their personal qualities, levels of confidence, knowledge and skill and the broader cultural and national frameworks of values, policies and laws. For example, an HIV/AIDS counsellor working in India would have a very different role from one working in the UK. The implications of a white counsellor meeting a black service user, or vice versa, will be different depending on the context. A Muslim youth development worker working in Australia, Canada, the Netherlands or UK will face a very different set of dilemmas and problems than she would in India. If we look briefly at some of the key ethical principles for social work we can see how the organisational and work setting changes the interpretation and implementation of these principles.

Confidentiality

- *HIV/AIDS counsellor* – confidentiality is a key focus of the counselling relationship and it is important that the counsellor can assure complete confidentiality (privacy) between herself and the service user except in circumstances where it is legally permitted or required that the counsellor disclose information (for example, where another is likely to be seriously harmed or where a court requires information, see Bond, 2000; Thomas et al., 1993). There is nevertheless potential for tensions and dilemmas in this role, precisely around when it is judged right to breach confidentiality (for example, if the service user refuses to disclose HIV status to a sexual partner).
- *Social worker/care manager for the elderly* – the limits of confidentiality are much broader and may include other members of the team and other health care professionals and service providers. If this particular social worker is unavailable or sick, then it would be expected that another social worker would consult the service user's file and continue with the work. The relationship between service user and worker is not a private one.
- *Community development worker* – while acknowledging the need to respect the confidentiality of certain personal information relating to individual residents, confidentiality might be regarded

as relatively unimportant in the context of residents working together collectively to achieve change.

- *Youth development worker* – this worker will take account of the importance of family and community in the context of the Muslim faith and culture. While recognising confidentiality as important as part of the relationship of trust with particular young people, this will be balanced with a concern for young people's welfare and safety and the needs of the wider group/community. There is potential for generational and cultural tensions, especially if the young people have grown up in a western country, straddling the different value systems.

Primacy of service user self-determination and the service user's interests

- *HIV/AIDS counsellor* – while the counsellor may need to ration time between one service user and another, and in exceptional cases consider the interests of others (for example, if a service user has not disclosed their HIV status to a partner), within these limits the counsellor can focus on the needs and interests of the service user. It will depend on the style of the particular counsellor and the nature of the service user's needs as to whether the counsellor respects the service user's own choices and decisions or adopts a more parentalist or directive style.
- *Social worker/care manager for the elderly* – this worker will need to keep in mind the needs and interests of other people as well as the service user – for example, any family carers, neighbours, service providers and other current and potential service users who will need resources. While the service user's own choices and interests may be respected as far as possible, there are many limitations on this.
- *Community development worker* – would see the promotion of individual self-determination or empowerment as part of the process of collective empowerment to achieve change. However, there may be conflicts between individual, group and community development (including sub-groups within the neighbourhood).
- *Youth development worker* – may be concerned to facilitate the spiritual development of each young person in the context of the teachings of Islam, focusing on a concern for the self-determination of young people as Muslim young people.

Distributive justice

- *HIV/AIDS counsellor* – except, as we have mentioned, for the rationing of time between service users, this worker does not have a direct role in distributing resources between individual service users. However, the worker may choose to campaign and draw to the attention of service providers and policy-makers the inadequacy of resources for this service user group in particular and the discrimination they face in society; indeed the social work codes include this as a principle.

- *Social worker/care manager for the elderly* – this worker does have a duty to distribute the resources of the agency fairly between individual service users and to manage them efficiently. In making a decision about what course of action to take, resourcing issues will be as important as service user choices and needs.

- *Community development worker* – will be concerned to achieve redistribution of resources (power, wealth, good housing) to residents as a group according to need, linked to a striving for equality of result, and may use campaigning and community action approaches.

- *Youth development worker* – may be concerned to get young people's voices heard in the organisational structures of the mosque, the wider Muslim community and in the neighbourhood more generally – challenging religious discrimination, racism and ageism as part of a broader movement for social change. This worker may be able to see herself quite clearly as an advocate for Muslim young people, although there is a lot of potential for tensions between young people, adults and the wider community.

These simplified examples do not explore the details of the potential tensions and dilemmas within each role (handling ethical conflicts and dilemmas is the subject of the next chapter). But these examples do indicate how the work setting – the type of agency and the role defined for the social worker – influence the extent to which a social worker may work more within one model than another. In the UK and many other western countries, there is an increasing shift towards the bureaucratic model within statutory social work, which we will now explore.

Growth of managerialism and authoritarianism: the case of the UK

Since the late 1980s in the UK there has been a growth in the production of quality standards, procedural manuals and assessment schedules in state-sponsored social work. This is particularly noticeable in the field of child protection, although it is a trend throughout social work and indeed the public, independent and private sector generally. This trend can be understood in the context of:

- *Consumerism* – a concern to offer a consistent standard of service, linked to service users' rights and quality assurance;
- *Managerialism* – which seeks greater control over the work of employees;
- *Authoritarianism* – which emphasises the social control function of practitioners;
- *De-professionalisation* – a process that seeks to characterise social workers as officials carrying out agency policy.

In child protection, these trends have been given added impetus by the series of public inquiries into child abuse cases where either children died in their homes or they were taken away from home unnecessarily and it was said that social workers should have acted differently. This led to a vast quantity of guidance and advice from central government about how to assess children thought to be at risk, how to monitor them and their families, how to conduct inter-agency case conferences, how to investigate suspected cases of child abuse and how to prepare evidence for court (for example, Department of Health, 1988, 1999).

Statutory agencies have child protection manuals that contain this kind of information and give detailed guidance on the procedures that social workers should follow. Harris (1987) notes the tendency that this encourages towards defensive social work, whereby social workers 'go by the book' and are as concerned about protecting themselves and the agency as they are about the interests of the service user. Howe (1992) talks of the 'bureaucratisation' of child care work, and McBeath and Webb (1990–1) note the technicist language of one of the first key books of guidelines produced by the Department of Health (*Protecting Children*, 1988). Cooper (1993, p. 45) warns that: 'Social workers who are simply agents of protection agencies may find it more difficult to operate beyond official procedures and guidelines arising from legislation, more difficult to use professional discretion in taking risks.' Lengthy recording schedules following a checklist approach have also been developed in relation to assessing and monitoring children in the looked-after system (Department of Health, 1995), which some have argued 'enhance the bureaucratic nature of being in public care' (Knight and Caveney, 1998, p. 29).

In the context of child protection work, Howe (1992, pp. 496–7) argues that a new perspective is emerging:

> Injury and neglect suffered by some children results in the demand that children should be protected; that protection is achieved by improving, standardising and prescribing full and proper methods of investigation and assessment; and that bureaucratic forms of organisation appear to be the best way of handling the ever more detailed and complex requirements of this new perspective.

King and Trowell (1992, p. 7) comment that social workers from both statutory and voluntary agencies 'find themselves spending less time working to support and advise parents, and offering services to help needy children, and more time investigating allegations of child abuse, collecting evidence and helping bring cases before the courts'.

Parton argues that in a time of increasing public concern about child abuse and limited resources for social work, the aim of social work is to predict those families that are 'dangerous' and therefore to protect children from abuse in these families by removing them (Parton, 1989, 1991, 1997, 1998; Parton and Small, 1989; Parton et al., 1997). Families that are not regarded as dangerous should be left alone. The assumption is that there is a scientific method that can predict with relative accuracy the levels of risk that children may be subject to in their families and home environments. As Alaszewski (1998, p. 142) comments, 'risk offers an alternative to need'. Most of the child protection manuals work on the basis of a checklist of predictors (for example, is there evidence of sustained, stable and sound family relationships; are there supportive networks; is the child generally well cared for?). However, the manuals do not suggest how each factor should be weighed against another, neither do they offer any statistical methods for calculating risk. This is because it would be a fairly meaningless exercise. Although it would be possible to ask social workers to place a numerical score against each predictor, and then to calculate an overall level of risk, it is doubtful whether this would actually help in predicting which children were most likely to be at risk of abuse.

Indeed, despite all these policies and procedures, there is still concern that the professionals involved with children at risk of harm or abuse are not collaborating sufficiently with each other; neither are they monitoring children and families intensively or systematically enough (Laming, 2003). This is leading to further re-organisation of services for children and young people, more systematic inter-professional working and the use of shared information technology systems to track the progress of individual children and record the concerns of all the professionals involved, including those in the fields of social work, health, education, youth justice and youth work, for example (Department for Education and Skills, 2003). While these are presented as 'benign' systems for enabling welfare agencies and professionals to prevent harm and promote child welfare, there are inevitable concerns about increasing surveillance systems, invasion of privacy and infringements of professional relationships of confidentiality (see Garrett, 2004).

To regard child welfare and protection purely as a technical exercise ignores the ethical questions about how much 'abuse' society is prepared to tolerate, balanced against how much interference in family life is thought to be justified. As was argued in Chapter 1, social workers are faced with trying to balance these contradictory, ambivalent and changing societal values. Their major role becomes one of surveillance and collecting evidence, rather than therapy with the families.

Major changes in approach also took place in the field of community care for adults in Britain, following the implementation of the National Health Service and Community Care Act in 1993 with its stress on assessment and care management (Payne, 1995). Detailed guidance from central government was provided (Department of Health Social Services Inspectorate, 1991a, 1991b), which has been developed into manuals and procedures about how to conduct assessments, plan care packages, draw up contracts with providers of services and monitor standards and quality. Again, the language is largely technical, standardised forms are often used and a 'procedural model' is invoked by agencies (Coulshed and Orme, 1998, p. 27). Although the views of service users and carers are to be taken into account, ultimately the decision regarding what services to provide and how depends on availability of resources and political and ethical decisions about priorities for types of service user groups and services. According to Lymbery (1998, p. 875) much of the work of the social worker within care management is limited by both time and resources, leading to 'a form of practice dominated by unimaginative, routinized, bureaucratic approaches'. Indeed, research by Lewis and Glennerster (1996, pp. 140–3) demonstrates increased levels of bureaucracy and managerial control and a shift in the balance of work from counselling to administration. While there is also evidence of empowering and creative social work taking place, which maintains a focus on the service user as a whole person in a community context, even the more optimistic commentators acknowledge that care management presents significant challenges for social workers both in maintaining their professional identity and integrity (Lloyd, 2002).

These changes in the field of child protection and community care represent major shifts in the role of social workers. We have already noted the emphasis on service users' rights, complaints, service user involvement, starting from service users' needs rather than available services and adopting multidisciplinary approaches, in Chapter 5. Some commentators argue that this represents a shift in attitude and behaviour on the part of social workers and other professionals amounting to 'a cultural revolution' (Audit Commission, 1992, p. 19). Indeed, Lymbery (2000, p. 123) argues that 'the implementation of community care has signalled a substantial setback for the professional project ... of social work'. Yet in some ways such thinking is much less revolutionary for social workers than is being suggested. First, the values of social work have always been about 'putting the service user first' and the current of 'anti-professionalism' within social work has always been strong. Second, despite the rhetoric about service user-centred, needs-led services, in a time of resource shortage the reality is that economy and efficiency are often going to come before meeting the particular preferences and needs of service users.

The real revolution is arguably in the role that social workers are increasingly taking on as assessors, inspectors, gatherers of evidence and managers of budgets and in the fragmentation of the role of generic social worker into specialist functions with different titles. The duties required by the agency or employer are being defined in increasing detail in order to meet the ever-changing requirements of central government for quality standards (see, for example, Department of Health, 1998). This leads at best to bureaucratic practice (which focuses primarily on issues of needs or risk assessment and resource allocation as determined by agency rules and procedures) and at worst to defensive practice (going by the book and denying personal responsibility). Such an approach to practice can be distinguished from the 'professional' model, which focuses more on the individual worker–service user relationship with guidance from the code of ethics and the 'radical' or 'committed' model, which stresses individual or societal change and does not separate out the personal from the professional or agency values (see Table 6.1). While there is an increasing emphasis on the 'technical–bureaucratic' model at the present time, there are constant tensions between all three and this is part of the reason why ethical dilemmas often arise in social work – because of the many layers of responsibilities involved. We have already noted that much social work often takes place in bureaucratic settings where social workers may be taking on both 'professional' and 'official' roles; this tension between bureaucracy and professionalism was noted in Chapter 4.

Ethics in bureaucracies: defensive, reflective and reflexive practice

While some of the new managerialist developments may have been designed to reduce bureaucracy and decentralise decision-making, the growth of centrally defined schedules and procedures has, in fact, increased the administrative approach that is one of the hallmarks of bureaucracies. According to Torstendahl (1991, p. 37) bureaucracy is 'the social subsystem of administrative work in a specific setting'. Although the new managerialist bureaucracies may have more of a flavour of a 'contract' culture, with some flatter and more decentralised management structures (Gray and Jenkins, 1999, pp. 211–12), more specialisation and interdisciplinarity (Mullender and Perrott, 1998, pp. 69–70) and a concern with consumer responsiveness (Hugman, 1998a, pp. 135–60), I would argue it still makes sense to characterise them as bureaucracies. One of the major concerns about professionals located in bureaucracies has been and still is that bureaucratic decision-making undermines moral responsibility. Rhodes (1986, pp. 134 ff.) suggests that bureaucracy is based on role and legal responsibility and encourages a split between personal and professional life – freeing employees from the demands of their personal moralities. For example, she says that:

> while you might *personally* wish to give welfare recipients more money, the organisation forbids it. (p. 136)

> You may be urged to place a child in a foster home rather than a residential treatment school, because the more expensive treatment plan is viewed as 'inefficient' and 'costly'. (p. 137)

She notes the contradictions between the individualised, caring concerns of social workers and the impersonal requirements of bureaucracies and argues that 'being a good worker may mean acting unethically' (p. 137). However, we need to ask whether it is, in fact, unethical to refrain from giving welfare recipients more money. First, if it is just a question of me personally 'wishing' to do this, is it a moral judgement at all? If this were to be a moral judgement, it would be stated in terms of the fact that welfare recipients ought to have more money. If we assume that moral judgements prescribe action and are universalisable, then it should commit me to action and it would mean that other people in other areas in similar situations should be given more money. Yet if I give these people more money, others may have less; it may not be fair. If I break the rules for distributing money, then chaos will ensue. I could argue that it is in the greatest interest of the greatest number of people to stick to the rules at present because I am in an organisation that works by rules and is dealing with many people. If I decide to do this, surely I would not be acting 'unethically'? I would essentially be working from utilitarian moral principles relating to justice and fairness. It would be unethical if I *unthinkingly* always followed all agency rules and procedures; or if I *knowingly* acted unethically, using the agency rules as an excuse.

There is a tendency to assume that questions around the distribution of resources, efficiency and cost are not ethical ones. They are and it is dangerous not to regard them as such. Seeking the cheapest service may not be an unethical decision, if it can be argued that this results in more people getting some level of service, rather than a few people getting good-quality service. It should be noted that Rhodes espouses a virtue-based ethical theory, which, while consistent as a theory of ethics, does not reflect the system of morality currently predominant in social work. Working in a bureaucracy does not inevitably mean acting 'unethically'; indeed, as du Gay (2000) argues in defence of bureaucracy, the impartial rules that are the hallmark of a bureaucracy play an important role in professional life. Such rules could be seen to be derived from utilitarian approaches to ethics that focus on the fair distribution of resources. In fact, it is vital to see such work as very much in the sphere of the ethical, rather than the purely technical. This enables us to debate the fairness of the bureaucratic rules and principles and to question the value of presuppositions and in whose interests they have been devised. Otherwise, there is the danger that we become 'defensive' practitioners. The ethical decisions regarding resource allocation or what is to count as child abuse may have been made elsewhere (by central government or by agency managers), but that does not absolve the social worker of the responsibility to challenge these decisions if necessary. For example, we need to guard against the preoccupation the bureaucratic approach encourages with the distribution of existing resources and think about arguing for more resources for social work service users. The social worker in a bureaucracy can and should still be both a 'reflective' and 'reflexive' practitioner. In summary, we may distinguish between defensive, reflective and reflexive practitioners as follows:

- *Defensive practitioners.* If we extend Harris's (1987) notion of defensive practice to the field of professional ethics, then defensive practitioners 'go by the book' and fulfil duties/responsibilities defined by the agency and the law. There is no need to take blame if the prescribed rules and procedures have been followed. Social workers are 'officials' or 'technicians'. Doing 'my duty' means fulfilling my obligations to the agency, rather than doing the morally right action; personal and agency values tend to be separated, and the latter tend to be adopted while in the role of social worker.

- *Reflective practitioners.* Building on Schön's (1983, 1987) notions of reflection on action (after the event) and in action (while doing), there has been an increasing recognition of the importance of reflective practice in social work (see Banks, 2003; Gould and Taylor, 1996; Martyn, 2000). Reflective practitioners are able to recognise and analyse ethical dilemmas and conflicts in their practice and consider how and why they arise (for example, through unequal power relationships with service users; contradictions within the welfare system; society's ambivalence towards the state welfare and social workers in particular). They are more confident about their own values and how to put them into practice; integrate knowledge, values and skills; learn from experience; are prepared to take risks and moral blame. There is a recognition that personal and agency values may conflict and that the worker as a person has a moral responsibility to make decisions about these conflicts. *Critical reflection,* as defined by Fook (2002, p. 43) involves a focus on issues of power and a redevelopment of practice and theory in relation to changing power structures to become more emancipatory.

- *Reflexive practitioners.* Often the terms 'reflective' and 'reflexive' are used interchangeably. However, as Fook (2002, p. 43) points out, 'reflexive' is also used to refer to a stance taken (it has often been used in relation to practitioners undertaking research) whereby the practitioner is able to locate herself in the picture and recognise how she both influences and is influenced by the people and events she is observing. Reflexivity may embrace reflection, but it is a more complex process, as Taylor and White (2000, pp. 6, 34–5) outline in their exploration of how knowledge is made and used in professional encounters. Reflexive practitioners are aware of the dominant professional constructions influencing their practice and subject their own knowledge and value claims to critical analysis. This may involve questioning received ideas and professional practices, analysing how truth claims are made, how professionals and service users perform as credible, reliable or morally adequate people or how form-filling prescribes action. *Critical reflexivity*, would focus on how dominant discourses construct knowledge and values and on the potential for challenging and changing existing power relations. Critical practice, as Adams et al. (2002, p. 309) stress, is transformational.

Conclusions

This chapter has discussed the many layers of often conflicting duties and broader responsibilities that social workers have to balance and choose between. It has been argued that the critically reflective and reflexive practitioner needs to be aware of how these conflicts arise, to make informed ethical judgements about which responsibilities have priority, while recognising how the ethical frameworks she is using are themselves constructed and contested. She may have to operate within several contradictory models of social work practice and be able to recognise and hold the tensions between them. If the social worker takes on one model to the exclusion of others, then important aspects of social work practice will be ignored. If the social worker regards herself exclusively as a 'professional', ignoring the constraints imposed by the employing agency, then she may become narrow and elitist. If she wholeheartedly takes on board the technical–bureaucratic model, she may become the defensive practitioner, mindlessly following agency rules. If she sees her own personal religious or political beliefs as paramount, then she may become unaccountable to her agency or to service users. To recognise and balance these layers of responsibilities is part of what it means to be a competent and ethically reflexive practitioner. We need to recognise that personal, professional, agency and societal values are interlocking, yet in tension.

putting it into practice

Exercise 6

Aims of the exercise – to show how the values of the individual, the agency and society may be similar and/or conflicting.

1. Think of the job that you are currently doing or one that you have done in the past:
   - What are your main *aims* in the job?
   - What *roles* do you play?
   - Describe your major *achievements* in this job.
   - What *values* do you think underpin your work in this job? (What you regard as your major achievements may help you think through what your values are.)
2. Now imagine looking at your job from the point of view of the agency you are working for or used to work for:
   - What do you think the agency's *aims* are?
   - What do you think is the agency view of the *role* you are playing?
   - What *achievements* do you think would be highly valued by the agency?
   - What *values* do you think underpin the agency's work?
3. Now imagine looking at your job from the point of view of society as a whole, or 'the public':
   - What do you think are the public perceptions of the *aims* of the job?
   - What *role* do you think the public regards you as playing?
   - What *achievements* do you think would be highly valued by the public?
   - What values do you think underpin public perceptions of your job?
4. Are there differences between your values and those of the agency and/or society? If so, why do you think this is the case?

Further reading

Banks, S. (2004a) *Ethics, Accountability and the Social Professions*, Basingstoke, Palgrave Macmillan. Chapter 2 discusses the relationship between the ethics of everyday life and professional ethics, while Chapter 6 explores aspects of the new managerialism in the light of interviews with professional practitioners.

Fook, J. (2002) *Social Work: Critical Theory and Practice*, London, Sage. A useful outline of a critically reflective and reflexive approach to social work practice, based within a clear theoretical framework with a focus on strategies for practice. This book covers issues of power, diversity, discourse, deconstruction, reconstruction and narrative approaches.

Harris, J. (2003) *The Social Work Business*, London, Routledge. This book examines the introduction of business thinking into social work and how this is impacting on the profession and service users. It is largely based on the UK experience, but the trends have wider relevance.

7 | Ethical problems and dilemmas in practice

This chapter will explore some of the ethical problems and dilemmas that arise in everyday social work practice in contexts where social workers have to make decisions. First, I will briefly outline a particular view of the nature of ethical decision-making in professional practice. I will then explore examples of problems and dilemmas that have been collected from both trainee and experienced social workers, in the light of the discussion in the previous chapters. All the case studies in this chapter are based on real accounts given by practitioners, either as written cases or in the course of interviews when they were specifically asked to recount examples of ethical problems and dilemmas. I have summarised their accounts, but tried to stay as close as possible to the language of the practitioners. All examples are from the UK, unless otherwise stated and some details have been changed in order to preserve anonymity.

Ethical judgements

Much of social work is concerned with making decisions about how to act in particular cases. For example:

> Carla Jones is an 87-year-old woman of Afro-Caribbean origin. She lives alone in a quiet street near the centre of a small town in southern Scotland. She is the only black person living in the street. She has support from a home care worker and daily visits from her only daughter, who has a full-time job and four young children. She has been diagnosed as having Alzheimer's disease and is becoming increasingly confused about times and dates, forgets to take her medication and has left her cooker turned on and wandered out of the house without any clothes on several times. Recently she became violent when her daughter tried to take her home on one of these occasions, causing her daughter to be admitted to hospital with severe cuts and bruises. The daughter and neighbours are increasingly concerned and have asked for an assessment by the

social worker, demanding that Ms Jones be admitted immediately to a psychiatric hospital. Ms Jones has hitherto refused to go to hospital for an assessment of her condition and believes that her daughter should spend more time with her.

The social worker, along with a medical practitioner and the others involved in this case, has to make a decision about what to do. One aspect of the decision may be a judgement that: 'It is morally wrong to commit this woman to hospital against her will.' As is apparent from our discussion in Chapters 2 and 3, there is considerable disagreement among ethical theorists not only about the nature of ethics, but also about how judgements are arrived at and justified and, indeed, whether ethical judgements are more akin to expressions of taste or feeling than rational prescriptions for action (for a more detailed discussion of different theories of ethics see Hudson, 1978; Lafollette, 2000). Nevertheless, in the context of professional ethics – where professionals have defined roles and responsibilities and deal with the distribution of public resources – notions of accountability, rationality and fairness are regarded as important aspects of decision-making. One view about the nature of ethical judgements that I think fits with the general context of the work of the welfare professions is now summarised. It articulates many of the preconditions for principle-based ethics, with an emphasis on rational justification with reference to principles (as articulated in Chapter 2). However, the importance of the particularity of situations, attitudes and emotions is also included, building on the discussions in Chapter 3:

1. Ethical judgements are about *human welfare* – for example the promotion of human happiness or the satisfaction of needs (Norman, 1998, pp. 218–20; Warnock, 1967, pp. 48–72). What counts as a 'human need' will be relative to a particular society or belief system and will change over time. This does not necessarily mean there are no universal values, but how they are implemented may vary according to time, place and circumstances (Ife, 1999, pp. 218–19).
2. Ethical judgements entail *action*, that is, they are prescriptive (Hare, 1952, 1963). If a social worker makes the moral judgement that the woman suffering from confusion ought not to be committed to hospital against her will, then the worker should be prepared to act on this, which might include making plans for her to stay at home and being prepared to argue the case to her family, neighbours and to professional colleagues.

3. Ethical judgements about particular cases take into account the *context of the situation*, including the particular relationships and responsibilities of the people involved. The relationship between mother and daughter will be a crucial one in the case of Ms Jones. The fact that Ms Jones is of Afro-Caribbean origin may be important in appreciating her expectations of her daughter and in considering whether the white neighbours may be less tolerant of her behaviour because she is black.

4. Nevertheless, an ethical judgement should exhibit *consistency* with previous and future judgements in the sense that it should apply to other people in similar circumstances. We would expect that the social worker would make the same judgement about another confused woman, unless it could be demonstrated that the situation was significantly different.

5. It makes sense to ask people to *justify* their ethical judgements. They may do so with reference to some general principles within their particular system of morality or to particular relationships and responsibilities. In the case of Ms Jones, the social worker might refer to a belief that 'all individuals have a right to decide for themselves what they want to do' (the principle of self-determination). This in turn might be justified with reference to the principle that 'all persons should be respected as rational and self-determining beings'. Ultimately a stage is reached where no further justification can be given and certain beliefs about the nature of human welfare and needs have to be taken as given. Alternatively, or in addition, the social worker might justify her judgement with reference to her particular relationship with Ms Jones, her understanding of Ms Jones' feelings, or her responsibilities as a social worker. In coming to a decision, the social worker may also have had a dialogue with Ms Jones and her daughter, with the doctor and perhaps the neighbours. Part of this dialogue may have been about listening to the stories and views of these people, questioning racist attitudes, family relationships and expectations and seeking consensus about a course of action. This is a very important process of justification in action, achieved through dialogue with others.

Ethical judgements in context

In considering how pracitioners make decisions when faced with situations that raise ethical issues, problems and dilemmas, there is a tendency to focus on the process of making a moral judgement and to see this primarily in terms of moral reasoning, as we have just outlined. However, as James Rest (1994, p. 22) comments, in the context of his study of moral psychology:

> There is widespread agreement that there are more components to morality than just moral judgement. The trick, however, is to identify more precisely what else there is in morality, and how all these pieces fit together.

Rest (1994, pp. 22–6) identifies four components of moral behaviour, of which moral judgement is just one. I will now summarise and elaborate upon these. Since Rest uses the term 'moral' rather than 'ethical' I will continue with his use of terminology (bearing in mind that in this book I am using the terms interchangeably):

1. *Moral sensitivity* – awareness of how our actions affect others. One of the most important moral qualities of a professional practitioner is that of empathy and the ability to perceive a situation as one of moral significance. This can be linked to what Blum (1994, pp. 30–61) calls 'moral perception' (see also Vetlesen, 1994, p. 6), which involves the use of the faculty of empathy (a disposition to develop concern for others) to see the morally relevant features of a situation ('the features that carry importance for the weal and woe of human beings involved'). For example, Vetlesen (1994, pp. 85–125) regards Eichmann's failure to see himself as responsible for following orders to kill Jews in Nazi Germany as a failure of moral perception (an emotional failure). In the case of Ms Jones, the social worker has to see the situation as not simply a case of implementing the law as contained in the Mental Health Act (1983) or following a mental health assessment schedule, but as involving Ms Jones's freedom to remain in her home, her feelings of dismay, discomfort and disruption.

2. *Moral reasoning or judgement* – the ability to make critical judgements regarding moral values and various courses of action (to judge which action is morally justifiable). The traditional view of moral reasoning would be the application of general moral principles by individual moral agents to particular cases through a rational, deductive process (Kohlberg, 1981, 1984). There are other versions, however, which work from particular cases ('casuistry') or start from the practical idea of 'reasonableness' (Toulmin, 2001), based on dialogue with others. I have already outlined some of the elements of this process in the previous section.

3. *Moral motivation* – placing moral values above competing non-moral values. Rest (1994, p. 24) gives the examples of Hitler and Stalin whose moral failures are less to do with deficiencies in awareness or reasoning, but rather because they set aside moral values in pursuit of other values. In a professional context this might include values such as self-actualisation or protecting the employing organisation.

4. *Moral character* – having certain personality traits, such as courage, perseverance and high self-esteem, that predispose us to act morally. Rest (1994, p. 24) comments that someone may be morally sensitive, make good moral judgments and put high priority on moral values, but 'if the person wilts under pressure, is easily distracted or discouraged, is a wimp and weak-willed' then moral failure occurs because of weak character. In the case of Ms Jones, the social worker may need to persevere quite strongly to persuade the daughter to accept that her mother can still be cared for at home and have to make extensive and time-consuming preparations to provide adequate support.

All these components are vital when considering how social workers and other professionals develop into ethically sensitive and competent practitioners. While moral reasoning or judgment is very important, the other components are equally so, although we often do not regard them as being part of the domain of ethics.

Moral sensitivity, motivation and character are less easily abstractable, observable or teachable than moral reasoning based on ethical principles. We often used de-contextualised cases in teaching professional ethics (Banks and Nyboe, 2003; Chambers, 1997) that focus more on the action taking place than on the motivations of the people concerned, their complex webs of prior relationships and the emotions generated. Situated ethics, ethics in practice, is deeply contextualised. The distinctions between the ethical, practical, technical, political; between the personal, professional, societal, religious; between the emotional, rational, affective are artifical, but nevertheless useful. So in the discussions of what we have already identified as the ethical dimensions of situations, we can further abstract from the situations and focus on principles at stake and the processes of moral reasoning that might be undertaken to come to decisions or be used to justify actions by the key moral agents involved. This does not mean that issues of sensitivity, motives and character are less important, just that they may not always feature highly in the accounts that people give. I have used accounts given by practitioners of real situations experienced in their practice. But the accounts they gave me were already highly selective, and would inevitably be constructed around what it was thought would be relevant to exemplify ethical problems and dilemmas (see Banks and Williams, 2006). In turning these accounts into shorter 'cases' suitable for discussion in an ethics text, I have inevitably created stories that highlight the ethical dimensions I think are important and relevant.

Developing the reflective and reflexive practitioner: case studies from trainee social workers

In discussing ethical dilemmas with trainee social workers, there is often an acute sense of confusion, anxiety and guilt around the decisions social workers have to make and the roles they play. This may arise from limited understanding of the nature of the social worker's role (that it is complex and contradictory), idealism, a lack of information about policies and procedures or simply an absence of opportunity to rehearse situations and learn from experience. An important part, therefore, of the education and training of social workers is to facilitate the development of skills in critical reflection.

Developing a capacity for critical reflection and reflexivity is much more than simply learning procedures or achieving particular 'competences'. As noted in the previous chapter, the notion of the helping professional as a reflective practitioner was developed particularly by Schön (1983, 1987) and is now an influential strand in the literature of the caring professions (see Gould and Taylor, 1996; Smith, 1994; Yelloly and Henkel, 1995). It is based on the notion of the practitioner reflecting on what is happening while in action and reflecting on what happened afterwards ('reflection in and on action'). According to Brookfield: 'Practitioners develop strategies, techniques, and habitual responses to deal with different kinds of situations, drawing chiefly on their acquired experience and intuitive understanding' (Brookfield, 1987, p. 156).

Part of the process of becoming a reflective and reflexive practitioner is the adoption of a critical and informed stance towards practice. This can only come about through doing the practice, reflecting on it through dialogue and questioning and changing the practice in the light of the reflection. It also involves being aware of the practitioner's own position of power and how dominant discourses construct the knowledge and values we use to describe and work with situations, policies and practice. This links to the concept of 'praxis' and the inseparability of theory and practice. Some commentators have argued that the social worker should be not only a reflective practitioner, but also a committed practitioner, working for change in society through her action (Ronnby, 1992). This fusion of reflection and action has been called 'praxis' – a concept that can be found in Aristotle and is developed in Marxist thinking and through the works of Paulo Freire. This moves beyond simply stating that values, knowledge and skill are inseparable to a normative statement about what the role of the social worker ought to be. If the social worker compartmentalises reflection (values and knowledge) from action (use of skill), she is, in fact, deceiving herself. She is in 'bad faith', as Sartre (1969, pp. 47–70) would say, because she is pretending that her action can be value free and purely 'technical'. She is denying her own responsibility as a moral agent for that action. For Freire, reflection without action results in 'mentalism' and action without reflection in 'activism'; and both are empty (Freire, 1972).

'Beginning' practitioners, or those with little experience, have obviously had less opportunity to gain experience and develop strategies and responses – or what Schön calls 'theories in use'. What a beginning practitioner may regard as an ethical dilemma – a choice between two equally unwelcome alternatives involving a conflict between ethical values (principles, relationships or qualities of character) – an experienced practitioner may not. For the experienced practitioner, it may be obvious that one alternative is less unwelcome than the other or that one value has priority over another, so she does not even conceptualise the decision as involving an ethical dilemma. This does not mean that ethical issues are not involved or that the situation should not be seen as involving an ethical problem, just that, strictly speaking, a dilemma is what confronts the worker before a decision is made. If the situation is familiar or the worker has a clear sense of which ethical principles, relationships or qualities of character have priority in this type of situation, then the situation will not be experienced as a dilemma, but simply a case of having to make a moral choice or decision. Thompson et al. (1994, pp. 4–5) distinguish between ethical problems and ethical dilemmas – arguing that an ethical problem usually has a solution or, at least, a *possible* solution. This seems to imply that a dilemma does not. However, I would argue that most of the time social workers do have to resolve dilemmas – in that they do have to take some action, even if this is deciding not to act, in which case they make a choice between the alternatives. This may be done either by making a random choice or, more usually, after a process of reflection and research that eventually leads the worker to decide that one course of action may be better than another and therefore is the right action.

Some of the anxieties around the ethical dilemmas experienced by trainee social workers seem to be based on the following:

1. low levels of confidence in their own status/position, especially vis-à-vis other professionals;
2. lack of power in relation to the supervisor/practice teacher during a fieldwork placement;
3. lack of clarity about the role of social worker, for example carer or controller, and rules attached to the role such as confidentiality;
4. limited experience and knowledge in a new situation;
5. narrow focus on the needs or rights of one individual service user, or on one issue, without seeing the complexity of the case;
6. the complexity of the situation is seen, but found to be overwhelming.

The following cases from trainee social workers illustrate the above points. These are all examples of ethical dilemmas experienced by trainee social workers either whilst undertaking fieldwork practice, or before they joined a social work training programme (that is, when they were unqualified workers or volunteers). It is important to remind readers that I am using the term 'value' in the context of discussions about ethics (as described in Chapter 1) to cover: ethical principles; virtues; commitments to particular others; to projects and to political and/or religious beliefs and ideals.

Low levels of confidence in status/position

Treatment of a resident in an institution. Susan was a 22-year-old woman living in a residential care home for people with cerebral palsy and related disabilities who was prone to spells of depression, which resulted in her crying a lot or refusing to communicate or eat. She communicated by means of a communication board attached to her wheelchair. The trainee social worker, who had worked in the home as an unqualified care worker for four months, was told by the other staff that Susan's behaviour was due to homesickness, a crush on a member of staff and a 'predisposition towards attention-seeking behaviour'. When Susan became upset, the policy was to take her to her room, shut the door and leave her there to calm down. When the care worker talked to Susan, she said she would like to get out of the home more often, meet more people and take a course at a local college. She asked the care worker to pass this information on at the next staff meeting. When the care worker did this, Susan's request was dismissed as 'playing up' and 'nagging susceptible new members of staff'. The care worker felt that there was a culture of running the home to suit the staff who spent a large part of their time smoking and drinking coffee, while residents watched TV or sat motionless in the corridors. The care worker commented afterwards: 'I was worried that I was rocking the boat too much, that I asked too many questions and that I refused to fit into the team and their way of doing things ... Nothing happened and shortly afterwards I left.'

This case is typical of many recounted by inexperienced workers who give accounts of feeling powerless to challenge or change what they consider to be bad practice in not meeting the needs or respecting the rights and dignity of individual service users. In this case it is a question of not fitting in with the team norms, in other cases (as in the case that follows) it may be fear of reprisals or of the power of the practice teacher or fieldwork supervisor to fail a student's placement. This case raises the question of how to challenge practice within a staff team, which may lead to making a complaint or even whistleblowing. For inexperienced workers, who are not confident of the expected 'standards' or how a complaints procedure may work and may be worried about reprisals, it is often difficult to take any action at all. They are left feeling that they ought to have acted, yet failed to do so. Seeking alliances with other workers, trainees and talking to college tutors may help in rehearsing the arguments and testing others' understandings of what counts as bad practice and how it can be challenged.

The care worker's comments that she 'did not fit in' and was 'rocking the boat' are ways of presenting herself as different from the rest of the staff. In her account she is performing the role of 'good and sensitive worker' in contrast to the other staff. I have given short extracts from this worker's own words, to indicate how practitioners construct accounts of themselves as morally good and sensitive.

Lack of power in relation to supervisor/practice teacher during a fieldwork placement

Black male student in an agency working mainly with women. Jim was a male student undertaking a fieldwork placement in an independent sector agency working with the families of children who have been placed in care. Jim sometimes described himself as 'black' (his father was originally from Kenya and his mother was English), and he said that this was one of the reasons the agency was keen to have him on placement (as there were no other black staff working there). He recounted how he had immediately been assigned the case of man from Botswana as it was thought the two men would 'have something in common'. He found the placement difficult as the majority of the people he worked with were women, whom he described as often vulnerable single parents. He felt it was potentially easy for them to get attached to him as a supportive young man. So he refused to do home visits on his own with 'vulnerable women'. However, his practice teacher (who was also male) would make visits on his own and expected Jim to do the same. Jim felt quite uncomfortable about this and other aspects of his practice teacher's work. In particular, he noticed that the practice teacher often made what Jim thought were inappropriate comments to female service users. Jim considered whether he should challenge his practice teacher and/or share his observations with the agency coordinator. He explained that he felt unable to do this for a number of reasons. The agency was small and a complaint might have a bad effect on the organisation and the delivery of much-needed services. The smallness of the agency also meant that there was no staff member other than the practice teacher who could assess Jim's practice. He also knew that when students had made complaints in the past, the issues had not been dealt with. Jim commented:

> I think it's also hard for a student to challenge a professional who's been in the job for a long time, because the student always feels 'what do I know?', or they feel like the professional is going to say 'what the hell do you know, you're a student?'.

In this case, a male student is giving an account of his attitudes and actions that suggests he is very aware of his gender and his own potential position of power in relation to female service users. This is placed in the context of an agency where the prevalent culture seems to condone what the student considers to be not only poor practice, but potentially dangerous and oppressive behaviour. However, because of his position as an inexperienced student, who is also black (although Jim did not mention this in the context of discussing his relationship with his supervisor), he felt unable to do anything. The direct quotation from Jim at the end of the summary shows him presenting himself as a person of inexperience, vulnerable to challenge. He adds strength to this characterisation by speaking in the voice of 'a student' (implying it is not just him that feels like this) and a supervisor, to whom he refers as 'a professional' (which emphasises the contrast with the unqualified student).

The issues in this case have some similarities with the first case, but also the added dimensions of race and gender. Jim was in the position of being not only inexperienced, but also a black student undergoing assessment in a predominantly white agency that had already demonstrated a very simplistic understanding of issues of ethnicity and an institutional blindness to sexist attitudes and behaviour. The feeling of powerlessness as a student is a very common one. One group of trainee students from Finland, discussing issues arising from their fieldwork practice, commented on the conflict between the idealism they gain during their studies and the realities of practice in the 'outside world'. It is not always clear what the standard of acceptable practice should be and sometimes students are indeed too idealistic. Yet they also see things with fresh eyes and can disturb a cosy complacency or, even worse, a seriously neglectful or abusive situation. As mentioned in relation to the first case, it is important that students feel able to raise issues such as those experienced by Jim, particularly with their college tutors, if not directly to the agency concerned. Structures for doing this in a confidential and supportive manner need to be in place. Otherwise poor and oppressive practice will remain unchallenged.

Lack of clarity about role

> *Mother who was working and claiming benefit.* A young mother was referred to a family centre because of feelings of social isolation. During a counselling session with her key worker discussing budgeting and the problems caused by spending any time away from her daughter, she revealed that she was claiming income support (a state benefit) and working nights as a cleaner. The key worker posed the following questions: 'Should I ignore it? By discussing it with her am I legally condoning it? Should the matter be reported to the Benefits Agency? Should the principle of confidentiality be upheld? Is the social worker an agent of the state?'

This trainee worker, having outlined the details of the case (which I have summarised) asks several questions at the end. These questions indicate that she is constructing this example as a dilemma or at least a difficult choice where she feels there is no one right answer. She presents herself as thoughtful, raising the issues and particularly as wondering about the extent to which she is 'an agent of the state'.

It appears that the worker is assuming that her responsibilities to the state extend more widely than they in fact do. She does not realise that if a service user has done or is doing something illegal the social worker does not automatically have to report this to the appropriate authority. Usually a social worker would only break confidentiality in these circumstances if a very serious crime were being committed or a life were in danger. While the social worker should not aid and abet a service user in an illegal pursuit, discussing the matter does not necessarily entail condoning it. In fact, the social worker can make it clear that what the service user is doing is illegal and cannot be condoned. Not only would the experienced practitioner be clearer about the law, but she would probably have had time to reflect on the complex and contradictory nature of the social worker's role and know when it was appropriate to adopt a social control role, an enabling role or a caring role. She might also ask the question 'whose dilemma is it anyway?' (Bond, 2000, p. 224) and realise that it is, in fact, the service user's own ethical dilemma, not the social worker's.

Limited experience and knowledge in a new situation

> *Child abuse disclosure to a volunteer.* A volunteer working in a day centre was approached by a 9-year-old girl with whom she had a good relationship, saying that her father had been hitting her and she was upset. She asked if the volunteer would sit in on a meeting between the girl and her parents. The centre manager encouraged the volunteer to go ahead and provided a room. The volunteer was given no guidance on procedure. She was asked to swear confidentiality by the father at the outset of the meeting. She commented afterwards: 'In my naivety I agreed, which I later found out was a mistake.' She was told about a variety of sexual and physical abuse and then faced a dilemma regarding what to do about this.

This trainee social worker is presenting herself as a naive volunteer. She is giving an account of a situation where she made a mistake. The dilemma here for the volunteer could be construed as a choice between respecting the confidence and keeping her promise to the girl (this could be linked to a Kantian approach) or breaking the confidence and discussing the matter with her line manager because of the serious harm that is being done to the girl (a utilitarian approach). A decision may be made by balancing the importance of respecting a confidence against what is in the girl's best interests – weighing up the immediate danger to the girl and the likelihood of the volunteer being able to persuade the girl to tell someone else. Alternatively, the volunteer may realise or discover that the agency she works for has a policy that all suspicions about child abuse must be reported to the line manager. She may decide that agency rules should always be followed or that this particular rule is an important one and it is in the interests of all that it is followed. Therefore the dilemma is resolved and she should tell her line manager.

For the experienced practitioner this case may not present a dilemma at all. First, the experienced practitioner would probably have said at the start that she could not promise confidentiality. However, assuming she had promised confidentiality because she knew the girl had something important to say and would not be able to say it otherwise, the experienced social worker would usually be much more aware of herself as an employee of an agency and would be familiar with agency rules and procedures and have worked out which ones it was important to follow. She may have worked out from past experience that confidentiality can never be absolute and in her view the best interests of the service user always come first.

The learning from this experience for the volunteer is that in similar circumstances next time she would start the meeting by explaining that any information she was given might be shared with the line manager. This might not stop her feeling anxious about sharing the information she was given, but she might perhaps feel less guilty about breaking a confidence.

Narrow focus on individual service user/one issue

> *Elderly couple and residential care.* Mr and Mrs Finch, aged 91 and 86, were admitted to residential care by the social work night duty team on a call from the warden of the sheltered accommodation where they lived. They were reported as being unable to cope with everyday domestic functions and Mrs Finch had had a fall in the night. There was pressure from the family, the warden and senior social work colleagues for them to be admitted permanently to

residential care. The trainee social worker stated that when she visited them: 'Mr and Mrs Finch were suffering from impaired memory function. They could not comprehend why they had been admitted to residential accommodation, but were categoric that they wanted to return home.' She felt that 'the couple should be allowed to return home on the basis of their individual right to choose'.

The trainee social worker in this case expresses her position using the language of social work ethics: 'their individual right to choose'. This case is presented as quite clear and unequivocal and the use of the word 'categoric' emphases the strong voice of the service users. The trainee social worker may well be right in this case – that the couple should be allowed to return home – but focusing on their right to choose (which links to Kantian ethical principles) is only one way of looking at the issue. She might consider the extent to which they are capable of making an informed choice, as well as taking into account the rights and needs of the warden and the family. It seems as though she sees herself principally in the role of advocate for the service users, whereas it is often the social worker's job to assess the whole situation and work for a solution in the best interests of all concerned (a more utilitarian approach). In stressing the principle of service user self-determination, there appears to be no dilemma here for the trainee social worker. Since she knows what is the morally right course of action, what she feels she is facing is a moral problem – of how to achieve this in the face of opposition. Others might see it as a dilemma – to be resolved by taking various other factors into account, such as whether the service users understand the risks attached to returning home and what level of support and responsibility is it fair to place on the warden.

Complexity of the situation is seen, but found to be overwhelming

Banning a particular newspaper in a residential home. At a staff meeting at a residential unit for drug users it was decided that the unit should stop buying newspapers published by News International. The reason for this was the dispute at the time between the printers' trade unions and this publisher. The union for public sector employees, to which the staff of the unit belonged, was supporting a boycott of these papers. The initial ban was just on newspapers from the unit's funds. Subsequently a ban was extended to residents buying a particular UK newspaper owned by this publisher, called the *Sun*, out of their own money on the grounds of not only the union dispute, but also its sexist, homophobic and racist stance and its distortions on the subject of AIDS. The trainee social worker reported that: 'What initially appeared to be a straightforward dilemma when the ban was introduced as a union issue soon became a complex and deeply disturbing problem for all concerned.'

The trainee social worker, in talking about this case, identifies it as 'complex and disturbing'. He raises a series of questions at the end of his account (not included here), including asking whether social workers are agents of change and, if so, where the limits of their responsibility to bring about change lie. He is presenting the case as one where complex ethical issues arise and he has been troubled by these. If the *Sun* is banned, what about television programmes and pornographic magazines? Have workers the right to impose their own values on residents? It was only after much reflection and discussion afterwards that this worker reports that he came to the view that the *Sun* should not be banned, but rather the issues regarding the dispute with the unions and the prejudiced and offensive nature of much of the material in the newspaper should be discussed with residents. This would entail treating the residents as capable of making their own choices and encouraging them to participate in decision-making. This case illustrates the dangers of an unquestioning radical stance, treating service users in a parentalist fashion (making judgements about what is best for them) and using them as part of a group of social workers' own political campaign. This worker engaged in a process of dialogue with colleagues and reflection himself in order to work out a course of action he felt was ethically justified in order to resolve the dilemma.

When are blame and guilt justified? Case studies from practitioners

In experienced practitioners, we would generally expect some clarity about their role as social workers, a certain confidence in acting on their own principles and an ability to hold complexity and contradiction in the work. Indeed, when senior social work practitioners were interviewed about ethical dilemmas in their work, their responses frequently referred to difficult cases involving ethical issues and problems (particularly around lack of suitable resources or threats to service users' well-being) rather than ethical dilemmas as such. A team manager in a childcare team told me of several difficult cases where other agencies had recommended courses of action with which she disagreed. Although she used the term 'ethical dilemma' frequently, it was clear that she knew what was the right course of action and was prepared to act on this. One of her examples is given at the end of this chapter, which highlights some of the value conflicts in multi-professional work in the field of health and social care.

Nevertheless, even the most experienced practitioners find themselves facing ethical dilemmas and have feelings of guilt about the choices and actions they take. Some of this guilt and blame is necessary – if we do what we know to be morally wrong, retreat into defensive practice or take a decision that turns out to have a bad outcome that we could have predicted if we had thought about it more deeply. Yet some of the guilt and blame is unnecessary and unproductive, as was discussed in Chapter 1. It is easy to see how it comes about, for the nature of a dilemma is that whatever decision is made there will be some unwelcome outcomes. Usually, there is a choice between two or more conflicting values or ethical principles, all of which we believe are important. If we can understand that this is the nature of the job and that, for example, in a particular case, we chose to break confidentiality because another overriding value relating to the welfare of the service user was more important, then we should not regard ourselves as having acted immorally. Rather, we have faced up to a difficult ethical decision. The following four case examples relate to two situations where social workers said they felt bad about the decisions they had made and wondered if they should have acted differently and two situations where the workers knew they had made hard or uncomfortable decisions, but still felt confident that they had made the right choice. In the two cases where the workers reported feeling confident about their decisions (one of which also resulted in a bad outcome), both workers felt very clear about where they stood on a particular issue – they had thought through their positions and accepted what the consequences of their actions might be. The four case examples can be categorised as follows (names and some details have been changed to preserve anonymity):

1. The worker felt guilty because a bad outcome occurred and he was aware of the dangers and wondered if he should have done more to prevent this.
2. The worker felt her actions were morally right, despite a bad outcome, because she stuck to a deeply held principle.

3. The worker felt guilty because he had to compromise an ethical principle to which he was committed.
4. The worker felt her actions were morally right, despite having to compromise one of her values, because another value had priority.

Worker felt guilty about a bad outcome

The following example was given to me by an approved psychiatric social worker and is a case where the social worker felt he did not act in the service user's best interests and felt guilty about this. The fact that there was a bad outcome to the case (the person died) no doubt exacerbated the feelings of guilt.

The service user's interests versus the constraints of the agency role. The social worker described a case where he felt the drugs administered by a psychiatrist had caused the physical health of a hospital patient, Mrs Baldwin, to deteriorate, culminating in death by pneumonia. Mrs Baldwin's family were concerned about whether she had been given the right treatment and whether the pneumonia had been picked up soon enough. The social worker commented: 'I thought it was the drugs that had caused her death. I didn't say it to the family. In the end you're working so much with other health professionals. I colluded.'

The social worker clearly felt quite bad about this case. He had been involved with admitting this woman to hospital originally for 28 days under the Mental Health Act (1983). The social worker felt this was the right decision. On going to hospital Mrs Baldwin became calmer, accepted her fate and agreed to take medication. But it soon became obvious to the social worker that the medication was affecting her physically. The social worker said he felt responsible for her, as he watched her condition deteriorate as she was shipped backwards and forwards between the psychiatric and general hospitals. He did not seem sure what he could or should have done: 'It is difficult to question consultants. You can only question whether hospital is the best place, not the diagnosis and treatment.'

In hindsight, he suggested that the point at which he could have done something was after the original 28-day period of detention in hospital ran out and was then renewed for six months. He did have a choice at this stage regarding whether to sign the documents as an approved social worker. However, he did feel Mrs Baldwin needed

> to be in hospital and trusted the hospital to pick up on any serious
> physical problems.

This case seems to have three stages. The first stage was the initial
committal to hospital, which the social worker felt was legally and
morally justified. The second stage was the time during the treatment, including the time when the application for compulsory detention in hospital had to be renewed, when he knew Mrs Baldwin was
deteriorating physically, but did not do anything about it. The third
stage was after her death when he had to decide whether or not to tell
the relatives the truth about his own feelings relating to the cause of
death. He commented that, with hindsight, perhaps he could have
acted differently at the second stage, but it would have been difficult.
Did he retreat into a kind of defensive practice? He acted within the
law and according to agency rules, but was he denying some moral
responsibility for the situation when he said that it was not his role
to question the diagnosis? It is always a difficult decision to go
beyond the agency-defined role – to risk going out on a limb, to
challenge another professional when it is not one's role to do so.

This is a good example of the type of tough dilemma often faced
by social workers, when no course of action has a good outcome.
The worker has to try to weigh up how much risk or harm to a
service user should be allowed before some action is taken. We can
understand the social worker's inaction in this case; perhaps we
would not blame him for Mrs Baldwin's death. However, we might
think perhaps his own feelings of blame and guilt are justified
because he did not do what he thought was in Mrs Baldwin's best
interests. The ethical issues here relate not just to the rights and
interests of the service user and the duties of professionals to
promote the welfare of service users, but to the summoning of the
courage and confidence to implement the right action. While it may
not be the social worker's role to question the diagnosis and treatment prescribed by a psychiatrist, the well-being of the service user
should be the joint concern of the various health and social care
professionals involved. This case illustrates the need for social
workers to assert themselves in multi-professional contexts and be
clear that they can and should voice professional opinions on all
aspects of service users' welfare.

The third stage of this case, when the question of what to say to
the relatives arose, is probably less problematic. Given the social
worker had signed the papers for the renewal of the detention in
hospital and had not challenged the consultant then or later, he no

doubt felt that it was not fair to mention his views about the drugs to Mrs Baldwin's family. The situation might have been different if the social worker had believed the psychiatrist to be incompetent and likely to put other patients at risk.

Worker did not feel guilty about a bad outcome because she stuck to a deeply held principle

The following example was given to me by a youth worker. It related to her previous experience as an unqualified worker in a voluntary sector youth club about 20 years ago. She felt the case described presented a moral dilemma and she had made a decision based on her belief in confidentiality and service user self-determination as absolute moral principles. Although the outcome of the situation was bad, she still felt she had made the morally right decision.

Confidentiality and service user self-determination versus the service user's interests. The youth worker was working in a busy youth club on a normal youth club evening. She was approached in the coffee bar by a 15-year-old girl, Jan, who was obviously in a state of distress. The youth worker took her into a quiet room. From that initial contact Jan swore the worker to secrecy. Jan revealed to the worker over several weeks that during the past year she had been raped four times by her father and was now pregnant by him. She had also decided to commit suicide as a way out of the situation. The youth worker talked through the issues with Jan, suggesting various options for help and that suicide was not the best way out. However, Jan continued to refuse to consider any professional help and insisted that the worker should not tell anyone. The youth worker respected her request for confidentiality. Jan did commit suicide.

This case relates to a youth worker, not a social worker, and to past practice in the voluntary sector. If the worker had been working for a UK social work agency or the majority of youth club settings at the present time, agency policy would require the worker to report any cases of suspected child abuse and would advise workers not to promise absolute confidentiality. The case would have been analogous to the one given earlier about the volunteer who promised confidentiality. However, in this case it seems there was no agency policy and the worker stuck to the principle of confidentiality because she personally believed it was an important one (this could be described as a Kantian approach). She did not feel she had any overriding duties to her agency or that she should adopt a different set of principles as a youth worker than she should in her everyday life – we might suggest that she was working within the committed practitioner model. She felt that the girl, at 15 years old, was capable of making her own decisions and should not be treated in a parentalist way. The youth worker, in spite of the girl's suicide, felt she had acted in accordance with her moral principles and therefore that her decision not to break the confidence was right.

This is a complex case to explore. For the majority of social workers and contemporary youth workers placed in such a situation, the decision about whether to break a confidence may hardly present a dilemma at all. Given it is a case of child abuse and there is even a slight risk of self-inflicted harm to the girl, a line manager or the statutory child protection services would be informed immediately. This would both cover the worker from feeling guilt if the girl did commit suicide and could be argued to be in the girl's best interests (utilitarian considerations). Other practitioners might see it as a dilemma, involving the weighing up of the importance of respecting the girl's right to confidentiality and to make her own decisions about her life against the likelihood of the girl committing suicide.

I am less concerned to consider what would have been the 'right' action in this case and more interested in the fact that this is a situation where a worker apparently did not feel guilty or responsible for a bad outcome. This type of worker is relatively rare in social work, partly because most social workers feel they have a right not to be burdened with the responsibility for someone's death and they adopt a much more utilitarian approach to moral decision-making by weighing up the possible outcomes of actions and being more prepared to take a parentalist view of what is in a service user's best interests. It is also partly because social work agencies (and many youth work agencies) have rules and procedures designed to ensure that an individual worker does not carry the total responsibility for the outcome of an intervention. Some people may feel that the youth worker should have acted differently and was at least partly to blame for the girl's death. The youth worker was in a position of responsibility in relation to the young people in the club and had a duty to promote their welfare; to adhere rigidly to a personally held principle of confidentiality may not have been appropriate in this context. Others may feel she was right, seeing her relationship with the girl in the context of a voluntary non-directive counselling role.

Worker felt guilty about compromising an ethical principle

The manager of a day centre for people with learning disabilities described a situation where he felt he had acted 'immorally'. The reason he described his action in this way was because he had made a decision that was contrary to one of the key principles that he believed was important for social work – namely, service user self-determination.

> *Service user self-determination versus the interests of the service user and others.* John, a 26-year-old man with learning disabilities who had been attending the day centre for some time, asked if he could walk to the centre on his own, rather than use the minibus provided by the social services department. Staff of the centre judged that he was capable of doing so and they thought that this would help him develop his life skills, self-confidence and independence. However, John's parents were extremely worried at this suggestion, feeling that John would not be able to cope. They stated categorically that they would not allow John to attend the centre if he had to make his own way there. The centre manager reluctantly agreed that John should continue to use the bus.

When the social worker who had been the centre manager was asked why he came to this decision, it became obvious that it was not that he lacked moral courage to take a risk or the integrity to hold onto his deeply held professional values, but rather that he was taking into account the views and feelings of John's parents, as well as what he thought would promote greater self-determination for John. He had taken account of the context of family relationships in which the decision had to be made and weighed up the consequences for John and his parents of insisting that John should walk to the day centre. Given that John relied on his parents for care, they had a right to have their views heard. Also it would not be in John's long-term interests if he stopped coming to the day centre or if his parents were excessively anxious. So this social worker had in effect gone through a process of weighing up the outcomes of the proposed change against the status quo and decided that the least harm would be done if the status quo were maintained. This social worker did not act 'unethically' – far from it – he actually exhibited moral sensitivity to the complexities of the situation and went through a very serious process of moral reasoning to come to the decision he did.

What this social worker's decision shows is that the principle of service user self-determination is not the only ethical principle, or even the paramount ethical principle for social work practice. Other principles such as promoting the good of the service user (which involves things other than self-determination) and promoting the general good (which involves people other than just the service user) are also important. If we accept utilitarianism as a theory of ethics, then these are ethical principles. If we continue to analyse this case in terms of principles, then this social worker could be described as facing an ethical dilemma involving a conflict between the principles of service user self-determination and the promotion of the greatest good of the greatest number of people. In order to resolve the dilemma he had to make a choice – and whichever choice he made would go against one of the principles. So it was not surprising that he was left feeling dissatisfied with the outcome. However, should he feel guilty that John was not allowed to exercise his freedom to walk to the day centre? Surely he should not, provided he felt he had done all he could to persuade and encourage the parents to allow a trial run. He may feel *regret* that John has not been allowed to walk to the centre, but not guilt. By reflecting on this and discussing it, will this worker feel any less guilty in the future? It is hard to say, but if he accepts that service user self-determination is not an absolute moral principle and that therefore it can be morally right to go against that principle, it might make it easier for him to understand the nature of the decisions he has to make.

Worker did not feel guilty because she clearly prioritised her values

This case is about the dilemmas expressed by a black practitioner working in a voluntary sector Asian women's project in a UK city. The project offered group work, educational opportunities and individual support to women who mainly came from various parts of India, Pakistan and Bangladesh. The worker herself was of Punjabi origin.

> *The needs of black children versus the 'betrayal' of the black community.* A woman of Punjabi origin moved into the area where the project was based from another part of the country. She was on her own, with five children under 6 years old, having fled a violent husband. She felt isolated as a newcomer, was given little support from the statutory services and found it hard to cope with the children. Her husband followed her and began harassing her. Some black professionals were providing her with limited support. In the course of her work, the worker at the Asian women's project discovered that the woman was locking up her children in her

house and going out, either to seek help or just for a break. The worker discussed this with her, explaining why it was not an appropriate thing to do and that the children were being put at risk. However, the woman continued to leave her children locked in the house. The worker had to warn the woman that if she continued to leave her children unattended at home she would have to report her to the statutory social work agencies and the implications of this might be that the children could be taken into care.

Finally the worker decided that she must inform the statutory social work agency because of the potential danger to the children. The worker found this a tough decision to make, because she felt that in the past the social work agency had treated black women very badly and had been insensitive to the complexities of cultural and gender issues. She said: 'It was a betrayal of the black community in a sense. In the past I had campaigned about the insensitivity of social services. But on this occasion I felt I had to do it because of the risk to the children.'

The worker in this case said she did not feel guilty about what she had done. She felt it was the right decision. Having explained to the woman on several occasions that she should not leave the children on their own and having worked with her trying to sort out her domestic and financial problems, she had given the woman due warning. This seems to be a case where the worker felt regret, but not guilt.

This case highlights some of the tensions felt by black workers in a professional position. This worker commented on how a large part of her job was trying to explain British laws to Asian women and the powers and roles of the various authorities and services. The women often found it hard to comprehend that neglect of and violence towards children were illegal. The statutory social work and other agencies generally were insensitive to the needs of the Asian women and were unwilling, or unable, to take into account the whole picture of a woman's life, including her religion and cultural background. The workers at the Asian women's project were in a sense mediating between the western and Asian cultures and values. Often their role was resented by members of the Asian community, particularly the men. The workers in the Asian women's project were concerned not just about balancing the needs and interests of different sections of the black community, but also about trying to adopt a committed/radical approach to practice and to work from a black feminist perspective. This particular worker commented that it was important for her to be very clear about her own values and about her professional commitments. While she had a strong commitment to help the Asian community, she was not prepared to cover up or ignore cases of family violence or neglect where women or children were at risk of harm. She said that she rarely felt guilt or self-blame about the actions she had taken, since she was clear where she stood. She commented that some black workers who were more ambivalent about their professional roles, particularly statutory social workers, seemed to have a tougher time.

Courage and commitment in multi-professional working: a team manager's case

All the cases examined thus far relate to whether or not a social worker should have felt blame or guilt about the outcomes of their decisions or actions. We have argued that it is important that social workers come to a considered decision. At the beginning of this chapter it was suggested that making a moral judgement in a profes-sional context should be regarded as an essentially rational process that can be justified by the social worker. In justifying decisions, it is often useful to make appeal to general and impartial principles, as we have done in the previous section. Yet part of the process of decision-making will also involve taking account of the particular-ities of the situation faced and the relationships with the people involved. What decision is made and whether it is implemented will also depend on the strength of commitment, integrity and deter-mination of the professionals involved. These factors are hard to encapsulate in brief case studies where the details of people's lives, relationships and the feelings and views of the social workers involved are not given. I will end the book by discussing just one example of a social work case that raised difficult ethical issues for the team manager and social worker involved and where some of the comments from the team manager are incorporated to contextualise the case. It highlights the problems and complexities of multi-professional working in cases regarded as 'high risk':

> At the age of 19 Tracey was convicted of infanticide, having stabbed to death a baby born after a concealed pregnancy. She was given a two-year non-custodial sentence, supervised by the probation service. Cynthia, a senior mental health social worker, worked with Tracey and her family for two years after this incident. At the age of 21 Tracey became pregnant again, to the same young

man as before, with whom she was now living. She phoned to tell Cynthia, who was now a team manager of a childcare team, very excited. According to Cynthia, 'this was a very different situation [from last time]'. Tracey's family and partner were very supportive and a childcare social worker in Cynthia's team made a positive assessment. Although Cynthia commented that 'there were obvious risks', particularly relating to the fact that Tracey had remained amnesiac about the events following the birth of her first child and Cynthia felt that 'the birth of this child might act as some kind of catalyst and we couldn't be sure what the reaction would be'. A plan was made for her to be admitted to the family unit of the local hospital for assessment following the birth. However, shortly before the birth was due, the decision was changed. A guardian *ad litem* was appointed to safeguard the interests of the baby. The medical staff, the probation officer and guardian decided that it was too risky to allow Tracey and the baby to be admitted to the family unit. According to Cynthia:

> At the last moment they pulled the plug and said: 'We're not prepared to have her on this ward.' The whole thing gathered a momentum of its own, where they were coming to conference suggesting that Group 4 [a security firm] should be involved, because of the risk she might pose to other mothers and children on the ward. This is a young woman who had been given a two-year probation sentence, not a custodial one, being treated, I felt, very respectfully by the courts and with a great deal of understanding and had worked incredibly well with us and had matured over that time ... All sorts of incredible things happened, like a professional forensic psychiatrist saw her for an hour, and said, you know, [the] health [professionals] were right ... This was a very dangerous situation.

Cynthia and the childcare social worker were left having to decide what to do at this point. She said: 'Both of us felt very strongly that it would have been completely wrong to have removed that child and for her [Tracey] not to have had a chance.'

Ethical issues involved

1. *Rights of the service user(s)* – the Kantian principle of respect for persons entails that a service user should be treated with respect and fairness and should be able to make decisions about her own

life provided she is capable of rational and self-determining action and the decision does not present a serious danger to herself or others. In this case, Tracey's ability to remain 'rational' after the birth is in question, which raises the issue of the risk to the baby once born and possibly other babies in the ward. It might be argued that the unborn baby should also be regarded as a 'service user' in this case, rather than just one of the 'others' involved. Certainly it would be the role of the social workers, as well as the guardian *ad litem*, to ensure that the rights of the unborn child were taken into account.

2. *The interests and welfare of the service user(s)* – what are the service users' best interests? The principle of promoting service user welfare arises here along with the question of whether we take account of Tracey's own view of her interests and welfare or what others think is best for her (parentalism). In the case of the unborn child, then we have to rely on what others think is best.

3. *The rights, interests and welfare of others* – who are the other parties involved (Tracey's partner, her parents, the other mothers and babies in the hospital ward, the hospital as a public institution, the professionals involved – from health, probation, social services, the guardian) and what are their rights and interests? The utilitarian principle of promoting the greatest good of the greatest number comes in here – which entails questions of distributive justice.

4. *Equality and justice* – how are pregnant young women, people with criminal convictions or psychiatric problems, regarded in society generally and how are they treated by powerful professionals? Is Tracey being unfairly discriminated against because of her past criminal conviction?

5. *Moral courage and professional integrity* – do the team manager and social worker have the moral strength to stand by their analysis of the situation and their commitment to respect the rights of the service user, in spite of strong pressures from other professionals? In a case like this where there is perceived to be a risk of harm to a child, then it is often easier to err on the side of caution.

6. *The relationship of care between professionals and service users* – the nature of the relationship between Tracey and the practitioners involved is an important feature in this case. We might wonder whether the social workers are more attentive to Tracey's needs, her moral qualities and her strengths than the health care staff who know her less well. What responsibilities do the various

professionals feel to the various people involved? Is it easier to feel responsibility towards a living person (Tracey) than to an unborn child?

How the issues arose

These issues arose because health and social care professionals have a duty to protect children. Their concern about the risks to Tracey's unborn child and to other babies she may come in contact with in the hospital leads them to propose strategies that circumscribe the freedom of choice and movement of Tracey, her partner and her family. Because there is no clear answer regarding how likely it is that any harm will occur, this creates a climate of uncertainty and anxiety and a concern among the health professionals and guardian about taking responsibility for a bad outcome. As Parton (1998, p. 21) suggests: 'Where the key concern is risk, the focus becomes, not making the *right* decision, but making a *defensible* decision.' The context in which this decision is being made can be understood in relation to the discussion in Chapter 6 of the increasing concern with risk assessment and risk management in the role of welfare professionals.

Lines of argument

There are a number of lines of argument that might be pursued by the social workers in coming to a decision and justifying it:

1. *Does Tracey have a right to look after her baby after its birth?* In normal circumstances the answer to this question would be 'yes'. But because she killed her first baby, this right may be overridden in the interests of the rights and welfare of the child. The extent to which this right is removed or limited will depend on the answer to the second question.
2. *Is Tracey likely to harm her baby after the birth?* This is where the different professionals involved either disagree on what the risk to the child would be, and/or disagree in terms of how much risk they are prepared to tolerate. The social workers feel they know Tracey pretty well and judge that she is ready and able to care for the baby. The team leader commented:

> Lots of things could weaken your resolve if we hadn't known the case as well as we did ... despite the fact that I'd joint worked with the psychiatrist for two years with the case, this forensic

psychiatrist 'expert' from London, you know, could make this judgement.

The other professionals seem to have greater doubts, however, with the forensic psychiatrist saying that it is a 'dangerous situation'. Furthermore, the guardian *ad litem* and the health professionals may have a lower tolerance of risk in this case than the social workers. Even if they all agree that the risk of harm to the baby in a supervised setting would be minimal, perhaps the guardian and health professionals see the worst case scenario (death of the baby) as so bad that they feel they cannot take responsibility for a decision which allows Tracey to be assessed in the hospital unit. The guardian certainly would be acting with the child's best interests at heart. The health professionals also seem concerned about risk of harm to other babies. As O'Sullivan (1999, p. 145) comments in discussing risk assessment in social work: 'One person's risk taking can be another person's hazard.'

3. *What is in Tracey's best interests?* If there is a grave danger of her harming her newborn baby, this would have serious consequences for her in that, apart from the emotional upset it would cause her, she would be likely to receive a custodial sentence. The safest option, therefore, might be to remove the baby at birth. However, if she is not given the chance to care for the baby from the time of its birth, she would not be able to bond with it and, if she was allowed to care for it subsequently, might find it difficult or be more likely to fail. It seems likely to be in Tracey's best interests to be well supervised and supported during the period after the birth, so that the baby does not have to be removed, and the risks of harm are minimised.

4. *What are the rights and interests of the unborn baby?* Clearly once the baby is born, it has a right to life, protection from harm and a safe environment. Whether this environment would best be provided by the mother and her family is the issue at stake. It could be argued that it is in the child's interests to have continuity of high-quality care that, if the mother is capable, might be best provided in the family of origin rather than in what might turn out to be a series of placements.

5. *What are the rights and interests of other parties involved?* Tracey's partner has some right to be involved in the decision-making process about the care of his child, although he does not seem to feature greatly in this case, apart from being described as

'supportive'. The parents are also described as 'supportive' by the team manager, but they were never assessed as potential alternative carers 'because there was a feeling that they could have prevented it, had been somehow involved in the event [the previous infanticide]'. A similar view seems to have been taken regarding Tracey's partner. The other parties who might be affected include the other mothers and babies in the hospital ward and this seems to have been a serious concern of the medical staff. By the same token, the social workers felt Tracey posed no risk to other people's babies. She had lived quite happily in the community for the past few years and had done babysitting for people. The health professionals involved were concerned not to have to take responsibility if anything went wrong. Their interests (which would involve protecting their own reputations, jobs, the hospital's credibility) were to minimise the risk.

6. *Is Tracey being treated fairly?* Cynthia, the team manager, said she felt at times as though there was a 're-trial' of Tracey taking place:

> I felt, strongly, that given that there'd been a court hearing, that this young woman had been convicted of her offence, that had to be our starting point. She was a Schedule 1 offender, she'd had this desperately awful incident in her past and we had to work from that premise. And we couldn't reconsider all the other possible dimensions of what might have happened on that occasion. But all the police files were got out again, the whole thing was trawled, which is not good for any pregnant young woman.

Cynthia is taking account of considerations of injustice and discrimination against Tracey on account of her past record. She does not feel this is warranted and is therefore prepared to stand up for Tracey.

7. *Professional judgement, autonomy and trust* – Cynthia and the social worker both have relationships with Tracey and judge that she is capable of looking after a baby. In this sense, they could be said to trust that, when offered the chance, she will not let them down; she will not behave in a way that is damaging to herself, her family or her child. Cynthia is an experienced social worker and is offering a considered judgement based on her experience and knowledge as a professional practitioner.

The decision

Cynthia decided to recommend that social services should supervise the young woman and child from the moment of birth 'because [the] Health [Service] wouldn't take that responsibility'. She commented that 'the social services director at the time was very unhappy that we were carrying that responsibility', adding that in this case, like many others, 'the stakes are so high'. In fact, the young woman and her partner coped very well with the child (who was three and a half years old at the time of the interview) and hence Cynthia felt vindicated. When asked what it was that made her feel so strongly that she was prepared to 'go out on a limb' in this case, she replied:

> I think it was the understanding of the individual person and the belief that she has qualities that were necessary to parent a child and indeed to protect the child, particularly with the support of her partner who'd been long term, and who absolutely knew what had happened before … But I think mainly, if I'd looked at that case on paper, I would have thought well, no wonder people are anxious, and it was mainly knowing and having assessed myself and then the new social worker having assessed the situation that gave me the confidence to feel that no way should she lose the opportunity to parent her child. But it is difficult … in the children and families team we have the luxury of knowing people fairly thoroughly before we have to make very far reaching decisions.

If we look at this case in terms of ethical principles, Cynthia was obviously concerned to respect Tracey as a person, to see her as an individual with the right and capacity to make her own choices and to promote her capacity to be self-determining by offering support (Kantian principles). There is no doubt that she was also concerned about the rights and interests of the unborn baby and other mothers and babies in the assessment unit, but she judged that the risks of harm to others (utilitarian considerations) were not sufficiently great to outweigh Tracey's rights and interests. But what enabled her to prioritise and implement her principles and duties in this way was her particular relationship with Tracey, her knowledge and understanding of her situation, her professional judgement about Tracey's capabilities, her sense of fairness and justice and her determination and commitment to support this person. In other words, Cynthia's qualities or 'virtues' and her relationship of care with Tracey were important features of this situation.

Conclusions

Discussion of these case examples shows the importance of critical reflection on social work practice and the need to understand the complexities and contradictions inherent in the role of social worker. This enables social workers to understand more clearly how and why ethical problems and dilemmas arise in practice and may enable them to be able better to defend themselves and the profession from moral attack and reduce some of the feelings of guilt, blame and anxiety in making difficult ethical decisions. Trainee social workers in particular experience a lot of confusion and anxiety about their roles, which can be reduced through reflection on ethical and value issues and relating them to social work practice.

The rapid changes taking place in the structure and organisation of social work services mean that it is even more important for practitioners to be clear about their value positions in order to resist the authoritarian, bureaucratising trends. These not only threaten professional identity and the traditional values based on respect for individual persons, but make it increasingly difficult to adopt more radical and committed forms of practice that challenge both the traditional Kantian values and the utilitarian principles of the bureaucratic model. It is also important to re-emphasise the importance of the face-to face relationship with service users based on empathy, care and trust, alongside a commitment to working for social justice and challenging the poverty, inequality and oppression that are an everyday feature of the lives of so many people with whom social workers come into contact in whatever parts of the world they are working.

---

putting it into practice

Exercise 7

Aims of the exercise – to encourage the reader to analyse her/his practice in terms of the ethical issues involved.

Using the format adopted for analysing the last case example in Chapter 7:

1. Briefly describe an ethical dilemma or problem experienced in your practice. Include reference to your feelings about the situation and the nature of your relationships with the people involved.
2. What were the ethical issues involved?
3. How did they arise?

4. What line of argument would you use to justify the course of action you took?

Further reading

Banks, S. and Nøhr, K. (eds) (2003) *Teaching Practical Ethics for the Social Professions*, Copenhagen, FESET. This book has a series of chapters written by authors from different European countries containing examples of a variety of techniques and approaches for teaching professional ethics, including methods of analysing cases, using drama, video and Socratic dialogue. The website of the European Social Ethics Project also has some examples of cases and questionnaires for use with students: http://www.dur.ac.uk/esep/.

Reamer, F. (1990) *Ethical Dilemmas in Social Service: A Guide for Social Workers*, 2nd edition, New York, Columbia University Press. This book contains discussions of a number of themes in social work ethics (ranging from truth-telling through government obligation to whistleblowing) and uses cases to illuminate the dilemmas and issues.

Rhodes, M. (1986) *Ethical Dilemmas in Social Work Practice*, Boston, MA, Routledge & Kegan Paul. Although this book was written some years ago now, it is very clearly written from a broadly virtue ethics orientation and uses case studies to discuss a range of themes including confidentiality, influencing and directing the client, dealing with bureaucracy, creating empathy and doing good.

References

Abbott, P. and Meerabeau, L. (1998) 'Professionals, Professionalization and the Caring Professions', in P. Abbott and L. Meerabeau (eds), *The Sociology of the Caring Professions*, London, UCL Press, pp. 1–19.

Abrioux, E. (1998) 'Degrees of Participation: A Spherical Model – The Possibilities for Girls in Kabul, Afghanistan', in V. Johnson, E. Ivan-Smith, G. Gordon, P. Pridmore and P. Scott (eds), *Stepping Forward: Children and Young People's Participation in the Development Process*, London, Intermediate Technology Publications, pp. 25–7.

Adams, R. (1999) *Personal Social Services: Clients, Consumers or Citizens?*, London, Longman.

Adams, R., Dominelli, L. and Payne, M. (2002) 'Concluding Comments: Facilitating Critical Practice', in R. Adams, L. Dominelli and M. Payne (eds), *Critical Practice in Social Work*, Basingstoke, Palgrave Macmillan, pp. 304–11.

Adams, R., Dominelli, L. and Payne, M. (eds) (1998) *Social Work: Themes, Issues and Critical Debates*, Basingstoke, Macmillan – now Palgrave Macmillan.

Adams, R., Dominelli, L. and Payne, M. (eds) (2005) *Social Work Futures: Crossing Boundaries, Transforming Practice*, Basingstoke, Palgrave Macmillan.

Ahmad, B. (1990) *Black Perspectives in Social Work*, Birmingham, Venture Press.

Akademikerförbundet SSR (1997) *Yrkesetiska Riktlinjer för Socionomer*, Stockholm, SSR.

Alaszewski, A. (1998) 'Health and Welfare: Managing Risk in Late Modern Society', in A. Alaszewski, L. Harrison and J. Manthorpe (eds), *Risk, Health and Welfare: Policies, Strategies and Practice*, Buckingham, Open University Press, pp. 127–53.

Aldridge, M. (1994) *Making Social Work News*, London, Routledge.

Allmark, P. (1995) 'Can There Be an Ethics of Care?', *Journal of Medical Ethics*, **21**: 19–24.

Amphlett, S. (1998) 'The Experience of a Watchdog', in G. Hunt (ed.), *Whistleblowing in the Social Services*, London, Arnold, pp. 65–93.

Aristotle (1954) *The Nichomachean Ethics of Aristotle*, translated by Sir David Ross, London, Oxford University Press.

Arnstein, S. (1969) 'A Ladder of Community Participation', *American Institute of Planners Journal*, (35): 216–24.

Arrington, R. (1998) *Western Ethics: An Historical Introduction*, Oxford, Blackwell.

Asociácia Sociálnych Pracovníkov na Slovensku (ASPS) (Association of Social Workers in the Slovak Republic) (1997) *The Code of Ethics for Social Workers in Slovakia*, Bratislava, ASPS.

Associação dos Profissionais de Serviço Social (APSS) (1994) *A Ética no Serviço Social – Principios e Valores*, Lisbon, APSS.

Association Nationale des Assistantes d'Hygiène Sociale, Assistantes Sociales et Infirmières Graduées du Luxembourg (1995) *Code de deontologie des professions d'assistant d'hygiène sociale et d'assistant social*, Luxembourg, ANAHSASIGL.

Association Nationale des Assistantes de Service Social (ANAS) (1994) *Code de Deontologie des Assistants de Service Social*, Paris, ANAS.

Association of Social Workers in Turkey (n.d.) *Ethical Principles and Responsibilities of Social Workers*, Ankara, Association of Social Workers in Turkey.

Association suisse des professionnels de l'action sociale (ASPAS) (1999) *Code de deontologie*, Berne, ASAS/SBS.

Audit Commission (1992) *The Community Revolution: Personal Social Services and Community Care*, London, HMSO.

Australian Association of Social Workers (AASW) (1994) *Code of Ethics*, Kingston, AASW.

Australian Association of Social Workers (AASW) (1999) *AASW Code of Ethics*, Kingston, AASW.

Baier, A. (1987) 'The Need for More Than Justice', in M. Hanen and K. Nelson (eds) *Science, Morality and Feminist Theory*, Calgary, University of Calgary Press, pp. 41–56.

Bailey, R. and Brake, M. (eds) (1975) *Radical Social Work*, London, Edward Arnold.

Bamford, T. (1990) *The Future of Social Work*, London, Macmillan – now Palgrave Macmillan.

Banks, S. (1990) 'Doubts, Dilemmas and Duties: Ethics and the Social Worker', in P. Carter, T. Jeffs and M. Smith (eds) *Social Work and Social Welfare Yearbook 2*, Buckingham, Open University Press, pp. 91–106.

Banks, S. (1995) *Ethics and Values in Social Work*, 1st edn, Basingstoke, Macmillan – now Palgrave Macmillan.

Banks, S. (1998a) 'Professional Ethics in Social Work – What Future?', *British Journal of Social Work*, **28**: 213–31.

Banks, S. (1998b) 'Codes of Ethics and Ethical Conduct: A View from the Caring Professions', *Public Money and Management*, **18**(1): 27–30.

Banks, S. (1999) 'Ethics and the Youth Worker', in S. Banks (ed.), *Ethical Issues in Youth Work*, London, Routledge, pp. 3–20.

Banks, S. (2001a) *Ethics and Values in Social Work*, 2nd edn, Basingstoke, Palgrave – now Palgrave Macmillan.

Banks, S. (2001b) 'Ethical Dilemmas for the Social Professions: Work in Progress with Social Education Students in Europe', *European Journal of Social Education*, (1): 1–16.

Banks, S. (2002) 'Professional Values and Accountabilities' in R. Adams, L. Dominelli and M. Payne (eds) *Critical Practice in Social Work*, Basingstoke, Palgrave Macmillan, pp. 28–37.

Banks, S. (2003) 'The Use of Learning Journals to Encourage Ethical Reflection During Fieldwork Practice', in S. Banks and K. Nøhr (eds), *Teaching Practical Ethics for the Social Professions*, Copenhagen, FESET, pp. 53–67.

Banks, S. (2004a) *Ethics, Accountability and the Social Professions*, Basingstoke, Palgrave Macmillan.

Banks, S. (2004b) 'Professional Integrity, Social Work and the Ethics of Distrust', *Social Work and Social Sciences Review*, **11**(2): 20–35.

Banks, S. (2005) 'The Ethical Practitioner in Formation: Issues of Courage, Competence and Commitment', *Journal of Social Work Education*, **24**(7): 737–53.

Banks, S. and Nyboe, N.-E. (2003) 'Writing and Using Cases', in S. Banks and K. Nøhr (eds), *Teaching Practical Ethics for the Social Professions*, Copenhagen, FESET, pp. 19–39.

Banks, S. and Williams, R. (1999) 'The Personal and the Professional: Perspectives from European Social Education Students', *Social Work In Europe*, **6**(3): 52–61.

Banks, S. and Williams, R. (2005) 'Accounting for Ethical Difficulties in Social Welfare Work: Issues, Problems and Dilemmas', *British Journal of Social Work*, **35**(7):1005–22.

Bauman, Z. (1992) *Intimations of Postmodernity*, London, Routledge.

Bauman, Z. (1993) *Postmodern Ethics*, Oxford, Blackwell.

Bauman, Z. (1995) *Life in Fragments: Essays in Postmodern Morality*, Oxford, Blackwell.

Bauman, Z. (1997) 'Morality Begins at Home – Or: Can there be a Levinasian Macro-Ethics?', in H. Jodalen and A. Vetlesen (eds), *Closeness: An Ethics,* Oslo, Scandinavian University Press, pp. 218–44.

Beauchamp, T. (1996) 'The Role of Principles in Practical Ethics', in L. Sumner and J. Boyle (eds), *Philosophical Perspectives on Bioethics*, Toronto, University of Toronto Press, pp. 79–95.

Beauchamp, T. and Childress, J. (1994) *Principles of Biomedical Ethics*, 4th edn, Oxford and New York, Oxford University Press.

Beauchamp, T. and Childress, J. (2001) *Principles of Biomedical Ethics*, 5th edn, Oxford and New York, Oxford University Press.

Beckett, C. and Maynard, A. (2005) *Values and Ethics in Social Work: An Introduction,* London, Sage.

Berry, L. (1988) 'The Rhetoric of Consumerism and the Exclusion of Community', *Community Development Journal*, **23**(4): 266–72.

Biestek, F. (1961) *The Casework Relationship*, London, Allen & Unwin.

Blaug, R. (1995) 'Distortion of the Face to Face: Communicative Reason and Social Work Practice', *British Journal of Social Work*, **25**: 423–39.

Bloxham, S. (1993) 'Managerialism in Youth and Community Work: A Critique of Changing Organisational Structures and Management Practice', *Youth & Policy*, (41): 1–12.

Blum, L. (1988) 'Gilligan and Kohlberg: Implications for Moral Theory', *Ethics*, **98**: 472–91.

Blum, L. (1994) *Moral Perception and Particularity*, Cambridge, Cambridge University Press.

Bond, T. (2000) *Standards and Ethics for Counselling in Action*, 2nd edn, London, Sage.

Boss, J. (1998) *Ethics for Life: An Interdisciplinary and Multi-Cultural Introduction*, Mountain View, CA, Mayfield.

Bouquet, B. (1999) 'De l'éthique personelle à une éthique profession-nelle', *EMPAN*, (36): 27–33.

Bowden, P. (1997) *Caring: Gender-Sensitive Ethics*, London, Routledge.

Bowie, N. (1999) *Business Ethics: A Kantian Perspective*, Oxford, Blackwell.

Bradshaw, P. (1996) 'Yes! There Is an Ethics of Care: An Answer for Peter Allmark', *Journal of Medical Ethics*, **22**: 8–12.

Brake, M. and Bailey, R. (eds) (1980) *Radical Social Work and Practice*, London, Edward Arnold.

Brandon, D. (1991) *Innovation without Change? Consumer Power in Psychiatric Services*, Basingstoke, Macmillan – now Palgrave Macmillan.

Braye, S. and Preston-Shoot, M. (1997) *Practising Social Work Law*, 2nd edn, Basingstoke, Macmillan – now Palgrave Macmillan.

Briskman, L. (2005) 'Pushing Ethical Boundaries for Children and

Families: Confidentiality, Transparency and Transformation', in R. Adams, L. Dominelli and M. Payne (eds), *Social Work Futures: Crossing Boundaries, Transforming Practice*, Basingstoke, Palgrave Macmillan, pp. 208–20.

Briskman, L. and Noble, C. (1999) 'Social Work Ethics: Embracing Diversity?', in B. Pease and J. Fook (eds), *Transforming Social Work Practice: Postmodern Critical Perspectives*, London, Routledge, pp. 57–69.

British Association for Counselling and Psychotherapy (BACP) (2001) *Statement of Fundamental Ethics for Counselling and Psychotherapy*, Rugby, BACP.

British Association of Social Workers (BASW) (1975) *A Code of Ethics for Social Work*, Birmingham, BASW.

British Association of Social Workers (1980) *Clients are Fellow Citizens*, Birmingham, BASW.

British Association of Social Workers (1983) *Effective and Ethical Recording*, Birmingham, BASW.

British Association of Social Workers (1989) *Rights, Responsibilities and Remedies*, Birmingham, BASW.

British Association of Social Workers (2002) *The Code of Ethics for Social Work*, Birmingham, BASW.

Brock, D. (1991) 'Decision-making Competence and Risk', *Bioethics*, 5(2): 105–12.

Brookfield, S. (1987) *Developing Critical Thinkers*, Milton Keynes, Open University Press.

Brown, H. and Smith, H. (1992) 'Assertion Not Assimilation: A Feminist Perspective on the Normalisation Principle', in H. Brown and H. Smith (eds), *Normalisation: A Reader for the Nineties*, London, Routledge, pp. 149–71.

Buber, M. (1937) *I and Thou*, trans. R. Gregor Smith, Edinburgh, T. & T. Clark.

Buchanan, A. and Brock, D. (1989) *Deciding for Others: The Ethics of Surrogate Decision Making*, Cambridge, Cambridge University Press.

Bulgarian Association of Social Workers (1999) *Code of Ethics*, Sofia, Bulgarian Association of Social Workers.

Burkitt, I. (1999) 'Relational Moves and Generative Dances', in S. McNamee, K. Gergen and Associates, *Relational Responsibility: Resources for Sustainable Dialogue*, Thousand Oaks, CA and London, Sage, pp. 71–80.

Burrage, M. and Torstendahl, R. (eds) (1990) *Professions in Theory and History: Rethinking the Study of the Professions*, London, Sage.

Butrym, Z. (1976) *The Nature of Social Work*, London, Macmillan – now Palgrave Macmillan.

Campbell, T. (1978) 'Discretionary Rights', in N. Timms and D. Watson (eds), *Philosophy in Social Work*, London, Routledge & Kegan Paul, pp. 50–77.

Canadian Association of Social Workers (CASW) (1994) *Code of Ethics*, Ottawa, CASW.

Caputo, J. (2000) 'The End of Ethics', in H. LaFollette (ed.), *The Blackwell Guide to Ethical Theory*, Oxford, Blackwell, pp. 111–28.

Central Council for Education and Training in Social Work (CCETSW) (1976) *Values in Social Work*, London, CCETSW.

Central Council for Education and Training in Social Work (1989) *Requirements and Regulations for the Diploma in Social Work*, London, CCETSW.

Central Council for Education and Training in Social Work (1995) *Assuring Quality in the Diploma in Social Work – 1: Rules and Requirements for the Diploma in Social Work*, London, CCETSW.

Chadwick, R. (ed.) (1994) *Ethics and the Professions*, Avebury, Aldershot.

Chambers, T. (1997) 'What to Expect from an Ethics Case (and What it Expects from You)', in H. Nelson (ed.), *Stories and Their Limits: Narrative Approaches to Bioethics*, New York and London, Routledge, pp. 171–84.

Chambon, A. (1994) 'Postmodernity and Social Work Discourse(s): Notes on the Changing Language of a Profession', in A. Chambon and A. Irving (eds), *Essays on Postmodernism and Social Work*, Toronto, Canadian Scholars' Press, pp. 63–75.

Chambon, A. and Irving, A. (eds) (1994) *Essays on Postmodernism and Social Work*, Toronto, Canadian Scholars' Press.

Clark, C. (1999) 'Observing the Lighthouse: From Theory to Institutions in Social Work Ethics', *European Journal of Social Work*, **2**(3): 259–70.

Clark, C. (2000) *Social Work Ethics: Politics, Principles and Practice*, London, Macmillan – now Palgrave Macmillan.

Clark, C. with Asquith, S. (1985) *Social Work and Social Philosophy*, London, Routledge & Kegan Paul.

Clarke, J. (2004) *Changing Welfare Changing States: New Directions in Social Policy*, London, Sage.

Clifford, D. (2002) 'Resolving Uncertainties? The Contribution of Some Recent Feminist Ethical Theory to the Social Professions', *European Journal of Social Work*, **5**(1): 31–41.

Community Care (1999–2000) 'Comment: A New Century of Uncertainty', *Community Care*, (1303), 16 December 1999–12 January 2000.

Consejo General de Colegios Officiales de Diplomados en Trabajo Social y Asistentes Socialies (n.d.) *Códigó Deontológico de la Profesión de Diplomada en Trabajo Social*, Madrid, Consejo General de Colegios Officiales.

Conselho Federal de Serviço Social (1993) *Social Worker Code of Professional Ethics*, Brasília, Conselho Federal de Serviço Social.

Cooper, D. (1993) *Child Abuse Revisited: Children, Society and Social Work*, Buckingham, Open University Press.

Cooper, D. (1998) *Ethics: The Classic Readings*, Oxford, Blackwell.

Corrigan, P. and Leonard, P. (1978) *Social Work Practice under Capitalism: A Marxist Approach*, London, Macmillan – now Palgrave Macmillan.

Coulshed, V. and Orme, J. (1998) *Social Work Practice*, 3rd edn, Basingstoke, Macmillan – now Palgrave Macmillan.

Crisp, R. (ed.) (1996) *How Should One Live? Essays on the Virtues*, Oxford, Oxford University Press.

Crisp, R. and Slote, M. (eds) (1997) *Virtue Ethics*, Oxford, Oxford University Press.

Croatia Association of Social Workers (2004) *Etički Kodeks Socijalnih Radnika*, Zagreb, Croatia Association of Social Workers.

Dalley, G. (1992) 'Social Welfare Ideologies and Normalisation: Links and Conflicts', in H. Brown and H. Smith (eds), *Normalisation: A Reader for the Nineties*, London, Routledge, pp. 100–11.

Dansk Socialrådgiverforening (1997) *Etiske Principper i Socialt Arbejde*, Copenhagen, Dansk Socialrådgiverforening.

Davis, M. (1999) *Ethics and the University*, London, Routledge.

Day, L. (1992) 'Women and Oppression: Race, Class and Gender', in M. Langan and L. Day (eds), *Women, Oppression and Social Work*, London, Routledge, pp. 12–31.

de Silva, P. (1993) 'Buddhist Ethics', in P. Singer (ed.), *A Companion to Ethics*, Oxford, Blackwell, pp. 58–68.

Deleuze, G. (1988) *Spinoza, Practical Philosophy*, San Francisco, City Lights.

Dent, M. (1999) 'Professional Judgement and the Role of Clinical Guidelines and Evidence-based Medicine (EBM): Netherlands, Britain and Sweden', *Journal of Interprofessional Care*, **13**(2): 151–64.

Department for Education and Skills (2003) *Every Child Matters*, London, DfES.

Department of Health (1988) *Protecting Children: A Guide for Social Workers Undertaking a Comprehensive Assessment*, London, HMSO.

Department of Health (1995) *Looking After Children: Good Parenting, Good Outcomes*, London, HMSO.

Department of Health (1998) *Modernising Social Services: Promoting Independence, Improving Protection, Raising Standards*, London, HMSO.

Department of Health (1999) *Framework for the Assessment of Children in Need and their Families (Consultation Draft)*, London, DoH.

Department of Health Social Services Inspectorate (1991a) *Care Management and Assessment: Managers' Guide*, London, HMSO.

Department of Health Social Services Inspectorate (1991b) *Care Management and Assessment: Practitioners' Guide*, London, HMSO.

Deutscher Berufsverband für Soziale Arbeit e. V. (DBSH) (1997) *Berufsethische Prinzipien des DBSH*, Göttingen, DBSH.

Deverell, K. and Sharma, U. (2000) 'Professionalism in Everyday Practice: Issues of Trust, Experience and Boundaries', in N. Malin (ed.), *Professionalism, Boundaries and the Workplace*, London, Routledge, pp. 25–46.

Dominelli, L. (1996) 'Deprofessionalising Social Work: Anti-Oppressive Practice, Competencies and Postmodernism', *British Journal of Social Work*, (26): 153–75.

Dominelli, L. (1997) *Anti-Racist Social Work*, 2nd edn, Basingstoke, Macmillan – now Palgrave Macmillan.

Dominelli, L. (2002) *Anti-Oppressive Social Work Theory and Practice*, Basingstoke, Palgrave Macmillan.

Dominelli, L. (2004) *Social Work: Theory and Practice for a Changing Profession*, Oxford, Polity Press.

Dominelli, L. and McLeod, E. (1989) *Feminist Social Work*, Basingstoke, Macmillan – now Palgrave Macmillan.

Donati, P. and Folgheraiter, F. (eds) (1999) *Gli operatori sociali nel welfare mix. Privatizzazione, pluralizzazione dei soggetti erogatori, managerialismo: il futuro del servo sociale?*, Trento, Italy, Erickson.

Downie, R. (1971) *Roles and Values*, London, Methuen.

Downie, R. (1989) 'A Political Critique of Kantian Ethics in Social Work: A Reply to Webb and McBeath', *British Journal of Social Work*, **19**: 507–10.

Downie, R. and Calman, K. (1994) *Healthy Respect: Ethics in Health Care*, 2nd edn, Oxford, Oxford University Press.

Downie, R. and Loudfoot, E. (1978) Aim, Skill and Role in Social Work', in N. Timms and D. Watson (eds), *Philosophy in Social Work*, London, Routledge & Kegan Paul, pp. 111–26.

Downie, R. and Telfer, E. (1969) *Respect for Persons*, London, Routledge & Kegan Paul.

Downie, R. and Telfer, E. (1980) *Caring and Curing*, London, Methuen.

Doyal, L. and Gough, I. (1991) *A Theory of Human Need*, Basingstoke, Macmillan – now Palgrave Macmillan.

du Gay, P. (2000) *In Praise of Bureaucracy: Weber, Organisation, Ethics*, London, Sage.

Dworkin, R. (1977) *Taking Rights Seriously*, Cambridge, MA, Harvard University Press.

Eastham, M. (2002) 'Vocation and Social Care', in M. Nash and B. Stewart (eds), *Spirituality and Social Care*, London, Jessica Kingsley, pp. 71–92.

Edmundson, W. (2004) *An Introduction to Rights*, Cambridge, Cambridge University Press.

Edwards, P. (1998) 'The Future of Ethics', in O. Leaman (ed.), *The Future of Philosophy: Towards the Twenty-First Century*, London, Routledge, pp. 41–61.

Edwards, S. (1996) *Nursing Ethics: A Principle-based Approach*, Basingstoke, Macmillan – now Palgrave Macmillan.

Ejaz, F. K. (1991) 'Self-determination: Lessons to be Learned from Social Work Practice in India', *British Journal of Social Work*, **21**: 127–42.

Etzioni, A. (1969) *The Semi-Professions and Their Organisation*, New York, Free Press.

Etzioni, A. (1995) *The Spirit of Community*, London, Fontana.

Etzioni, A. (1997) *The New Golden Rule: Community and Morality in a Democratic Society*, New York, Basic Books.

Exworthy, M. and Halford, S. (eds) (1999) *Professionals and the New Managerialism in the Public Sector*, Buckingham, Open University Press.

Farley, M. (1993) 'Feminism and Universal Morality', in G. Outka and J. Reeder (eds), *Prospects for a Common Morality*, Chichester, Princeton University Press, pp. 170–90.

Feinberg, J. (1973) *Social Philosophy*, Englewood Cliffs, NJ, Prentice Hall.

Fellesorganisasjonen for Barnevernpedagoger, Socionomer og Vernepleiere (FO) (1998) *Yrkesetiske prinsipper og retningslinjer*, Oslo, FO.

Fook, J. (2002) *Social Work: Critical Theory and Practice*, London, Sage.

Foucault, M. (1984) 'On the Genealogy of Ethics: An Overview of Work in Progress', in P. Rabinow (ed.), *The Foucault Reader*, Harmondsworth, Penguin, pp. 340–72.

Foucault, M. (1999) 'Social Work, Social Control, and Normalization:

Discussion with Michael Foucault', in A. Chambon, A. Irving and L. Epstein (eds), *Reading Foucault for Social Work*, New York, Columbia University Press, pp. 83–97.

Frankena, W. (1963) *Ethics*, Englewood Cliffs, NJ, Prentice Hall.

Franklin, B. (1989) 'Wimps and Bullies: Press Reporting of Child Abuse', in P. Carter, T. Jeffs and M. Smith (eds), *Social Work and Social Welfare Yearbook*, Milton Keynes, Open University Press, pp. 1–14.

Freidson, E. (1994) *Professionalism Reborn: Theory, Prophecy, and Policy*, Chicago, University of Chicago Press.

Freidson, E. (2001) *Professionalism: The Third Logic*, Cambridge, Polity Press.

Freire, P. (1972) *Pedagogy of the Oppressed*, London, Penguin.

Galper, J. (1980) *Social Work Practice: A Radical Perspective*, Englewood Cliffs, NJ, Prentice Hall.

Garrett, P. (2004) 'The Electronic Eye: Emerging Surveillant Practices in Social Work with Children and Families', *European Journal of Social Work*, **7**(1): 57–71.

General Social Care Council (2002) *Codes of Practice for Social Care Workers and Employers*, London, GSCC.

Gewirth, A. (1996) *The Community of Rights*, Chicago, Chicago University Press.

Gibbs, L. and Gambrill, E. (2002) 'Evidence-based Practice: Counter-Arguments to Objectors', *Research in Social Work Practice*, **12**(3): 452–76.

Gilligan, C. (1982) *In a Different Voice: Psychological Theory and Women's Development*, Cambridge, MA, Harvard University Press.

Gilligan, C., Rogers, A. and Brown, L. (1990) 'Epilogue', in C. Gilligan, N. Lyons and T. Hanmer (eds), *Making Connections*, Cambridge, MA, Harvard University Press, pp. 314–34.

Gould, N. and Taylor, I. (eds) (1996) *Reflective Learning for Social Work*, Aldershot, Arena.

Graham, M. (1999) 'The African-Centred Worldview: Developing a Paradigm for Social Work', *British Journal of Social Work*, **29**: 251–67.

Graham, M. (2002) *Social Work and African-centred Worldviews*, Birmingham, Venture Press.

Gray, A. and Jenkins, B. (1999) 'Professions, Bureaucracy, and Social Welfare', in J. Baldock, N. Manning, S. Miller and S. Vickerstaff (eds), *Social Policy*, Oxford, Oxford University Press, pp. 191–217.

Greenwood, E. (1957) 'Attributes of a Profession', *Social Work*, **2**(3): 44–55.

Groenhout, R. (2004) *Connected Lives: Human Nature and an Ethics of Care*, Lanham, MD, Rowman and Littlefield.

Habermas, J. (1990) *Moral Consciousness and Communicative Action*, trans. C. Lenhardt and S. Nicholsen, Cambridge, MA, MIT Press.

Hall, C., Sarangi, S. and Slembrouck, S. (1997) 'Moral Construction in Social Work Discourse', in B.-L. Gunnarsson, P. Linell and B. Nordberg (eds), *The Construction of Professional Discourse*, London, Longman, pp. 265–91.

Hall, C., Juhila, K., Parton, N. and Pösö, T. (eds) (2003) *Constructing Clienthood in Social Work and Human Services: Interaction, Identities and Practices*, London, Jessica Kingsley.

Halmos, P. (1978) *The Faith of Counsellors*, London, Constable.

Hanford, L. (1994) 'Nursing and the Concept of Care: An Appraisal of Noddings' Theory', in G. Hunt (ed.), *Ethical Issues in Nursing*, London, Routledge, pp. 181–97.

Hare, R. M. (1952) *The Language of Morals*, Oxford, Clarendon Press.

Hare, R. M. (1963) *Freedom and Reason*, Oxford, Clarendon Press.

Harris, J. (2003) *The Social Work Business*, London, Routledge.

Harris, N. (1987) 'Defensive Social Work', *British Journal of Social Work*, **17**: 61–9.

Harris, N. (1994) 'Professional Codes and Kantian Duties', in R. Chadwick (ed.), *Ethics and the Professions*, Aldershot, Avebury, pp. 104–15.

Harvey, D. (1990) *The Condition of Postmodernity*, Oxford, Blackwell.

Hayes, D. (2005) 'Social Work with Asylum Seekers and Others Subject to Immigration Control', in R. Adams, L. Dominelli and M. Payne (eds), *Social Work Futures: Crossing Boundaries, Transforming Practice*, Basingstoke, Palgrave Macmillan, pp. 182–94.

Healy, K. (2005) *Social Work Theories in Context: Creating Frameworks for Practice*, Basingstoke, Palgrave Macmillan.

Healy, L. (2001) *International Social Work: Professional Action in an Interdependent World*, New York and Oxford, Oxford University Press.

Hekman, S. (1995) *Moral Voices, Moral Selves: Carol Gilligan and Feminist Moral Theory*, Cambridge, Polity Press.

Hollis, M. and Howe, D. (1990) 'Moral Risks in the Social Work Role: A Response to Macdonald', *British Journal of Social Work*, **20**: 547–52.

Holm, J. and Bowker, J. (eds) (1994) *Making Moral Decisions*, London, Continuum.

Holmes, J. (1981) *Professionalisation – A Misleading Myth? A Study of the Careers of Youth and Community Work Courses in England and Wales from 1970 to 1978*, Leicester, National Youth Bureau.

Hong Kong Social Workers Association (1998) *Code of Practice*, Hong Kong, HKSWA.

Horne, M. (1999) *Values in Social Work*, 2nd edn, Aldershot, Wildwood House.

Houston, S. (2003) 'Establishing Virtue in Social Work: A Response to McBeath and Webb', *British Journal of Social Work*, **33**: 819–24.

Howe, D. (1991) 'Knowledge, Power and the Shape of Social Work Practice', in M. Davies (ed.), *The Sociology of Social Work*, London, Routledge.

Howe, D. (1992) 'Child Abuse and the Bureaucratisation of Social Work', *The Sociological Review*, **40**(3): 491–508.

Hudson, W. (1978) *Modern Moral Philosophy*, London, Macmillan – now Palgrave Macmillan.

Hugman, R. (1991) *Power in Caring Professions*, London, Macmillan – now Palgrave Macmillan.

Hugman, R. (1998a) *Social Welfare and Social Value*, Basingstoke, Macmillan – now Palgrave Macmillan.

Hugman, R. (1998b) 'Social Work and De-professionalization', in P. Abbott and L. Meerabeau (eds), *The Sociology of Caring Professions*, 2nd edn, London, UCL Press, pp. 178–98.

Hugman, R. (2005) *New Approaches in Ethics for the Caring Professions*, Basingstoke and New York, Palgrave Macmillan.

Humphries, B. (2004) 'An Unacceptable Role for Social Work: Implementing Immigration Policy', *British Journal of Social Work*, (34): 93–107.

Hunt, G. (ed.) (1998) *Whistleblowing in the Social Services: Public Accountability and Professional Practice*, London, Arnold.

Hursthouse, R. (1997) 'Virtue Theory and Abortion', in D. Statman (ed.), *Virtue Ethics: A Critical Reader*, Edinburgh, Edinburgh University Press, pp. 227–44.

Hursthouse, R. (1999) *On Virtue Ethics*, Oxford, Oxford University Press.

Husband, C. (1995) 'The Morally Active Practitioner and the Ethics of Antiracist Social Work', in R. Hugman and D. Smith (eds), *Ethical Issues in Social Work*, London, Routledge, pp. 84–103.

Ife, J. (1997) *Rethinking Social Work: Towards Critical Practice*, Melbourne, Longman.

Ife, J. (1999) 'Postmodernism, Critical Theory and Social Work', in B. Pease and J. Fook (eds), *Transforming Social Work Practice: Postmodern Critical Perspectives*, London, Routledge, pp. 211–23.

Ife, J. (2001) *Human Rights and Social Work: Towards Rights-based Practice*, Cambridge, Cambridge University Press.

Illich, I. et al. (1977) *The Disabling Professions*, London, Marion Boyars.

Interfaith Network for the UK (2004) *Connect: Different Faiths, Shared Values*, London, Interfaith Network for the UK, in association with Timebank and The National Youth Agency, available at: http://www. interfaith.org.uk.

International Federation of Social Workers (IFSW) (1990) *Social Workers in the European Community: Training–Employment– Perspectives 1992*, Brussels, IFSW.

International Federation of Social Workers (IFSW) (1994) *The Ethics of Social Work – Principles and Standards*, http://www.ifsw.org/4.4. pub.html, accessed 10.08.05.

International Federation of Social Workers (2000) 'Definition of Social Work', http://www.ifsw.org/publications, accessed 31.03.05.

International Federation of Social Workers (IFSW) and International Association of Schools of Social Work (IASSW) (2004) *Ethics in Social Work, Statement of Principles*, Berne, IFSW and IASSW, http://www.ifsw.org/GM-2004/GM-Ethics.html, accessed 10.08.05.

Irish Association of Social Workers (IASW) (1995) *Code of Ethics of the Irish Association of Social Workers*, Dublin, IASW.

Irving, A. (1994) 'From Image to Simulacra: The Modern/Postmodern Divide in Social Work', in A. Chambon and A. Irving (eds), *Essays on Postmodernism and Social Work*, Toronto, Canadian Scholars' Press, pp. 21–32.

Jackson, J. (1994) 'Common Codes: Divergent Practices', in R. Chadwick (ed.), *Ethics and the Professions*, Aldershot, Avebury, pp. 116–24.

Jameson, F. (1991) *Postmodernism or, The Cultural Logic of Late Capitalism*, London, Verso.

Japanese Association of Social Workers, Japanese Association of Social Workers in Health, Japanese Association of Certified Social Workers and Japanese Association of Psychiatric Social Workers, Joint Committee on Ethics (2004) *Code of Ethics of Social Workers (Draft)*, Tokyo, JASW et al.

Jeffs, T. and Smith, M. (1994) 'Young People, Youth Work and a New Authoritarianism', *Youth and Policy*, (53): 1–14.

Johnson, T. (1972) *Professions and Power*, London, Macmillan – now Palgrave Macmillan.

Johnson, T. (1984) 'Professionalism: Occupation or Ideology?', in S. Goodlad (ed.), *Education for the Professions: Quis Custodiet ... ?*,

Guildford, Society for Research into Higher Education and National Foundation for Educational Research/Nelson.

Jordan, B. (1975) 'Is the Client a Fellow Citizen?', *Social Work Today*, **6**(15): 471–5.

Jordan, B. (1989) *The Common Good: Citizenship, Morality and Self-Interest*, Oxford, Blackwell.

Jordan, B. (1990) *Social Work in an Unjust Society*, Hemel Hempstead, Harvester.

Jordan, B. (1991) 'Competencies and Values', *Social Work Education*, **10**(1): 5–11.

Kant, I. (1964) *Groundwork of the Metaphysics of Morals*, New York, Harper & Row.

King, M. and Trowell, J. (1992) *Children's Welfare and the Law: The Limits of Legal Intervention*, London, Sage.

Knight, T. and Caveney, S. (1998) 'Assessment and Action Records: Will they Promote Good Parenting?', *British Journal of Social Work*, **28**: 29–43.

Koehn, D. (1994) *The Ground of Professional Ethics*, London, Routledge.

Koehn, D. (1998) *Rethinking Feminist Ethics: Care, Trust and Empathy*, London, Routledge.

Kohlberg, L. (1981) *Essays on Moral Development: Volume 1, The Philosophy of Moral Development: Moral Stages and the Idea of Justice*, New York, Harper & Row.

Kohlberg, L. (1984) *Essays on Moral Development: Volume 2, The Psychology of Moral Development*, San Francisco, Harper & Row.

Kuhse, H. (1997) *Caring: Nurses, Women and Ethics*, Oxford, Blackwell.

Kutchins, H. (1991) 'The Fiduciary Relationship: The Legal Basis for Social Workers' Responsibilities to Clients', *Social Work*, **36**(2): 106–13.

Lafollette, H. (ed.) (2000) *The Blackwell Guide to Ethical Theory*, Oxford, Blackwell.

Laming, H. (2003) *The Victoria Climbie Inquiry*, London, The Stationery Office.

Langan, M. (2000) 'Social Services: Managing the Third Way', in J. Clarke, S. Gewirtz and E. McLaughlin (eds), *New Managerialism, New Welfare?* London, Sage/Open University Press, pp. 152–68.

Langan, M. and Lee, P. (eds) (1989) *Radical Social Work Today*, London, Unwin Hyman.

Lansdown, G. (1995) 'Children's Rights to Participation: A Critique', in

C. Cloke and M. Davies (eds), *Participation and Empowerment in Child Protection*, London, Pitman, pp. 19–38.

Larson, M. (1977) *The Rise of Professionalism: A Sociological Analysis*, Berkeley, CA, University of California Press.

Le Grand, J. and Bartlett, W. (eds) (1993) *Quasi-Markets and Social Policy*, Basingstoke, Macmillan – now Palgrave Macmillan.

Leighton, N. (1985) 'Personal and Professional Values – Marriage or Divorce?', in D. Watson (ed.), *A Code of Ethics for Social Work: The Second Step*, London, Routledge & Kegan Paul, pp. 59–85.

Leonard, P. (1997) *Postmodern Welfare: Reconstructing an Emancipatory Project*, London, Sage.

Levinas, E. (1984) *Justifications de l'éthique*, Bruxelles, Edition de l'Université de Bruxelles.

Levinas, E. (1989) 'Ethics as First Philosophy, translated by Seán Hand', in S. Hand (ed.), *The Levinas Reader*, Oxford, Blackwell, pp. 75–87.

Levinas, E. (1997) 'On Buber, Marcel, and Philosophy', in H. Jodalen and A. Vetlesen (eds), *Closeness: An Ethics*, Oslo, Scandinavian University Press, pp. 27–44.

Levy, C. (1976) *Social Work Ethics*, New York, Human Sciences Press.

Levy, C. (1993) *Social Work Ethics on the Line*, Binghampton, NY, Haworth Press.

Lewis, J. and Glennerster, H. (1996) *Implementing the New Community Care*, Buckingham, Open University Press.

Lister, R. (1991) 'Citizenship Engendered', *Critical Social Policy*, (32): 65–71.

Lloyd, M. (2002) 'Care Management', in R. Adams, L. Dominelli and M. Payne (eds), *Critical Practice in Social Work,* Basingstoke, Palgrave Macmillan, pp. 159–68.

Løgstrup, K. (1997) 'On Trust', in H. Jodalen and A. Vetlesen (eds), *Closeness: An Ethics*, Oslo, Scandinavian University Press, pp. 71–89.

Long, A. and Harrison, S. (1996) 'Evidence-based Decision-making', *Health Service Journal*, **106** (11 January): pp. 8–11.

Lorenz, W. (2001) 'Social Work Responses to "New Labour" in Continental European Countries', *British Journal of Social Work*, **31**: 595–609.

Lukes, S. (1987) *Marxism and Morality*, Oxford, Oxford University Press.

Lund, B. (1999) '"Ask Not What Your Community Can Do for You": Obligations, New Labour and Welfare Reform', *Critical Social Policy*, **19**(4): 447–62.

Lymbery, M. (1998) 'Care Management and Professional Autonomy:

The Impact of Community Care Legislation on Social Work with Older People', *British Journal of Social Work*, **28**: 863–78.

Lymbery, M. (2000) 'The Retreat from Professionalism: From Social Worker to Care Manager', in N. Malin (ed.), *Professionalism, Boundaries and the Workplace*, London, Routledge, pp. 123–38.

Lyotard, J.-F. (1984) *The Postmodern Condition: A Report on Knowledge*, trans. G. Bennington and B. Massumi, Manchester, Manchester University Press.

McBeath, G. and Webb, S. (1990–1) 'Child Protection Language as Professional Ideology in Social Work', *Social Work & Social Sciences Review*, **2**(2): 122–45.

McBeath G. and Webb, S. (1991) 'Social Work, Modernity and Post Modernity', *Sociological Review*, **39**(4): 745–62.

McBeath, G. and Webb, S. (2002) 'Virtue Ethics and Social Work: Being Lucky, Realistic, and not Doing one's Duty', *British Journal of Social Work*, **32**: 1015–36.

McDermott, F. (1975) 'Against the Persuasive Definition of Self-determination', in F. McDermott (ed.), *Self-Determination in Social Work*, London, Routledge & Kegan Paul, pp. 118–37.

Macdonald, G. (1990) 'Allocating Blame in Social Work', *British Journal of Social Work*, **20**: 525–46.

McFarlane, S. (1994) 'Buddhism', in J. Holm and J. Bowker (eds), *Making Moral Decisions*, London, Continuum, pp. 17–40.

Machin, S. (1998) 'Swimming Against the Tide: A Social Worker's Experience of a Secure Hospital', in G. Hunt (ed.), *Whistleblowing in the Social Services: Public Accountability and Professional Practice*, London, Arnold, pp. 116–30.

MacIntyre, A. (1985) *After Virtue: A Study in Moral Theory*, 2nd edn, London, Duckworth.

MacIntyre, A. (1999) *Dependent Rational Animals: Why Human Beings Need the Virtues*, London, Duckworth.

Mackenzie, C. and Stoljar, N. (eds) (2000) *Relational Autonomy: Feminist Perspectives on Autonomy, Agency and the Social Self*, Oxford, Oxford University Press.

McNamee, S., Gergen, K. and Associates (1999) *Relational Responsibility: Resources for Sustainable Dialogue*, Thousand Oaks, CA and London, Sage.

Malin, N. (2000) 'Professionalism and Boundaries of the Formal Sector: The Example of Social and Community Care', in N. Malin (ed.), *Professionalism, Boundaries and the Workplace*, London, Routledge, pp. 7–24.

Marshall, T. (1963) 'Citizenship and Social Class', in *Sociology at the Crossroads and Other Essays*, London, Heineman, pp. 67–127.

Marshall, T. (1972) 'Value Problems of Welfare-Capitalism', *Journal of Social Policy*, **1**: 15–30.

Martyn, H. (ed.) (2000) *Developing Reflective Practice: Making Sense of Social Work in a World of Change*, Bristol, The Policy Press.

Marx, K. and Engels, F. (1969) 'Manifesto of the Communist Party', in L. Feuer (ed.), *Marx and Engels: Basic Writings on Politics and Philosophy*, Glasgow, Collins/Fontana, pp. 43–82.

Mayer, J. and Timms, N. (1970) *The Client Speaks*, London, Routledge & Kegan Paul.

Mendus, S. (1993) 'Different Voices, Still Lives: Problems in the Ethics of Care', *Journal of Applied Philosophy*, **10**(1): 17–27.

Mill, J. S. (1972) *Utilitarianism, On Liberty, and Considerations on Representative Government*, London, Dent.

Millerson, G. (1964) *The Qualifying Associations: A Study in Professionalisation*, London, Routledge & Kegan Paul.

Milner, J. (2001) *Women and Social Work: Narrative Approaches*, Basingstoke, Palgrave – now Palgrave Macmillan.

Mintzberg, H. (1979) *The Structuring of Organisations*, Englewood Cliffs, NJ, Prentice Hall.

Moffet, J. (1968) *Concepts of Casework Treatment*, London, Routledge & Kegan Paul.

Moon, D. (1988) 'Introduction: Responsibility, Rights and Welfare', in D. Moon (ed.), *Responsibility, Rights and Welfare: The Theory of the Welfare State*, Boulder, CO, Westview Press, pp. 1–15.

Mullaly, B. (1997) *Structural Social Work: Ideology, Theory, and Practice*, Ontario, Oxford University Press.

Mullender, A. and Perrott, S. (1998) 'Social Work and Organisations', in R. Adams, L. Dominelli and M. Payne (eds), *Social Work: Themes, Issues and Critical Debates*, Basingstoke, Macmillan – now Palgrave Macmillan, pp. 67–77.

Mullender, A. and Ward, D. (1991) *Self-Directed Groupwork: Users Take Action for Empowerment*, London, Whiting & Birch.

Nagel, T. (1976) 'Moral Luck', *Proceedings of the Aristotelian Society*, Supplementary volume, **L**: 137–51.

Nagel, T. (1979) 'The Fragmentation of Value', in T. Nagel, *Mortal Questions*, Cambridge, Cambridge University Press, pp. 128–41.

National Association of Social Workers (NASW) (1999) *Code of Ethics*, Washington, DC, NASW.

National Federation of Social Workers in Romania (2004) *Ethical Code of the Profession of Social Worker*, Mamamures, National Federation of Social Workers in Romania.

Nederlandse Vereniging van Maatschappelijk Werkers (NVMW) (1999) *Beroepscode voor de maatschappelijk werker*, Utrecht, NVMW.

New Zealand Association of Social Workers (NZASW) (1993) *Code of Ethics*, Dunedin, New Zealand, NZASW.

Noddings, N. (1984) *Caring: A Feminine Approach to Ethics and Moral Education*, Berkeley and Los Angeles, University of California Press.

Noddings, N. (2002) *Starting at Home: Caring and Social Policy*, Berkeley and Los Angeles, University of California Press.

Norman, R. (1998) *The Moral Philosophers*, Oxford, Clarendon Press.

O'Connor, J. (1973) *The Fiscal Crisis of the State*, New York, St Martin's Press.

O'Neill, O. (2002) *Autonomy and Trust in Bioethics*, Cambridge, Cambridge University Press.

O'Sullivan, T. (1999) *Decision Making in Social Work*, Basingstoke, Macmillan – now Palgrave Macmillan.

Oakley, J. and Cocking, D. (2001) *Virtue Ethics and Professional Roles*, Cambridge, Cambridge University Press.

Offe, C. (1984) *Contradictions of the Welfare State*, London, Hutchinson.

Okin, S. (1994) 'Gender Inequality and Cultural Difference', *Political Theory*, **22**: 5–24.

Ordine Nazionale Assistenti Sociali (2002) *Codice deontologico dell'Assistente Sociale*, Rome, ONAS.

Osborne, T. (1998) 'Constructionism, Authority and the Ethical Life', in I. Velody and R. Williams (eds), *The Politics of Constructionism*, London, Sage, pp. 221–34.

Outka, G. and Reeder, J. (eds) (1993) *Prospects for a Common Morality*, Chichester, Sussex, Princeton University Press.

Österreichischer Berufsverband Diplomierter Sozialarbeiterinnen (OBDS) (2004) *Ethische Standards – Berufspflichten für Sozialarbeiterinnen*, Salzburg, OBDS.

Øvretveit, J. (1997) 'How Patient Power and Client Participation Affects Relations Between Professions', in J. Øvretveit, P. Mathias and T. Thompson (eds), *Interprofessional Working for Health and Social Care*, Basingstoke, Macmillan – now Palgrave Macmillan, pp. 79–102.

Pardeck, J., Murphy, J. and Choi, J. (1994) 'Some Implications of Postmodernism for Social Work Practice', *Social Work*, **39**(4): 343–6.

Parsons, T. (1959) 'The Professions and Social Structure', in *Essays in Social Theory*, New York, Free Press.

Parton, N. (1989) 'Child Abuse', in B. Kahan (ed.), *Child Care*

Research, Policy and Practice, London, Hodder & Stoughton/Open University, pp. 55–79.

Parton, N. (1991) *Governing the Family: Child Care, Child Protection and the State*, Basingstoke, Macmillan – now Palgrave Macmillan.

Parton, N. (1994) 'The Nature of Social Work under Conditions of (Post) Modernity', *Social Work and Social Sciences Review*, **5**(2): 93–112.

Parton, N. (1997) 'Child Protection and Family Support: Current Debates and Future Prospects', in N. Parton (ed.), *Child Protection and Family Support: Tensions, Contradictions and Possibilities*, London, Routledge, pp. 1–24.

Parton, N. (1998) 'Risk, Advanced Liberalism and Child Welfare: The Need to Rediscover Uncertainty and Ambiguity', *British Journal of Social Work*, **28**: 5–27.

Parton, N. (1999) 'Reconfiguring Child Welfare Practices: Risk, Advanced Liberalism, and the Government of Freedom', in A. Chambon, A. Irving and L. Epstein (eds), *Reading Foucault for Social Work*, New York, Columbia University Press, pp. 101–30.

Parton, N. (2002) 'Postmodern and Constructionist Approaches to Social Work', in R. Adams, L. Dominelli and M. Payne (eds), *Social Work: Themes, Issues and Critical Debates,* 2nd edn, Basingstoke, Palgrave Macmillan, pp. 237–46.

Parton, N. (2003) 'Rethinking Professional Practice: The Contributions of Social Constructionism and the Feminist "Ethics of Care"', *British Journal of Social Work*, **33**: 1–16.

Parton, N. and O'Byrne, P. (2000) *Constructive Social Work: Towards a New Practice*, Basingstoke, Macmillan – now Palgrave Macmillan.

Parton, N. and Small, N. (1989) 'Violence, Social Work and the Emergence of Dangerousness', in M. Langan and P. Lee (eds), *Radical Social Work Today*, London, Unwin Hyman, pp. 120–39.

Parton, N., Thorpe, D. and Wattam, C. (1997) *Child Protection, Risk and the Moral Order*, Basingstoke, Macmillan – now Palgrave Macmillan.

Payne, H. and Littlechild, B. (eds) (2000) *Ethical Practice and the Abuse of Power in Social Responsibility: Leave No Stone Unturned*, London, Jessica Kingsley.

Payne, M. (1989) 'Open Records and Shared Decisions with Clients', in S. Shardlow (ed.), *The Values of Change in Social Work*, London, Routledge, pp. 114–34.

Payne, M. (1995) *Social Work and Community Care*, Basingstoke, Macmillan – now Palgrave Macmillan.

Payne, M. (2005) *Modern Social Work Theory*, 3rd edn, Basingstoke, Palgrave Macmillan.

Pease, B. and Fook, J. (1999) 'Postmodern Critical Theory and Emancipatory Social Work Practice', in B. Pease and J. Fook (eds), *Transforming Social Work Practice: Postmodern Critical Perspectives*, London and New York, Routledge, pp. 1–22.

Picht, W. (1914) *Toynbee Hall and the English Settlement Movement*, London, G. Bell and Sons.

Pierson, C. (1998) *Beyond the Welfare State? The New Political Economy of Welfare*, Oxford, Polity Press.

Pinker, R. (1990) *Social Work in an Enterprise Society*, London, Routledge.

Plamenatz, J. (1966) *The English Utilitarians*, Oxford, Blackwell.

Plant, R. (1970) *Social and Moral Theory in Casework*, London, Routledge & Kegan Paul.

Ragg, N. (1977) *People Not Cases*, London, Routledge & Kegan Paul.

Ramon, S. (ed.) (1991) *Beyond Community Care: Normalisation and Integration Work*, London, Macmillan – now Palgrave Macmillan.

Raphael, D. (1981) *Moral Philosophy*, Oxford, Oxford University Press.

Rauner, D. (2000) *They Still Pick Me Up When I Fall: The Role of Caring in Youth Development and Community Life*, New York, Columbia University Press.

Rawls, J. (1973) *A Theory of Justice*, Oxford, Oxford University Press.

Rea, D. (1998) 'The Myth of the Market in the Organisation of Community Care', in A. Symonds and A. Kelly (eds), *The Social Construction of Community Care*, Basingstoke, Macmillan – now Palgrave Macmillan, pp. 199–207.

Reamer, F. (1990) *Ethical Dilemmas in Social Service*, 2nd edn, New York, Columbia University Press.

Reamer, F. (1999) *Social Work Values and Ethics*, 2nd edn, New York, Columbia University Press.

Rest, J. (1994) 'Background: Theory and Research', in J. Rest and D. Narváez (eds), *Moral Development in the Professions: Psychology and Applied Ethics*, Hillsdale, NJ, Lawrence Erlbaum Associates, pp. 1–26.

Rhodes, M. (1986) *Ethical Dilemmas in Social Work Practice*, Boston, MA, Routledge & Kegan Paul.

Rice, D. (1975) 'The Code: A Voice for Approval', *Social Work Today*, 18 October: 381–2.

Roger, J. (2000) *From a Welfare State to a Welfare Society: The*

Changing Context of Social Policy in a Postmodern Era, Basingstoke, Macmillan – now Palgrave Macmillan.

Ronnby, A. (1992) 'Praxiology in Social Work', *International Social Work*, **35**: 317–26.

Ronnby, A. (1993) 'The Carer Society and Ethics', unpublished paper, Department of Social Work and Humanities, Mid-Sweden University, Östersund.

Rosenau, P. (1992) *Post-modernism and the Social Sciences: Insights, Inroads, and Intrusions*, Princeton, NJ, Princeton University Press.

Ross, W. (1930) *The Right and the Good*, Oxford, Clarendon Press.

Rossiter, A., Prilleltensky, I. and Walsh-Bowers, R. (2000) 'A Postmodern Perspective on Professional Ethics', in B. Fawcett, B. Featherstone, J. Fook and A. Rossiter (eds), *Practice and Research in Social Work: Postmodern Feminist Perspectives*, London, Routledge, pp. 83–103.

Russian Union of Social Educators and Social Workers (2003) *The Ethical Guideline of Social Educator and Social Worker*, Moscow, Union of Social Educators and Social Workers.

Sandel, M. (1998) *Liberalism and the Limits of Justice*, 2nd edn, Cambridge, Cambridge University Press.

Sartre, J.-P. (1969) *Being and Nothingness*, translated by Hazel Barnes, London, Methuen.

Schön, D. (1983) *The Reflective Practitioner. How Professionals Think in Action*, New York, Basic Books.

Schön, D. (1987) *Educating the Reflective Practitioner. Towards a New Design for Teaching and Learning in the Professions*, San Francisco, Jossey-Bass.

Seedhouse, D. (1998) *Ethics: The Heart of Health Care*, Chichester, Wiley.

Sevenhuisen, S. (1998) *Citizenship and the Ethics of Care: Feminist Considerations on Justice, Morality and Politics*, London, Routledge.

Shah, N. (1989) 'It's Up to You Sisters: Black Women and Radical Social Work', in M. Langan and P. Lee (eds), *Radical Social Work Today*, London, Unwin Hyman, pp. 178–91.

Shaw, M. and Martin, I. (2000) 'Community Work, Citizenship and Democracy: Re-making the Connections', *Community Development Journal*, **35**(4): 410–3.

Shaw, W. (1999) *Contemporary Ethics: Taking Account of Utilitarianism*, Oxford, Blackwell.

Siegrist, H. (1994) 'The Professions, State and Government in Theory and History', in T. Becher (ed.), *Governments and Professional*

Education, Buckingham, Society for Research into Higher Education and Open University Press, pp. 3–20.

Singapore Association of Social Workers (n.d.) *Code of Ethics of the Singapore Association of Social Workers*, Singapore, SASW.

Singer, P. (ed.) (1993) *A Companion to Ethics*, Blackwell, Oxford.

Slote, M. (1992) *From Morality to Virtue*, New York, Oxford University Press.

Smart, J. and Williams, B. (1973) *Utilitarianism: For and Against*, Cambridge, Cambridge University Press.

Smith, D. (ed.) (2004) *Social Work and Evidence-Based Practice*, London, Jessica Kingsley.

Smith, M. (1994) *Local Education: Community, Conversation, Praxis*, Buckingham, Open University Press.

Smith, R. (2005) *Values and Practice in Children's Services*, Basingstoke, Palgrave Macmillan.

Sociálních Pracovníku České Republiky (1995) *Etický Kodex*, Prague, SPCR.

Solomon, R. (1992) *Ethics and Excellence*, Oxford, Oxford University Press.

Solomon, R. (1997) 'Corporate Roles, Personal Virtues: An Aristotelian Approach to Business Ethics', in D. Statman (ed.), *Virtue Ethics: A Critical Reader*, Edinburgh, Edinburgh University Press, pp. 205–6.

Soulet, M.-H. (ed.) (1997) *Les transformations des métiers du social*, Fribourg, Editions Universitaires Fribourg Suisse.

South African Association of Black Social Workers (SABSWA) (n.d.) *Code of Ethics*, Johannesburg, SABSWA.

Southon, G. and Braithwhaite, J. (2000) 'The End of Professionalism?', in C. Davies, L. Finlay and A. Bullman (eds), *Changing Practice in Health and Social Care*, London, Sage, pp. 300–7.

Spicker, P. (1988) *Principles of Social Welfare*, London, Routledge.

Stalley, R. (1978) 'Non-Judgmental Attitudes', in N. Timms and D. Watson (eds), *Philosophy in Social Work*, London, Routledge & Kegan Paul, pp. 91–110.

Statman, D. (1997) 'Introduction to Virtue Ethics', in D. Statman (ed.), *Virtue Ethics: A Critical Reader*, Edinburgh, Edinburgh University Press, pp. 3–41.

Stèttarfèlag íslenskra félagsráðgjafa (n.d.) *Code of Ethics for Social Workers*, Reykjavik, Stèttarfèlag íslenskra félagsráðgjafa.

Swanton, C. (2003) *Virtue Ethics: A Pluralistic View*, Oxford, Oxford University Press.

Taylor, C. (1989) *Sources of the Self: The Making of Modern Identity*, Cambridge, Cambridge University Press.

Taylor, C. and White, S. (2000) *Practising Reflexivity in Health and Welfare*, Buckingham, Open University Press.

Taylor, D. (1989) 'Citizenship and Social Power', *Critical Social Policy*, (26): 19–31.

Thomas, T., Noone, M. and Rowbottom, T. (1993) *Confidentiality in Social Services*, London, CCETSW.

Thompson, I., Melia, K. and Boyd, K. (1994) *Nursing Ethics*, 3rd edn, Edinburgh, Churchill Livingstone.

Thompson, N. (1993) *Anti-Discriminatory Practice*, Basingstoke, Macmillan – now Palgrave Macmillan.

Thompson, N. (2000) *Understanding Social Work: Preparing for Practice*, London, Macmillan – now Palgrave Macmillan.

Timms, N. (1983) *Social Work Values: An Enquiry*, London, Routledge & Kegan Paul.

Toren, N. (1972) *Social Work: The Case of a Semi-Profession*, Beverley Hills, CA, Sage.

Torstendahl, R. (1991) *Bureaucratisation in Northwestern Europe 1880–1985: Domination and Governance*, London, Routledge.

Toulmin, S. (2001) *Return to Reason*, Cambridge, MA, Harvard University Press.

Tronto, J. (1993) *Moral Boundaries: A Political Argument for an Ethic of Care*, London, Routledge.

United Nations (1959) *Declaration of the Rights of the Child*, reprinted in P. Newell (1991) *The UN Convention and Children's Rights in the UK*, London, National Children's Bureau, pp. 182–3.

Urmson, J. (ed.) (1975) *The Concise Encyclopedia of Western Philosophy and Philosophers*, London, Hutchinson.

Veatch, R. (1999) 'Abandoning Informed Consent', in H. Kuhse and P. Singer (eds), *Bioethics: An Anthology*, Oxford, Blackwell, pp. 523–32.

Velody, I. and Williams, R. (eds) (1998) *The Politics of Constructionism*, Sage, London.

Vetlesen, A. (1994) *Perception, Empathy and Judgment: An Inquiry into the Preconditions of Moral Performance*, University Park, PA, Pennsylvania State University Press.

Warnock, G. (1967) *Contemporary Moral Philosophy*, London, Macmillan – now Palgrave Macmillan.

Warnock, M. (1998) *An Intelligent Person's Guide to Ethics*, London, Duckworth.

Watson, D. (1985) 'What's the Point of a Code of Ethics for Social Work', in D. Watson (ed.), *A Code of Ethics for Social Work: The Second Step*, London, Routledge & Kegan Paul, pp. 20–39.

Webb, S. and McBeath, G. (1989) 'A Political Critique of Kantian Ethics in Social Work', *British Journal of Social Work*, vol. 19, pp. 491–506.

Webb, S. and McBeath, G. (1990) 'A Political Critique of Kantian Ethics in Social Work: A Reply to Prof. R. S. Downie', *British Journal of Social Work*, **20**: 65–71.

Webb, S. (2001) 'Some Considerations on the Validity of Evidence-based Practice in Social Work', *British Journal of Social Work*, **31**(1): 57–79.

Webb, S. (2002) 'Evidence-based Practice and Decision-analysis in Social Work', *Journal of Social Work*, **2**(1): 45–63.

White, S. and Stancombe, J. (2003) *Clinical Judgement in the Health and Welfare Professions: Extending the Evidence Base*, Maidenhead, Open University Press.

Whitley, C. (1969) 'On Duties', in J. Feinberg (ed.), *Moral Concepts*, Oxford, Oxford University Press, pp. 53–9.

Wicclair, M. (1991) 'Patient Decision-making Capacity and Risk', *Bioethics*, **5**(2): 91–104.

Wilding, P. (1982) *Professional Power and Social Welfare*, London, Routledge & Kegan Paul.

Wilkes, R. (1981) *Social Work with Undervalued Groups*, London, Tavistock.

Wilkes, R. (1985) 'Social Work: What Kind of Profession?', in D. Watson (ed.), *A Code of Ethics for Social Work: The Second Step*, London, Routledge & Kegan Paul, pp. 40–58.

Wilmot, S. (1997) *The Ethics of Community Care*, London, Cassell.

Yelloly, M. and Henkel, M. (eds) (1995) *Learning and Teaching in Social Work: Towards Reflective Practice*, London, Jessica Kingsley.

Younghusband, E. (1981) *The Newest Profession: A Short History of Social Work*, Sutton, Surrey, IPC Business Press Ltd.

Index